Eminent Educators

Eminent Educators
Studies in Intellectual Influence

MAURICE R. BERUBE

Contributions to the Study of Education,
Number 76

GREENWOOD PRESS
Westport, Connecticut • London

Library of Congress Cataloging-in-Publication Data

Berube, Maurice R.
    Eminent educators : studies in intellectual influence / Maurice R.
Berube.
    p. cm. — (Contributions to the study of education, ISSN 0196–707X
; no. 76)
    Includes bibliographical references and index.
    ISBN 0–313–31060–2 (alk. paper)
    1. Dewey, John, 1859–1952. 2. Gardner, Howard. 3. Gilligan,
Carol, 1936–   . 4. Ogbu, John U. 5. Educators—United States
Biography. 6. Progressive education—United States. 7. Education—
Philosophy. I. Title. II. Series.
LB875.D5B47 2000
370´.1—dc21   99–29555

British Library Cataloguing in Publication Data is available.

Library of Congress Catalog Card Number: 99–29555
ISBN: 0–313–31060–2
ISSN: 0196–707X

First published in 2000

Greenwood Press, 88 Post Road West, Westport, CT 06881
An imprint of Greenwood Publishing Group, Inc.
www.greenwood.com

Printed in the United States of America

The paper used in this book complies with the
Permanent Paper Standard issued by the National
Information Standards Organization (Z39.48-1984).

10 9 8 7 6 5 4 3 2

Copyright Acknowledgments

Grateful acknowledgment is given for permission to quote from the following sources:

Chapter 3, "John Dewey and The Abstract Expressionists," first appeared in *Educational Theory* 48, no. 2 (spring 1998): 211–27.

John Dewey, "To Conscience," *The Poems of John Dewey,* edited by Jo Ann Boydston. Copyright (1977) by the Center for Dewey Studies, reprinted by permission of the publisher Southern Illinois University Press.

In a Different Voice by Carol Gilligan. Copyright © 1982, 1993 by the President and Fellows of Harvard College. Reprinted by permission of Harvard University Press.

Abstract Expressionism in America by William C. Seitz. Copyright © 1983 by the President and Fellows of Harvard College. Reprinted by permission of Harvard University Press.

From *To Open Minds.* Copyright © 1989 by Howard Gardner. Reprinted by permission of Basic Books, a member of Perseus Books, L.L.C.

From *Multiple Intelligences: The Theory in Practice.* Copyright © 1993 by Howard Gardner. Reprinted by permission of Basic Books, a member of Perseus Books, L.L.C.

From *Leading Minds: An Anatomy of Leadership.* Copyright © 1995 by Howard Gardner. Reprinted by permission of Basic Books, a member of Perseus Books, L.L.C.

Every reasonable effort has been made to trace the owners of copyright materials in this book, but in some instances this has proven impossible. The author and publisher will be glad to receive information leading to more complete acknowledgments in subsequent printings of the book and in the meantime extend their apologies for any omissions.

For Clair

To Conscience

"Arouse! Fight on! Combat and conquer;
Evil are the forces."
I have struggled and am tired
Of this road embriared;
Let things take their courses.

I have fought and got no gain;
Toiled and been passed by
By all save would and pain;
Others work and take their joy;
Now, stern comrade, so shall I,
Sick, sick, of thy endless employ.

Shall I never know pleasure?
Never know rest from strain?
Let me sail a sea of azure

Wave on wave of pleasure
Turn from treading this path of rocks
With no drug for bruise save its stain.

Give me rest for I am tired;
Nor ask me how I reconcile
My coward's choice of pleasured ease
With ideals that once inspired.

Comrade conscience, cease thy talk—
Your part but talk as mine was strife—
While I do take this flowered walk
And daily with sweet soft things alluring.
Rested mayhap, I'll resume thy hard life
Of search, stern comrade, for things enduring.

John Dewey
The Poems of John Dewey (1977)

Contents

Preface

The impetus for this book was a deep desire to write biography. After eight books, some quantitative policy studies, others on educational history, I decided to attempt some form of biography. However, the idea of concentrating one's intellectual efforts—and stamina—on one subject proved forbidding. I was not prepared to devote a decade or more to one figure whom, quite possibly, I would come to detest after such a Herculean effort. Moreover, as the novelist Joyce Carol Oates has so ably pointed out, most biography today concentrates on the warts of a person's life, or as she put it, creates a new genre of "pathobiography." This study is an intellectual history of the thinking of major researchers and has biographical data only as it illuminates their thought.

In discussing my writing plans with a colleague at my university, I was given the solution to my problem. He had wanted to do the first biography of Carl Rogers, the humanist psychologist. However, his editor persuaded him to consider a shorter version, an "appreciation." Thus, this volume is an "appreciation." I concentrate on those intellectual figures whom I consider to have had the greatest influence on American education in this century. The model for my study is Lytton Strachey's classic portrait of the Victorian age *Eminent Victorians*. Strachey selected his subjects for irony's sake: Cardinal Manning, Florence Nightingale, Dr. Matthew Arnold, and General Gordon.

I also chose four figures: John Dewey, a philosopher and the father of modern American education; two psychologists, Howard Gardner and Carol Gilligan; and one anthropologist, John Ogbu. All but Dewey are still living and writing and conducting research. The difficult part of this study for me was how to focus on a main theme. Strachey attempted to portray an age through representative figures: a famed cleric, a celebrated nurse, a famous general, and an intellectual literary critic. Only one was a practicing intellectual. I also toyed with the idea of the influence of organizational men and women—the Horace Manns, Terrell Bells, and the civil rights leaders who shaped and defined American education from a political and policy perspective. However, I settled on intellectual leaders and their influence as my focal point since few intellectual histories have been written on American educational thinkers.

And as is the case with historical and qualitative research, the thesis further developed as I became more immersed in the historical data. That subtext is that my four figures—John Dewey, Howard Gardner, Carol Gilligan, and John Ogbu—best represented the legacy of progressive education, which I have come to believe is what distinguishes American education from education in the rest of the world.

The progressives sought to educate children in four dimensions: intellectual ability, moral character, social sense (seeking to improve society), and aesthetic sense. John Dewey, the most eminent of the progressives, preached all four goals so successfully. Here he is represented by two: intellectual and aesthetic; Gardner illustrates the intellectual with his redefinition of intelligence; Gilligan, the moral, by her concern for the moral development of girls; and Ogbu, the social, by his research on the education of African Americans. Moreover, Gardner and Gilligan are in varying measures the intellectual heirs of John Dewey. They have been influenced by his educational philosophy.

The final organizing point of this study is that my subjects have shaped indelibly American education for the better. As the first chapter on leadership indicates, leadership—in all its aspects including intellectual influence—must itself have a moral component, to improve society for the good. I believe that there is not any question that my subjects have influenced American education for the good.

Acknowledgments

There are a number of people that I am indebted to in the preparation of this study. Clair T. Newbold was not only instrumental in writing chapter 5 on Carol Gilligan but also reviewed the chapters on Howard Gardner and the final chapter on an "intellectual legacy." I thank her for her valuable participation.

I am grateful to Professors Carol Gilligan and John U. Ogbu for permitting me to interview them. Also, I would be remiss in not acknowledging those individuals who first noticed the importance of my subjects and introduced their thinking to me. Dr. Cheryl Evans first acquainted me with Howard Gardner; my daughter, Katherine Bérubé, showed me Gilligan's studies; and Dr. Carlton Brown, President of Savannah State College, introduced me to the work of John Ogbu. Clay Vaughan of the Old Dominion University Library was an invaluable resource. I thank them all.

Thanks again to my editors, especially Arlene Belzer and copyeditor Sally Hemingway.

— 1 —

In Search of Leadership

Intellectual Leadership—"Ideas as Moral Power"
 —James MacGregor Burns

This study seeks to flesh out the turning points in American public school education through biographical portraits of the major change agents combined with a policy analysis of their impact. By combining biography with policy analysis, the student of the history of education may be provided with a human face in the defining moments of education.

A few caveats are in order. First, this study deals only with public school education, which is the bedrock of education in the United States. I did look in some detail in this study at private or parochial education or higher education, but for the most part the greatest change and innovation has occurred at the school level and in the public sector.

Second, I am not submitting a new definition of leadership. For one thing, scholars and school practitioners still have yet to reach a consensus on what leadership is specifically and how it can be programmed, if at all. Nevertheless, there is an idea of what leadership is, although one must rely on the broadest of generalizations.

Finally, one must guard against the temptation to read history as a prelude to future social engineering. Arguably, one of the most misleading quotes was philosopher George Santayana's admonition that those who do not pay heed to the past are doomed to repeat it. Many historians now realize that each historical era, incident, and/or person is rooted in a unique matrix. Egypt's history is not that of Rome's; the New York School of Abstract Expressionists were quite distinct from the Parisian Impressionists; the American educational philosopher John Dewey had little in common with the scholastic St. Thomas Aquinas and the scholarum. In short, first and foremost, history exists for itself.

Why then pursue a study of history? One reason is to gain a fuller understanding of ourselves. As the psychologist Carl Jung discovered, each person has a collective subconscious of mankind's history. The student of history then learns his/her place in the universe. Understanding the past enables us to understand the present and perhaps the future.

WHAT IS LEADERSHIP?

One approaches the study of leadership cautiously. There is no consensus among either scholars or practitioners about crucial concepts basic to the idea of leadership. There is no clear definition of what constitutes leadership. Does leadership entail a moral component that transforms society for the good, as the most important of American leadership scholars argue? Can leadership be taught, programmed in individuals through institutes and workshops, as many popular manuals imply? Is it a combination of the right person at the right time making the right decisions?

Nevertheless, despite unsettled issues concerning leadership, the public has shown a great demand for books on this subject. In 1981, Bass reviewed no less than 4,725 leadership books.[1] Joseph C. Rost counted 132 such books published in the United States in the 1980s alone.[2] Yet, in his 1993 analysis, *Leadership for the Twenty-First Century*, Rost confidently declared that no precise definition of leadership had been reached in previous studies. Indeed, one reads each new leadership study with the warning that none has to date encapsuled the concept of leadership. Nonetheless, undaunted, each leadership author offers his/her idea of what leadership is and how one can realize its secrets.

However, there is a consensus about what leadership is not. Some leadership scholars argue that most studies and manuals confuse leadership with management. They maintain that management is not leadership. In his review of leadership studies since the 1930s, Rost pointed out that "a consistent view of leadership" mistakenly views "leadership as good management."[3] Indeed, Warren Bennis and Burt Nanus in their 1985 study, *Leaders: The Strategies for Taking Charge*, pinpointed the problem. They cited "more than 350 definitions of leadership" which "don't agree with each other."[4] They concluded that "leadership is the most studied and least understood topic of any in the social sciences."[5] What passes for the study of leadership in American schools of business, they argued, is no more than courses in micromanagement. "What's needed is not *management* education," they maintained, "but *leadership* education."[6] And despite the plethora of definitions of leadership, Bennis and Nanus offered their own "new theory of leadership."[7]

Indeed, when the political scientist, James MacGregor Burns, published his classic 1978 study, *Leadership*, which was to influence the next generation of leadership scholars, he concluded that leadership remained "one of the most observed and least understood phenomena on earth."[8] Although Burns bemoaned the fact that "no central concept of leadership has yet emerged," he attributed the lack of a clear definition of leadership to a situation of academic isolation whereby "scholars have worked in separate disciplines."[9] Since Burns's indictment of academia, a host of multidisciplinary leadership studies programs have emerged on college campuses both at the graduate and undergraduate levels.

HISTORY OF THE IDEA OF LEADERSHIP

The concept of leadership is a relatively modern term. Although some evidence suggests that the word "leader" first appeared in the Western world around the year 1300, serious commentary on the idea of "leadership" belongs to nineteenth-century England and the rise of the British Parliament.[10] Since then, the idea of leadership has undergone many interpretations, often reflecting the historical matrix of the time.

The first fully developed definition of leadership involved the Great Man/Great Woman theory at the end of the nineteenth century. One fine example is Lytton Strachey's satirical portrayal of Victorian society in his classic study *Eminent Victorians*. Strachey reviews the era in terms of those towering individuals who shaped the age, such as Florence Nightingale, General Charles Gordon, and Matthew Arnold. The Great Man/Great Woman theory rested on the interpretation that superior individuals, acting almost alone, rise to the historical occasion and make history. The Great Man/Great Woman theory developed when a primitive industrial capitalism was dominated by Captains of Industry. It was a time when Social Darwinism and Rugged Individualism were popular ideas.

With the economic depression of the 1930s, a new interpretation of leadership emerged. This concept stressed the social interactions of a leader with groups and movements. By the 1950s, scholars looked to the personal qualities of the leader, studying the leader's psychological traits, revealing the influence of the now established field of psychology. This concept was enhanced by the 1960s as scholars looked also at behavior theory in addition to psychological traits. Situational theory was emphasized in the

1970s—that is, the right person at the right time. Nevertheless, during those last two decades, according to Rost, there were a number of leadership scholars who defined leadership in terms of influence.

By the 1980s, the Great Man/Great Woman theory reemerged. This coincided with economic decline in the United States. The key was to become excellent once again and revive a dormant United States economy. Best-selling books on how to revive the American economy had such titles as Thomas J. Peters's *In Search of Excellence* (1982). Public school reformers who sought to fine-tune education to restore American economic primacy by raising academic standards dubbed their movement "the excellence reform movement." And the key to a revitalization of the economy was the leader. Rost observed that: "Taking its cue from the past, the 1980s saw leadership recast as great men and women with certain preferred traits influencing followers to do what the leaders wish in order to achieve group/organizational goals that reflect excellence defined as some kind of higher-level effectiveness."[11]

Some scholars in the 1980s argued that influence was synonymous with leadership. "Influence," Rost observed, "is probably the most used word in the leadership definitions of the 1980s."[12]

The concept of influence in these writers is used in either one of two ways: (1) synonymous with the concept of leadership or (2) as a component of a larger definition of leadership. Indeed, it is in the latter sense of the term that Rost, himself, offered his own four-part version of what consists of leadership. For Rost, influence—defined as persuasion—is the first of four "essential" variables of leadership; the other three are followers, a "mutual purpose," and "real changes."[13] But first the "relationship is based on influence."[14]

Those scholars who equate leadership with influence measured it by the impact on society. (This study has much in common with their approach.) Nevertheless, other scholars reject leadership as influence because "the concept was too political and slippery" since it is "very difficult to do an empirical study of influence."[15] One senses that by "empirical study" these scholars imply a quantitative, statistically measured methodology. A qualitative approach employing historical and policy analysis methodology would be the more appropriate methodology and is accepted among the more enlightened social science researchers.

DOES LEADERSHIP HAVE TO BE MORAL?

One of the key questions concerning a definition of leadership is whether a leader must effect change for the good. In short, does leadership have to be moral? The question is perplexing and has a long history.

Niccolò Machiavelli's *The Prince*, posthumously printed in 1532, shocked the Renaissance world with his advocacy of a *realpolitik* that suspended moral principles. Closer to our day, leadership scholars confronted the evil of "leaders" such as Adolf Hitler and Stalin. Were Hitler and Stalin "leaders" or mere evil actors passing on a historical stage?

Perhaps the most profound examination of leadership and the moral good was political scientist James MacGregor Burns seminal book simply titled *Leadership*. Burns deeply influenced the generation of leadership scholars who followed him. For example, nearly all of the scholars discussed in these pages acknowledged their debt to Burns directly or indirectly. Rost dedicated his book to Burns, "who changed my whole way of thinking about leadership," and Burns supplied a favorable foreword to the book.[16]

The educator Thomas J. Sergiovanni in his work *Value-Added Leadership* credited Burns's influence as being "seminal."[17] Warren Bennis and Burt Nanus in their leadership study claimed that their "new theory" of leadership owed much to "John Gardner . . . and James MacGregor Burns for their intellectual *inspiration*."[18] Howard Gardner, the developmental psychologist and father of the theory of multiple intelligences, acknowledged Burns "for the original suggestion that I write about leadership." Gardner's 1995 book, *Leading Minds: An Anatomy of Leadership*, is in the Burns tradition.[19] Stephen Covey's best-selling books on leadership revealed how well he has mastered Burns's *Leadership*. And Gary Wills's 1994 study, *Certain Trumpets: The Call of Leaders*, confronted Burns's provocative definition of leadership.

Burns's great contribution is his definition of leadership, which included a moral component. He defined leadership as having three variables: first, "the crucial variable is purpose"; second, leaders must induce "followers to act for certain goals"; and third, "transforming leadership ultimately becomes *moral*."[20] He is insistent on the moral dimension of leadership. "Transforming leadership," he argued, "occurs [when] . . . leaders and followers raise one another to higher levels of motivation and morality."[21] Again, he maintained that "leadership is a process of morality to the degree that leaders engage with followers on the basis of shared motives, values and goals."[22] Burns flatly declared that "*moral leadership* concerns me most."[23] He viewed intellectual leadership in terms of "ideas as moral power."[24] He criticized those scholars who "regard value as corrupting the critical sense; they argue for moral detachment. But moral detachment is itself at best a moral value and one hostile to the concerns of the free mind."[25]

The problem of leadership as evil strikes at the core of what truly constitutes leadership. Must true leadership transform society for the good as

Burns argued? Or are the Hitlers of the world also leaders since they had goals shared by followers?

Wills confronted the Hitler problem. Wills's "aim is to destroy Hitler" as a leader, although "Hitler's followers shared, at some level, his goals."[26] "Hitler's enormities," he concluded, "arouse hatred in me."[27] For Wills, then, Hitler is not a true leader.

Similarly, Covey dismissed Hitler as being an authentic leader. According to Covey, Hitler lacked a "moral compass" and "violated compass principles."[28] "The German Nazis," Covey declared had "shared values, but these violated basic principles."[29] In short, Covey agreed with Burns that leadership must have a moral component.

Sergiovanni reflected his intellectual debt to Burns on moral leadership. "Does the leader model beliefs, live purses, exemplify standards?" Sergiovanni asked.[30] Sergiovanni argued that "bureaucratic theories of leadership are secular" when the "unique response is of the spirit . . . (and) . . . moral leadership taps the spirit."[31]

Gardner makes a distinction. He believed that one can be a leader and pursue evil although Gardner has an interest in "the moral aspects of leadership."[32] Departing from Burns, Gardner adopted a "value neutral" position regarding the "moral dimensions of leadership," although he was more interested in "the moral aspects of leadership."[33] Gardner found his variables for leadership "to be as characteristic of reprehensible leaders— the Hitlers and the Stalins—as of leaders whom we might wish to praise."[34]

The moral question was first posed by Niccolò Machiavelli in his slim volume, *The Prince*. A high-ranking Florentine government official who was deposed, Machiavelli wrote *The Prince* as a treatise on government and leadership that he hoped would restore him to favor from the very people who had him removed—the Medicis. With the death of the Medicis, his book became moot and *The Prince* was not published until after Machiavelli's death.

The Prince introduced a new concept to government and leadership: *realpolitik*. It was government and leadership as it was actually played, suspended from moral constraints. Machiavelli foresaw that he had departed "radically from the procedures of others" when it "seemed more suitable . . . to search after the effectual truth of the matter rather than its imagined one."[35]

The Prince eventually became a classic—part of the Western canon of great books—and has remained controversial to the present. Machiavellian scholar Peter Bondanella observed that *The Prince* "has become a mainstay of courses on the great books" and "continues to stimulate heated debate and controversy."[36]

Twenty-seven years after its publication, the Roman Catholic Church placed *The Prince* on its index of forbidden hooks. In Elizabethan England, where the term Machiavellian was introduced, nearly four hundred derogatory references to the book were made. A U.S. Random House dictionary defined Machiavellian as "being or acting in accordance with the principles of governance in Machiavelli's *The Prince*, in which political expediency is placed above morality."[37]

Machiavelli sought a "unified Italian state guided by the principles of political realism" to replace the smaller city-states that existed.[38] Political realism often meant pursuing any means to achieve the higher end. "If a prince wishes to maintain the state," Machiavelli wrote, "he is often obliged not to be good."[39] The health of the state, he tells us,

> depends on whether cruelty be well or badly used. Well used are those cruelties (if it is permitted to speak well of evil) that are carried out in a single stroke, done out of necessity to protect oneself, and are not continued but are converted into the greatest possible benefits for the subjects. Badly used are those cruelties which, although being few at the outset, grow with the passing of time instead of disappearing.[40]

In short, this is *realpolitik* as practiced to our day. Burns sidestepped the moral implication of *The Prince* by labeling it "satire."[41]

Burns was not altogether mistaken. *The Prince* lends itself to alternate interpretations. Bondanella argued that "we may also absolve the author of *The Prince* from being 'Machiavellian.'"[42] For Bondanella, Machiavelli "is subtler than some moralists have appreciated."[43] As a case in point, the Machiavelli scholar argued that the idea that the end justifies the means was a "gross mistranslation" of Machiavelli.[44] A more exact translation has Machiavelli saying that "in the actions of all men . . . one must consider the final result."[45] Still, Bondanella conceded that despite the more accurate translation "the concept is of moral interest" and that "no amount of historical scholarship succeeded in explaining away the moral issues."[46]

CAN LEADERSHIP BE TAUGHT?

It was also Burns who raised the quintessential question: "Can *leadership* be taught?"[47] The answer is not self-evident. Nonetheless, nearly everyone who has written about leadership—scholars, practitioners, and popularizers—assumed that when one reads their work an understanding of the dynamics of leadership will lead to an ability to lead.

Burns criticized the many popular how-to manuals as no less than texts offering "salesman's tricks" to "manage and manipulate other persons rather than to lead them."[48] Unfortunately, Burns equivocated on whether leadership can be taught, and does not give a clear answer.

The how-to manuals have taken many forms from *The Prince* to equally scholarly works such as those presented by Burns and Sergiovanni. They range from the scholarly to the simplistically mundane, such as Dale Carnegie's bestseller of all time, *How To Win Friends and Influence People*. The genre keeps replenishing itself. Witness the publication in one year of the serious study by Howard Gardner, *Leadership*, and the more breezy account of professional football coach Bill Parcell's *Finding a Way to Win: The Principles of Leadership, Teamwork and Motivation*. One concludes that leadership is a concept that belongs to everyone.

Machiavelli's *The Prince* had the how-to approach in mind. Approximately half of the brief chapters deal with his version of the traits of the leader. Machiavelli characterized the ideal leader as one who was generous, loyal, not hated or subject to flattery, managed advisors wisely, was esteemed by followers, and employed cruelty only as a temporary measure for the greater good. To Machiavelli these characteristics would result in leadership.

The other crucial ingredient of leadership is vision. And the other half of *The Prince* deals with Machiavelli's vision of the ideal Italian state. In his study of leadership, educator Thomas J. Sergiovanni stressed that the key to leadership is vision. In his 1990 book, *Value-Added Leadership: How to Get Extraordinary Performance in School*, Sergiovanni concluded that "the concept of vision gets a great deal of play in leadership."[49] He echoed Warren Bennis's observation that argued "vision to be critical" in leadership.[50] However, one struggles to perceive how vision can be programmed, thus questioning whether leadership can be taught.

Although a flawed study, *Value-Added Leadership* performed a useful task in applying leadership and management analysis to the realm of public education. Rost placed Sergiovanni among the leadership scholars in the excellence movement. Correspondingly, Sergiovanni was a cheerleader for excellence school reform, arguing for national standards to restructure public education for the best and brightest in order to compete economically with foreign nations.

Sergiovanni defined leadership as "extraordinary performance" in the public schools that "builds upon sound management ideas that have served well in the past."[51] These ideas are culled from "a synthesis of traditional management and social science studies and recent studies of successful school and corporate cultures."[52] However, Rost, in his assessment of *Value-Added Leadership*, concluded that Sergiovanni failed to clearly demark the shifting line between management and leadership. For him, Sergiovanni "has no clear definition of leadership."[53]

In addition to the literature on leadership, Sergiovanni drew on examples of "extraordinary performance" from public education and the business world. He argued that "there are enough examples of successful schools to make this a hopeful time . . . [so that] . . . the challenge we face is to make the exception the rule."[54] In that statement, one can summarize much of the history of American public education. American school leaders have been uniquely obsessed throughout our history with innovation and experimentation. Their underlying assumption is that one can convert the exception to become the rule; the successful experiment in one school can be transplanted to other schools. Never mind that few of these experiments have succeeded in the long run. A constant emphasis on innovation and change characterizes American public education.

Sergiovanni's argument runs thin when he substituted principles from the world of business to that of public education. Indeed, his writing is rife with business language. For example, he wrote that value-added leadership asks school administrators "to seek a fair return . . . for . . . investments . . . in the form of financial, psychological, social and educational benefits."[55] The ideas are right but the language is not. Moreover, the book has a plethora of success stories from the world of business complete with admiring portraits of business leaders such as H. Ross Perot. Indeed, Sergiovanni wanted to do for education what Thomas J. Peters and Robert Waterman Jr. accomplished in their bestseller on business management, *In Search of Excellence*—namely, provide a wake-up call to America's corporate chiefs.

Perhaps Sergiovanni's main deficiency is to inexorably link business with education. His provocative thesis that "when corporate America shines, the schools also shine . . . and deteriorating worker commitment in corporate America . . . [has] . . . paralleled declines in schooling" is a serious misreading of American educational history.[56] Certainly, some of our finest hours in school reform—progressive education and equity reform of the 1960s—had little to do with American business. On the other hand, the Revisionist educational historians of the 1970s and other radical educators, such as Henry Giroux and Stanley Aronowitz in the 1980s, explored the link between business and education. They concluded that, for the most part, the interests of the corporate world did not coincide with that of public education and in many instances, were, in fact, detrimental to schooling.

Another important attempt to instruct was William G. Cunningham and Donald Gresso's *Cultural Leadership: The Culture of Excellence in Education*. Published in 1993, the book was read by President Bill Clinton. *Cultural Leadership* joined several management and leadership concepts together to provide a recipe for educational improvement (for example, Edward Deming's Total Quality Management program with Sergiovanni's values and Bennis and Nanus' views on vision as part of leadership). Although Cunningham and Gresso make a notable package to be applied to the excellence school reform movement in education, the book's strength, like Sergiovanni's *Value-Added Leadership*, is essentially as a primer for good management. There *are leadership* concepts presented but no clear definition differentiating leadership from management.

However, Cunningham and Gresso make a strong contribution to the literature. They applied the concept of organizational culture to education, first developed by Terence E. Deal and Allen A. Kennedy in their 1982 study, *Corporate Cultures: The Rites and Rituals of Corporate Life*. An organization's culture becomes crucial in an organization's effectiveness. Deal and Kennedy defined culture as a "system of informal rules that spells out how people are to behave most of the time."[57] Cunningham and Gresso similarly define an organization's culture as "an informal understanding of the 'way we do things around here'. Culture is a powerful but ill-defined conceptual thinking within the organization that expresses organizational values, ideals, attitudes, and beliefs."[58]

Deal and Kennedy observed that "every business—in fact, every organization—has a culture."[59] Moreover, they added that "values are the bedrock of any corporate culture."[60] Cunningham and Gresso moved beyond that concept to argue that the "first step" in leading/managing an organization is "developing the vision for the organization."[61] Both sets of authors hark back to Burns when maintaining that the leader or manager must first *transform* the organization's culture to improve its effectiveness. "Culture," Deal and Kennedy declared, "is *the* barrier to change."[62] And Cunningham and Gresso devoted their final chapter to "transforming school culture."[63] Interestingly, neither set of authors included a moral component in their leadership/management program. Moreover, neither book presented *cultural* leaders from the world of literature, arts, and academia.

Another scholarly approach to programming leadership is Howard Gardner's 1995 analysis, *Leading Minds: An Anatomy of Leadership*. (Gardner, who achieved fame with his theory of multiple intelligences a decade earlier, is featured as an intellectual leader in this study.) Like other scholars, Gardner employed a biographical case study approach to flesh out his theory of leadership.

He is concerned that his analysis be taken seriously as a means to teach prospective leaders. He concluded in *Leading Minds* that there are "three lessons that are relevant for the proper training of leaders."[64] Potential leaders should learn the "enduring features of leadership," which Gardner noted in the "stories" of his subjects, confront "new trends" as they develop, and educate the whole public on what constitutes leadership.[65] "The 'best' leadership training *for* potential leaders," he argued, "is the best training *about* leadership for all. . . ."[66] Gardner's reasoning for the latter is that "the larger society remains ignorant about leadership . . . [which] . . . testifies to the continuing orphan status of leadership. . . ."[67] However, like the type of scholar that he is, Gardner's prescription for leadership deals with large ideas rather than operational specifics.

Gardner defined leadership as influence. He wrote: "Churchill exerted his influence in a direct way. . . . Einstein exerted his influence in an indirect way. . . . Einstein and Churchill mark two ends of a continuum that denotes the capacity of a person . . . to *influence* other people. (Indeed, I could have termed this study *"An Examination of Influence"* [emphasis added].)[68]

Moreover, Gardner subscribed to the Great Man/Great Woman theory of leadership. He professed "little sympathy for those who challenge the 'great person' theory of leadership."[69] And in a previous study of creativity—*Creative Minds*—he stated that "there is a sense—for which I do not apologize—in which this study of creativity reflects the 'great man/great woman' view of creativity."[70]

Gardner's profiles are grouped into six distinct camps. There are case studies of intellectuals, mainstream politicians, confrontational political figures, military leaders, corporate executives, and religious leaders.[71] Three of his figures—Martin Luther King Jr., Eleanor Roosevelt, and Pope John XXIII—were also selected by Gary Wills in his leadership book.

Moreover, Gardner examined his subjects through the "identity" prism of Erik Erikson, the psychoanalyst whose theories of identity formation were popular in the 1950s. "I owe a special debt to my own mentor," Gardner declared, "the late psychoanalyst Erik Erikson who in many ways inspired this study."[72]

Consequently, Gardner found that the leaders he studied fully developed their identities as they had their impact on society. For example, we read that Martin Luther King Jr. was a "story of identity" whereby "King helped to provide a sense of identity for blacks."[73] The physicist J. Robert Oppenheimer "presented a far more elemental story of identity" in his leadership of scientists than as a scientist himself.[74] The anthropologist Margaret Mead had no less a task than to confront "her Western Audience with the universal question of Who Are We?"[75] And the chapter on British Prime Minister Margaret Thatcher is simply entitled: "Margaret Thatcher: A Clear Sense of Identity."[76]

Interwoven with identity theory and Great Man/Great Woman theory, Gardner noted prominent variables associated with the leadership of his subjects. The most important of these are family background, the supporting role of family and peers, and "the cognitive strengths or intelligences exhibited by leaders."[77] Among Gardner's other contributions to leadership scholarship is his idea of "risk" associated with leaders. In his "stories," there is a historical rise and fall of the leaders in their lifetimes, suggesting that a leader is never one forever. Gardner's main weakness is his downplaying of the historical moment. One must stress that leaders are those who rise to the great historical moment. Without major historical challenges there are no leaders, just managers. Like the rise and fall of the influence of a great leader in his/her lifetime, not all eras in the various domains give rise to great leaders.

Gardner stated that "ever since childhood, I have been fascinated with politics and history."[78] Nevertheless, as an intellectual leader himself, Gardner is on surer footing in *Leading Minds* when analyzing intellectual leaders. Correspondingly, he reveals in his discussion of these leaders much of his own style as a seminal thinker. The three intellectuals he selected—Mead, Oppenheimer, and Robert Maynard Hutchins—have much in common with Gardner. First, they developed as leaders—and their identities—at a young age. Mead was thirty when her classic study, *Coming of Age in Samoa*, was published, and Robert Maynard Hutchins was the same age when he assumed the presidency of the University of Chicago. Gardner was not far behind when, at forty, his book, *Frames of Mind: The Theory of Multiple Intelligences*, made him widely known. These intellectuals would be what today are known as "public intellectuals," having crossed over from the world of the scholarly to that of the general public. Mead, Oppenheimer, and Hutchins became famous not only to those within their academic fields, but also each was "virtually a household name in literate America."[79] Such has also been the case with Gardner.

Part of the reason that these academics became celebrated to America at-large is that they addressed their message to the widest possible audience as well as to specialists within their field. For Gardner, Mead's *Coming of Age in Samoa* was "directed at two separate audiences . . . [being] . . . addressed to the general public as well as to her anthropological colleagues."[80] Oppenheimer's work with the development of the atomic bomb became public knowledge, and Hutchins's definition of the American university was complemented by his speaking out on "a wide range of matters of public concern."[81]

What were their contributions that made them intellectual leaders? For Gardner, both Mead's and Hutchins's impact was in the realm of ideas, whereas Oppenheimer succeeded as a intellectual administrative leader. Gardner assessed Mead's influence as two-fold: first, she "made the word *culture* and the concept of 'cultures' part of the American lexicon."[82] Second, Gardner argued that Mead "combatted the widespread belief that 'we' are special and superior to other cultural groups."[83] This nonelitism is echoed by Gardner's work.

Hutchins's influence was embodied, in Gardner's opinion, with an "emerging philosophy of education" that is being debated to this day.[84] Hutchins's vision of the "central mission" of the university was based on the Great Books of Western Civilization. Hutchins advocated a role for the American university whereby the "major texts from Western thought and literature" would be taught—"works that would be today considered "the canon.'"[85] Although Gardner is sympathetic to each of his subjects in *Leading Minds*, he seemed especially drawn to Hutchins and Mead, both of whom could be considered opposites of the political spectrum—Hutchins, the conservative, and Mead, the radical thinker. Gardner's own *weltanschaung* carries within it this dichotomy.

In Oppenheimer's case, Gardner is less enthusiastic. Perhaps like Greek tragedy, Gardner saw in Oppenheimer's "story" the tragic fate that could occur if the intellectual exceeded his/her limits. Oppenheimer's contribution was as the administrative leader who was able to successfully manage other scientists, who successfully developed the Atomic bomb in the Manhattan Project. Gardner quotes the Nobel Prize–winning physicist, Hans Bethe, who worked in the Manhattan Project, as saying that Oppenheimer's "leadership . . . [was] . . . to get a lot of prima donnas to work together."[86] Gardner concluded that "by unanimous consent Oppenheimer proved a brilliant success as the scientific director of the Manhattan Project"[87]—despite the opinion of his friend, physicist I. I. Rabi, who observed "that most of his [Oppen-heimer's] ideas came from others."[88] Indeed, Gardner's "own guess is that the single biggest obstacle to Oppenheimer's immortality as a pure scientist was his lack of scientific nerve."[89]

Oppenheimer's Greek tragedy began when he became an advocate of disarmament at a time of cold war hysteria. This led to a congressional loyalty hearing. In Gardner's opinion, Oppenheimer had been "unques-tionably a man of the left" who "displayed a sensitivity to injustice, sup-ported radical causes, and strove to build a better social world."[90] With the rise of McCarthyism and a conservative foreign policy, Oppenheimer was seen as disloyal. In 1954 he was declared a security risk and the Atomic Energy Commission withdrew his security clearance.

CULTURAL LEADERS

One of the problems with leadership scholarship is the narrow academic disciplines of the leadership scholars. Most of these academics are from the fields of business and political science, and their books are full of re-search and/or case studies from these sectors. Most simply ignore the pro-found transforming contributions of intellectuals and artists. In short, leadership scholars reflect their narrow disciplines so far as cultural lead-ership is concerned.

Let us examine the mass newsweekly *Time* magazine as a case in point. Each year since 1927, *Time* editors select a *Man (Person) of the Year* as "the one person or thing that has made the greatest impact in the world in a given year."[91] Regrettably, the editors have bestowed that honor almost wholly on political figures, bypassing the world of culture. No intellectual, poet, novelist, painter, or musician—among other cultural trailblazers—have graced *Time's* annual cover (although they have appeared on weekly issues). For Henry Luce, founder and owner of *Time*, the real world was exclusively political. This narrow application of leadership, of people who have "made the greatest impact in the world in a given year," reflected deep intellectual lag. In truth, a number of intellectuals and artists have been among the most important in their worldwide impact.

Time served a steady diet of the politically powerful, some of whom—Hitler, Stalin, and Deng Xiaoping—qualified for their mismanagement of history and would be disqualified as leaders under Burns's code of moral leadership. Included were second- and third-rate presidents of the United States (for example, Eisenhower, Nixon, Carter, Reagan, and Bush). Worse still, *Time* offered a roll call of marginal leaders (Owen D.

Young, Harlow Curtice, Hugh S. Johnson) whose names have entered the dustbin of history.

Nor did *Time* editors select the great modern thinkers of the century— Einstein, Freud, and Dewey in the modern era—much less artists or thinkers in the post-modern era. There were only two *Time* annual covers acknowledging intellectual achievement. One credited U.S. scientists of 1960 in the wake of Sputnik and the arms race; the other, in 1982, heralded "The Computer," prompting speculation that *Time* was more comfortable with artificial intelligence. *Time* selections reflected mainstream opinion of what constitutes leadership.

Even Burns suffered from an exclusively political view of leadership. Although he began *Leadership* by invoking the titans of twentieth-century modernism, "Freud and Einstein, Shaw and Stravinsky, Mao and Gandhi, Churchill and Roosevelt," he relegated leadership mainly to politics.[92] Burns's chapter on intellectual leadership was devoted to scrutinizing French and English intellectuals of the eighteenth century and their impact on American founding fathers as well as on their respective societies.

Burns was quite firm in dissociating intellectualism from intellectual leadership. According to Burns, the academic in the ivory tower was light years away from the intellectual whose purpose it was to restructure society. "The concept of intellectual *leadership* brings in the role of *conscious purpose* drawn from values. The intellectual may be a mandarin; the intellectual leader can not be. Intellectual leadership is *transforming* leadership."[93]

Indeed, Burns was quick to point out that the French "*philosophes* were *hommes engagé.*"[94] Burns viewed those eighteenth-century French thinkers as active in social change. "The portrait of the remote and withdrawn thinker," he observed, "has been as overdrawn as that of the starving poet in the garret."[95] The *philosophes* undermined the French monarchy. "Forty-three editions of Voltaire's forbidden *Candide,*" he noted, "were printed before the Revolution."[96]

Burns cited James Madison as an "intellectual leader" who derived much of his political principles from seventeenth century English philosophers on liberty. He credited Madison's *Federalist Papers* on checks and balances in the following manner: "So sagaciously did Madison state the problem, so compellingly did Hamilton, Adams, and the others conceive, execute, and defend their strategy, that later generations have spoken of an explosion of political genius in 1776 and [especially] 1787."[97] Ever the professor of political science, James MacGregor Burns missed a golden opportunity to apply his brilliant analysis to cultural leaders.

Part of the problem with recognizing cultural leaders is defining leadership. Is a painter's impact on the collective human psyche merely *influence*? Does such a painter need followers within and beyond his/her discipline?

Gary Wills expanded the definition of leadership in his 1994 study *Certain Trumpets: The Call of Leaders*. Wills argued that "we unduly limit ourselves when we look mainly to elected officials to give us leadership" since "there are many important forms of guidance—spiritual, intellectual, artistic."[98]

For Wills, as well as Burns and other mainstream leadership scholars, the key is *followers*. Wills emphasized this in his definition of leadership: "a goal *shared* by leaders and followers.[99] Wills chose Socrates as his intellectual leader despite the fact that "he wrote nothing."[100] For Wills, Socrates "was an *intellectual* leader . . . because he used the mind and its powers as the principal instruments of moral action."[101] Wills argued that Socrates was a "highly original man who made a deep impact on many Athenians" because of his "fierce moral quest . . . for self-knowledge."[102] Socrates' "break with Athenian morality" in the name of a higher morality resulted in his imprisonment and death for allegedly "making delinquents of (Athenian) youth" with his quest for self-knowledge, which threatened the status quo.[103]

In considering Socrates as an intellectual leader, Wills attempted to more clearly demark the line between intellectual influence and leadership. In this regard, he was only partially successful. Wills failed to fully grasp the concept of intellectual/artistic influence as leadership. Wills argued that: "Intellectual distinction, at its purest, disregards followers. It seeks the truth for its own sake, apart from its impact on others' lives. . . . [It is] . . . a less exacting but more accessible truth, one more to be disseminated than discovered. The best intellectual work is done by the first route, but *leadership* is only made possible by the second. . . . Intellectual leadership is not the highest form of intellectual activity."[104]

As his antitype to Socrates, Wills presented Ludwig Wittgenstein whom he ranked as "the most influential philosopher of this century."[105] Yet, Wills did not consider Wittgenstein an intellectual leader because "he personally *led* few even of his small group of students."[106] Indeed, Wills discounted such intellectual giants as Freud and Einstein, although he said "we are influenced by the impact of their theories" for lack of activist followers.[107] Wills concluded that "intellectual *leadership* is as rare as intellectual *influence* is common."[108]

Wills applied his definition of cultural leadership to Martha Graham, the great choreographer of ballet. He maintained that: "An artist can be successful, important and influential without being a leader. . . . Yet there *are* artists who are also leaders—those who attract followers precisely to advance their arts as part of a cause."[109] For Wills, Martha Graham was such an artistic leader.

THE POPULARIZATION OF LEADERSHIP

Popular books and manuals revealing the "secrets" of leadership comprise a growing industry. The modern forerunner of such popular manuals was Dale Carnegie's *How to Win Friends and Influence People*, published in 1937. To date, Carnegie's book has sold over fifteen million copies worldwide establishing the book as the most successful of all leadership manuals.

One can trace a direct line from Carnegie to Stephen Covey's immensely popular 1989 book, *The 7 Habits of Highly Effective People*, which has been on the *New York Times* paperback bestseller list for "Advice, How-to and Miscellaneous" category since 1991. President Bill Clinton has consulted the book for ideas.

In addition to the printed word, both Carnegie and Covey's books are available in audiocassette. Covey is the reader for his text. Warren Bennis offers two of his books on audiocassette, *On Becoming a Leader* and *Reinventing Leadership*, both read by him. Another offering is *The Prince*, read by actor Fritz Weaver. Moreover, some of these popularized manuals were listed in the "Bibliography and Resources" handout as a reading list for school superintendents distributed at the 1994 convention of the Association of American School Administrators.

Unfortunately, the popular manuals have the effect of confusing serious inquiry and leadership. Like the Carnegie and Covey tomes, they are a rehash of existing leadership and management ideas imbedded in homilies on personal growth. America has had a long history of obsession with personal growth. It is part of the American myth, the Horatio Alger concept, that one can rise from one's circumstances by perfecting one's character for either worldly success and/or personal happiness. Personal growth is a correlate of American individualism and self-reliance. One can readily understand why psychologist Carl Rogers found a receptive audience in America for his human potential movement. Along with leadership/management books, books on personal growth are a staple of America's reading diet. The archetypical American assumption is that one can will oneself to success, irrespective of societal forces, discrimination, or brutalizing poverty. It is an assumption that does not survive scrutiny. Nevertheless, it is an idea that dies hard in the American mind.

Perhaps no one captured that aspect of the American character better than F. Scott Fitzgerald in his classic novel, *The Great Gatsby* (1925). Jay Gatsby was a man who sought to recapture a romantic dream through the pursuit of worldly success. He erroneously believed that his newfound wealth, albeit obtained through the shady world of 1920s prohibition, would regain him the love of his youth, the rich Daisy, who had once spurned him.

At Gatsby's funeral, his father, the narrator, Nick Carraway, Gatsby's neighbor, and four or five servants are the only mourners present. Gatsby's father shows Nick a "ragged old copy" of a cowboy book the young Gatsby read.[110] On the last flyleaf page, the youngster had written his regimen for self-improvement. The first section, titled "Schedule," included rising early, exercising, studying, elocution practice, and playing sports. The "Schedule" spanned 6 A.M. to 9 P.M.—a full day. Next were written "General Resolves." These numbered six and included "no more smoking," "a bath every day," "save . . . $3.00 per week," "be better to parents," and "read one improving book or magazine per week."[111]

Proudly Gatsby's father declared that "it just shows you" that "Jimmy was bound to get ahead" since "he always had some resolves" and was "improving his mind."[112] The small party is joined at the cemetery by Owl Eyes, the only one of the hundreds that had gathered at Gatsby's famous Saturday parties. When he realized that he is the only person from those parties at the cemetery, Owl Eyes pronounced final judgment on Gatsby. "The poor son–of–a–bitch," Owl Eyes said. With superb irony, Fitzgerald critiques the myth of self-improvement and the pursuit of worldly "success."[113]

I read *How to Win Friends and Influence People* in 1947 as a young man approaching my fourteenth birthday. Since I lived with my aunt after having been orphaned at ten and was about to enter a new school and neighborhood, I thought the book could help me make friends. I can't recall its having any effect on me or improving my social relations. Re-reading it now nearly a half century later, I am puzzled by the fact that it is still published.

How to Win Friends and Influence People is the poor man's Machiavelli, minus the satire. Dale Carnegie's manual is a simplistic presentation of mostly dated anecdotes, heavily weighted toward the business world, with a simple maxim at the end of each chapter. The intent is to learn these maxims so that one can easily manipulate others to either gain their friendship or lead them toward a specified goal.

Given the format, one has to wonder at the book's enormous success. Originally published by Simon and Schuster in 1937 with a modest press run, the book became an all time bestseller. One can only conclude that the book's popularity is due to two major factors. One is that the title immediately sells itself to a prospective reader, certainly a thirteen-year-old schoolboy seeking to stabilize his life. The other is that the book offers— as many other leadership bestsellers do—an easy, painless and quick recipe for popularity and leadership.

Dale Carnegie was a poor midwestern farmboy who was so ashamed of his poverty while at college that he contemplated suicide at the age of eighteen. He solved his social problem by becoming a debater at college. His working life was a series of ups and downs but his public speaking enabled him to be a very good salesman. Later he would attend the American Academy of Dramatic Arts in New York and try the stage. The public speaking and the acting background gave him the experience to become perhaps the first motivational speaker in America. He offered his services on effective speaking to corporate America.

Carnegie's success made him expand his subject to human relationships and leadership. He sought to provide a text to his popular course. *How to Win Friends and Influence People* was to be that text. He instructed his readers before reading the book to follow nine suggestions "to get the most out of the book."[114] Among these were: "read every chapter twice before going to the next one"; "underscore each important idea"; "review the book each month"; "keep notes in the back of this book showing how and when you applied these principles."[115] This is the stuff of Gatsby.

For making friends, the principles consist of "six ways to make people like you."[116] These bromides include: "smile"; "be a good listener"; "talk in terms of the other person's interests"; and "make the other person feel important."[117] This advice is outer-directed. Unlike Covey, there is scant mention of character or a moral compass.

Continuing his emphasis on self-effacement, Carnegie proposed that in order to "be a leader" one must know "how to change people without giving offense or arousing resentment."[118] Like Covey, the book has a plethora of anecdotes from business. In re-reading this text, it is difficult to accept some of Dale Carnegie's stories at face value. For example, he related that Andrew Carnegie, the ruthless captain of the steel industry at the turn of the century, "learned early in life that the only way to influence people is to talk in terms of what the other person wants."[119] The history of labor strife in the steel industry belies Dale Carnegie's assertion.

Moreover, despite revisions by his wife and daughter after his death, *How to Win Friends and Influence People* has many examples that are painfully dated. Consider Carnegie's observation that "many people who go insane find in insanity a feeling of importance that they were unable to achieve in a world of reality."[120] Surely, in an era of scholarship on the brain and genetic codes, culture, and stress, Carnegie's description of mental illness is laughable.

Still, Carnegie struck a deep chord in business as well as the general public. His seminars on leadership were extremely popular even at the depth of the Depression of the 1930s. *How to Win Friends and Influence People* tapped into the insatiable hunger for self-improvement and success in the American psyche. Nevertheless, books such as *How to Win Friends and Influence People* promise more than they can deliver. By simplifying the complexities of leadership and the dynamics of human potential, they, in effect, perform more of a disservice than a service.

Stephen R. Covey is arguably America's most celebrated popularizer of ideas of personal growth and leadership. Unlike F. Scott Fitzgerald in *The Great Gatsby*, Covey approached the subject of personal growth with the messianic zeal of a true believer, enwrapped in religious faith. A Mormon, Covey is an adjunct professor of management at Brigham Young University (where he received his doctorate), and chairman of the Covey Leadership Center and the Institute for Principle-Centered Leadership. Like Dale Carnegie, he is in much demand as a speaker in the corporate sector. Unlike Carnegie, his "expertise" ranges from seminars to business executives to counseling on marital and family relationships with books such as *Spiritual Roots of Human Relationships*, *The Divine Center*, and *Marriage and Family Insights*. An indication of Covey's mindset, he subtitled *The Seven Habits of Highly Effective People: Restoring the Character Ethic*. Covey would have an easy answer to why Jay Gatsby never *really* succeeded: Gatsby had a flawed character. That is essentially Covey's message: one must go beyond improving one's self in mind and body to improving one's soul. (Interestingly, the 1996 paperback version seeks to have it both ways: a front cover with an "advertising" subtitle of *Powerful Lessons in Personal Change*, and a flyleaf inside with the original subtitle.)

Covey's reason for writing *The Seven Habits of Highly Effective People* was that, of nine children, a son was doing "poorly academically . . . socially was immature . . . and athletically was small, skinny, and uncoordinated."[121] The boy's lack of success resulted in negative effects "on his self-esteem."[122] Covey's answer to these worldly problems, of course, is a spiritual renewal. One is prompted to observe that perhaps the only true religion in America has been Calvinism with its interlocking of spirituality with worldly success, the latter being a visible sign of the former.

At the time Covey was already embarked on leadership and personal effectiveness studies. He was working on his doctoral dissertation in the mid-1970s "reviewing 200 years of success literature."[123] From this review, Covey culled his ideas on personal growth and first tried them out on his son. Covey's ideas bore fruit and soon his son "began to blossom, at his own pace and speed" so that the son "became outstanding as measured by standard social criteria—academically, socially and athletically."[124] One must assume that Covey and his wife were able to induce the son to restore his character.

Covey is forthright. He presented his "Principle-Centered Paradigm as follows: "The Character Ethic is based on the fundamental idea that there are *principles* that govern human effectiveness—natural laws in the human dimension that are just as real, just as unchanging and unarguably "there" as laws such as gravity are in the physical dimension. . . . These principles are a part of most every major enduring religion, as well as enduring social philosophies and ethical systems."[125] That is the core of Covey's message. Its fundamental weakness is when one reverses this Calvinistic idea: Does one's lack of worldly success imply an immoral character?

Nor is Covey—like Dale Carnegie—above advocating manipulation. He warned his readers that "If I try to use human influence strategies and tactics of how to get other people to do what I want, to work better, to be more motivated, to like me and each other—while my character is fundamentally flawed, marked by duplicity and insincerity—then, in the long run, I cannot be successful."[126] In short, in order to manipulate others for whatever end, one must have "basic goodness" which "gives life to technique."[127]

Covey's vastly popular seven habits promise a quick fix formula for success. They are:

Habit 1. Be Proactive

Habit 2. Begin with the End in Mind

Habit 3. Put First Things First

Habit 4. Think Win/Win

Habit 5. Seek First To Understand, then To Be Understood

Habit 6. Synergize

Habit 7. Sharpen the Saw

Covey blended self-help advice with management stratagems. The seven habits read as if they were sermons from a pulpit, and indeed, Covey's religious background and spiritual faith seep through. There is a Panglossian ring to the book because Covey failed to fully recognize the dark burden the unfortunate in our society confront through discrimination and poverty. *The Seven Habits of Highly Effective People* is addressed to a large middle-class audience who want to further maximize their existing advantages.

Consider Covey's simplistic view of life. Covey informed us that "there are actually . . . three theories of determinism widely accepted . . . to explain the nature of man."[128] These are: "*Genetic determinism* basically says your grandparents did it to you. . . . *Psychic determinism* basically says your parents did it to you. . . . *Environmental determinism* basically says your boss is doing it to you—or your spouse, or that bratty teenager, or your economic condition, or national policies.[129]

For Covey, the fault lies in ourselves and the remedy is to become "proactive," become the masters of our fate and captains of our soul. The key is will. It is the "power of independent will" Covey argues, "that really makes effective self-management possible."[130] The language of the successful person is "I control. . . . ," "I can create. . . . ," "I choose," "I prefer," and "I will."[131] The bottom line is whether one is willing to pay the price for success. Ignored are personal attributes such as intellect, physical and emotional stamina one may or may not possess, as well as societal factors, such as poverty, racism, and sexism that constrain many.

The Seven Habits of Highly Effective People reflects a political conservatism that is nostalgic of the mythical American past of rugged individualism. Consequently, it is not surprising that Covey admiringly quotes such conservatives as Winston Churchill and George Bush, and conservative Senators Jake Garn and Orrin Hatch endorse the book. For Covey these seven nuggets of wisdom are applicable to both the realm of personal growth and management of an organization.

Nonetheless, Covey recognized the parameters of leadership theory. "Leadership," he correctly argued, "is not management."[132] For leadership he wrote, "We are more in need of a vision or destination and a compass (a set of principles or directions)."[133] Indeed, Covey's basis for leadership was, like Burns's, a "moral compass."[134] Covey, then, has grasped two of the essentials of modern day leadership theory—the need for vision grounded in a moral principle.

Consequently, Covey further explored the insights he gathered from his review of the literature of leadership and management theory in his 1991 book, *Principle-Centered Leadership*. The book is comprised of part leadership theory, part recasting Edward Deming's Total Quality Management with its fourteen points, and part offering advice for personal growth in dealing with family problems. In other words, lessons learned in leadership can be applied to all facets of life. In *Principle-Centered Leadership*, three main concepts emerge. First, leadership principles are immutable and eternal, similar to the natural laws espoused by medieval scholastic philosophers. Second, these principles apply to individuals seeking personal growth. And third, these principles govern management of organizations.

Covey described these principles as follows: "principles are self-evident, self-validating natural laws. They don't change or shift. . . . Principles apply at all times in all places. They surface in the form of values, ideas, norms, and teachings that uplift, ennoble, fulfill, empower, and inspire people. . . . Principles, unlike values, are objective and eternal."[135]

Like the lay preacher that he is, Covey admonished us to "center our lives and our leadership of organizations and people on certain 'true north' principles."[136] Success, he warned "is predicated upon certain *inviolate principles*—natural laws in the human dimension."[137] The key is character. One cannot influence people—that is, lead others—while "my *character* is flawed."[138] In short, "principle-centered leadership is practiced from the inside out."[139] Then Covey joined his seven habits of highly effective people to Deming's fourteen points for good management.

From his seven habits, there are "seven deadly sins—wealth without work, pleasure without conscience, knowledge without character, business without morality, science without humanity, religion without science, and politics without principle."[140] His strategies for personal growth include "thirty methods of influence"; "eight ways to enrich marriage and family relationships," and advice on "making champions of your children."[141] There's an overarching tendency of popularizers to offer the reader numerology.

In summary, Covey offered a reprise of leadership and management ideas with personal growth. His books were written with a mass audience in mind. Indeed, few, if any readers, may go on to have a transforming impact on society. Whereas *The Prince* was written for an actual prince in the spirit of a modern day policy analyst sending a memorandum to his political superior, Covey offered feel good notions on leadership and personal development to a mass audience. One asks: Can millions of leaders be created?

Perhaps the greatest travesty of leadership manuals has been Bob Briner's *The Management Methods of Jesus: Ancient Wisdom for Modern Business*. Published in 1996 by Thomas Nelson, a Bible publisher, the book resembled a small prayerbook: 7½ inches by 5½ inches, 114 pages in length divided into one and a half page "chapters," fifty-one in number. *The Management Methods of Jesus* is written simply, with each "chapter" idea rooted in a New Testament story, highlighted by a boxed moral—for example, "A plan puts you in charge of your energies and activities."[142] *The Management Methods of Jesus* is not the first attempt at portraying Christ as a businessman. In the 1920s, Bruce Barton's novel, *The Man Nobody Knew*, portrayed Jesus as a salesman.

Bob Briner is a salesman of sporting events. He has had a thirty-five-year career as a sports publicist and marketeer and, at the time of writing *The Management Methods of Jesus*, was president of Pro Serv television. He described himself to a reporter from the *New York Times* as "a Bible believing Christian."[143] His business manual was written in the overheated tone of a born-again Christian. One wonders: Has there ever been an athletic coach who was an atheist?

The Management Methods of Jesus is a serious misreading of the life of Christ. Briner reduced to simplistic terms a Jesus whose purported "example" is the bottom line of every business—namely, profit. As Briner phrases it, "As corporate managers . . . our job is not to preserve capital but to grow it."[144] Unlike Covey with his deep spiritual roots advocating character improvement in order to achieve transforming moral change, Briner set his sights lower. He misunderstood both religion and business. Surely, Christ was a great leader for the moral good and for many a divine leader. Serious study of the Divine *and* historical Jesus provides much inspirational guidance in all walks of life. (Research on the historical Jesus has only been underway in the past generation among theological scholars from the major religions.) Briner's *The Management Methods of Jesus* is worlds away from such a study. "The all-time greatest management entrepreneur is Jesus Christ. . . . [He] . . . reigns supreme as the greatest manager the world has ever known. Take the life and teaching of Jesus out of any mystical or spiritual context, and you will see that it is packed full of wisdom highly relevant to my world and yours—the world of business."[145]

Many of Briner's leadership ideas reflect those in the serious leadership literature. For example, chapter 1 deals with vision: "Have A Plan." We are told that Jesus had "a master plan" (read: *vision*) and "adhered to it unfailingly," which was "a major reason for his success."[146] Moreover, Briner noted that the manager (read: *leader*) had to be prepared ("Jesus prepared for *thirty years* before beginning to execute his plan"); "choose your own associates" (although Christ picked Judas, which prompted Briner to comment "I wish that I had been successful in selecting the right employee

eleven out of twelve times"); "share the glory"; "be a risk taker"; "be an inspirational leader"; "set priorities"; "prepare for tough times"; and "prepare for your successors." In short, Briner rehashes much that is in the
various popular manuals in one form or another and factors it through the
New Testament.

The Management Methods of Jesus departs from the sober leadership terrain in its Biblical examples. In his sensible advice to prospective
leader/managers to "practice good public relations," Briner called the
prophet John the Baptist no less than "the most successful advance man
ever" who was "without a doubt, the most carefully chosen advance man
of all time."[147] Moreover, we are told that Jesus "saw the need to add one
more top-level person to his organization."[148] That person was Paul, who
was to become "an executive recruiter, an organizational fundraiser, an
opener of new branches, and, most important, a faithful and prolific dis-
seminator of the organization's message."[149] Thus, Briner argued, that
Jesus accomplished "one of the most brilliantly successful hires in the an-
nals of human organizational history."[150] *Moral*: "When you hire a quality
person from your competitor, you accomplish two things: You strengthen
your organization, and you weaken the competition."[151]

Unfortunately, this small manual gets worse. Corporate managers are
advised to follow Jesus' "example" and "stay in touch with real people"
who are "leading real lives."[152] In the same vein, corporate managers
would do well to "eat with the troops" as Jesus did not only at the Last
Supper but also on many different occasions.[153] And following Covey's admonition to "sharpen the saw," Briner follows suit by arguing that the executive "take real vacations . . . in which you truly do get away from the
office" since "Jesus got his sleep . . . [even at] . . . times when everyone else
was awake."[154]

Unfortunately Briner revealed a more unchristian side to his persona,
one that is autocratic and suspicious of intellectuals. "Jesus did not run a
democratic organization," we are told.[155] Indeed, Briner rants at "nonau-
thoritarian leadership . . . lauded at every turn."[156] And he attacks "tweedy
talk show academics who have never met a payroll" who argue that "it is
not politically correct to insist on absolutes."[157]

One could continue but the point has been made: the insatiable desire of
the American public for knowing about leadership—no matter how ba-
nal—has no limits. Moreover, the connection between business—capitalism—and religion has been painstakingly established by a number of
scholars. One of the first was the British economic historian, R. H. Tawney,
who described the relationship of the emergence of Protestantism with the

rise of industrial capitalism in his 1926 book, *Religion and the Rise of Capitalism*. Tawney noted the change in theology of the Calvinist Puritans from the medieval Catholic scholastics as industrialism began to take root.

He described the Puritan as follows: "Convinced that character is all and circumstances nothing, (the Puritan) sees in the poverty of those who fall by the way, not as a misfortune to be pitied and relieved, but a moral failing to be condemned, and in riches, not an object of suspicion . . . but the *blessing* which rewards the triumph of energy and will." (Emphasis added.)[158]

In that one paragraph we read much of the assumptions of the American popularizers of leadership, for example, the Coveys and the Briners.

SUMMARY

What can we conclude about leadership? First, the literature suggests that much of what is written about leadership is actually concerned with management. There is nothing wrong with good management studies or, for that matter, popular manuals on micromanagement techniques. Solid work in that area is bound to enhance the effectiveness of organizations.

On the other hand, leadership is quite another matter. It is the extraordinary performance that is rooted in a long-term vision of society. Leaders equipped with vision can see beyond the programming of the past to be able to transform the unexpected—in short, the future. Moreover, great leaders appear only during great eras. The rest is management, which is not an inferior goal in itself.

Third, leadership requires a moral perspective. Leadership must transform society for the good. Someone who impacts society with evil consequences—a Hitler—has not provided leadership. Finally, leaders also come from the intellectual and artistic world as well as business, politics, and education.

Still, there are unresolved questions. Can leadership be taught? Probably not, but the jury is still out on that question. There is not enough research to provide a definitive answer. Perhaps the study of leadership properly belongs to the historian and/or the philosopher.

Although the definitions of leadership vary, one can distill general concepts from the literature. Within this leadership matrix, we shall examine the lives and analyze the impact of educational leaders in our history who have transformed American education for the better.

The confusion about the parameters of influence is illustrated by *Time* magazine's 1996 list of the twenty-five "most influential people in

America."[159] As a counterpart to this list, *Time* also added a list of the "most powerful people in America."[160] The influential list is culturally and ethnically diverse. Carol Gilligan, the subject of chapter 5, is represented, as are African Americans Nobel Laureate Toni Morrison and sociologist William Julius Wilson. This list also includes architect Frank Gehry and "human potential guru" Stephen Covey, whose message *Time* rates as "unremarkable," but a "packaging of common sense" that "has pushed his circle of influence toward the global."[161]

Yet *Time* does not equate influence with power. The editors argue that "influence is not the same as power." They define power narrowly in terms not of ideas but of political and economic power. *Time*'s "ten most powerful" consist of "ten white guys in suits."[162] Only three are political: President Bill Clinton, former Speaker of the House Newt Gingrich, and Chairman of the Federal Reserve, Alan Greenspan. The other seven are chief executive officers of major corporations, such as Bill Gates of Microsoft and Michael Eisner of Disney. *Time* editors consider that influence—ideas—"are sometimes powerful" but that "in the organizational flow chart of American life" they are on the sidelines. Yet the editors concede that "influential ideas . . . will be detected and eventually embraced by those in power" thus strengthening a democratic society "from the close interplay between power and influence."[163] *Time* editors ignore the paradigm concept that insists that major ideas are ahead of their time and they cut against the grain of a mainstream society intent on preserving the status quo. The truth is that, in short, ideas are power.

NOTES

1. Joseph C. Rost, *Leadership for the Twenty-First Century* (Westport, Conn.: Praeger, 1993), p. 4.

2. Ibid., p. 69.

3. Ibid., p. 10.

4. Warren Bennis and Burt Nanus, *Leaders: The Strategies for Taking Charge* (New York: Harper & Row, 1985), p. 4.

5. Ibid., p. 20.

6. Ibid., p. 27.

7. Ibid., p. 3.

8. James MacGregor Burns, *Leadership* (New York: Harper & Row, 1978), p. 2.

9. Ibid., p. 3.

10. Rost, *Leadership for the Twenty-First Century*, p. 38.

11. Ibid., p. 91.

12. Ibid., p. 9.

13. Ibid., pp. 102–3.

14. Ibid., p. 103.

15. Ibid., p. 30.

16. Ibid., pp. xi–xii.

17. Thomas J. Sergiovanni, *Value-Added Leadership* (San Diego: Harcourt Brace Jovanovich, 1990), p. xiii.

18. Bennis and Nanus, *Leaders*, p. ix.

19. Howard Gardner, *Leading Minds: An Anatomy of Leadership* (New York: Basic Books, 1995), p. 18.

20. Burns, *Leadership*, pp. 19–20.

21. Ibid., p. 20.

22. Ibid., p. 39.

23. Ibid., p. 4.

24. Ibid., p. 141.

25. Ibid.

26. Gary Wills, *Certain Trumpets: The Call of Leaders* (New York: Simon and Schuster, 1994), p. 19.

27. Ibid.

28. Stephen R. Covey, *Principle-Centered Leadership* (New York: Simon and Schuster, 1991), p. 95.

29. Ibid.

30. Sergiovanni, *Value-Added Leadership*, p. 28.

31. Ibid.

32. Gardner, *Leading Minds*, p. 297.

33. Ibid.

34. Ibid.

35. Niccolò Machiavelli, *The Prince* (New York: Oxford University Press, 1984), p. 52.

36. Peter Bondanella, "Introduction," Machiavelli, *The Prince*, p. ix.

37. *The Random House Dictionary of the English Language* (New York: Random House, 1967), p. 859.

38. Machiavelli, *The Prince*, p. xvi.

39. Ibid., p. 65.

40. Ibid., pp. 32–33.

41. Burns, *Leadership*, p. 445.

42. Bondanella, "Introduction," Machiavelli, *The Prince*, p. xiii.

43. Ibid.

44. Ibid., p. xii.

45. Ibid., p. xiii.

46. Ibid., p. xii.

47. Burns, *Leadership*, p. 448.

48. Ibid., p. 447.

49. Sergiovanni, *Value-Added Leadership*, p. 20.

50. Ibid.

51. Ibid., p. 3.

52. Ibid.

53. Rost, *Leadership for the Twenty-First Century*, p. 82.

54. Sergiovanni, *Value-Added Leadership*, p. 3.

55. Ibid., p. 3.

56. Ibid., p. 2.

57. Terrence E. Deal and Allen A. Kennedy, *Corporate Cultures: The Rites and Rituals of Corporate Life* (Reading, Mass.: Addison-Wesley, 1982), p. 15.

58. William G. Cunningham and Donald W. Gresso, *Cultural Leadership: The Culture of Excellence in Education* (Boston: Allyn and Bacon, 1993), p. 20.

59. Deal and Kennedy, *Corporate Cultures*, p. 4.

60. Ibid., p. 21.

61. Cunningham and Gresso, *Cultural Leadership*, p. 78.

62. Deal and Kennedy, *Corporate Cultures*, p. 159.

63. Cunningham and Gresso, *Cultural Leadership*, pp. 259–76.

64. Gardner, *Leading Minds*, p. 302.

65. Ibid., pp. 302–3.

66. Ibid., p. 304.

67. Ibid.

68. Ibid.

69. Ibid., p. 295.

70. Howard Gardner, *Creating Minds* (New York: Basic Books, 1993), p. 37.

71. Gardner, *Leading Minds*.

72. Ibid., p. 18.

73. Ibid., pp. 210, 220.

74. Ibid., p. 97.

75. Ibid., p. 82.

76. Ibid., p. 225.

77. Ibid., p. 21.

78. Ibid., p. x.

79. Ibid., p. 72.

80. Ibid., pp. 72–73.

81. Ibid., p. 126.

82. Ibid., p. 80.

83. Ibid., p. 82.

84. Ibid., p. 117.

85. Ibid.

86. Ibid., p. 96.

87. Ibid.

88. Ibid., p. 93.

89. Ibid.

90. Ibid., p. 94.

91. *New York Times*, December 20, 1993, p. A20.

92. Burns, *Leadership*, p. 1.

93. Ibid., p. 142.

94. Ibid., p. 145.

95. Ibid.

96. Ibid., p. 147.

97. Ibid., p. 156.

98. Wills, *Certain Trumpets*, p. 323.

99. Ibid., p. 19.

100. Ibid., p. 162.

101. Ibid., p. 168.

102. Ibid., pp. 166–67.

103. Ibid., pp. 162, 167.

104. Ibid., pp. 160–63.

105. Ibid., p. 105.

106. Ibid., p. 172.

107. Ibid., p. 160.

108. Ibid.

109. Ibid., p. 197.

110. F. Scott Fitzgerald, *The Great Gatsby* (Cambridge, Eng.: University of Cambridge Press, 1995), p. 134.

111. Ibid., p. 135.

112. Ibid.

113. Ibid., p. 136.

114. Dale Carnegie, *How to Win Friends and Influence People* (revised ed.) (New York: Pocket Books, 1982), p. xxv.

115. Ibid.

116. Ibid., p. 112.

117. Ibid.

118. Ibid., p. 203.

119. Ibid., p. 34.

120. Ibid., p. 120.

121. Stephen R. Covey, *The Seven Habits of Highly Effective People* (New York: Fireside, 1990), p. 16.

122. Ibid., p. 17.

123. Ibid., p. 15.

124. Ibid., p. 20.

125. Ibid., pp. 33, 34.

126. Ibid., p. 21.

127. Ibid.

128. Ibid., p. 67.

129. Ibid., pp. 67–68.

130. Ibid., pp. 147–48.

131. Ibid., p. 78.

132. Ibid., p. 101.

133. Ibid.

134. Ibid., p. 94.

135. Covey, *Principle-Centered Leadership*, p. 19.

136. Ibid., p. 18.

137. Ibid.

138. Ibid., p. 17.

139. Ibid.

140. Ibid., pp. 87–93.

141. Ibid., pp. 118, 130, 144.

142. Bob Briner, *The Management Methods of Jesus: Ancient Wisdom for Modern Business* (Nashville, Tenn.: Thomas Nelson, Inc., 1996), p. 1.

143. *New York Times*, March 16, 1996, p. 10.

144. Briner, *The Management Methods of Jesus*, p. 69.

145. Ibid., pp. xi–xii.

146. Ibid., p. 1.

147. Ibid., pp. 31, 32.

148. Ibid., p. 7.

149. Ibid., p. 8.

150. Ibid.

151. Ibid., p. 10.

152. Ibid., p. 41.

153. Ibid., p. 96.

154. Ibid., p. 27.

155. Ibid., p. 15.

156. Ibid., p. 17.

157. Ibid.

158. R. H. Tawney, *Religion and the Rise of Capitalism* (New York: Harcourt, Brace and Co., 1926), p. 230.

159. *Time*, June 17, 1996, p. 53.

160. Ibid., p. 83.

161. Ibid., p. 77.

162. Ibid., p. 160.

163. Ibid.

2

John Dewey:
American Genius

At the end of every blind alley we seem to find Dewey.
                                                    —Richard Rorty

At the height of his fame and influence, John Dewey was proclaimed by the University of Paris-Sorbonne in 1930 as "the most profound and complete expression of American genius."[1] Sixty-five years later the British political philosopher, Alan Ryan, would call Dewey "one of the greatest of twentieth century philosophers."[2] Dewey's profound influence dominated intellectual thought for the first half of the twentieth century. Now, once again, Dewey's thought is on the ascendance. "Over the past twenty years," Ryan observed, "Dewey has become fashionable ... [since] ... Dewey seems to epitomize a time when intellectuals could talk to the public ... [and the] ... 1990s are turning out to be astonishingly like the 1890s."[3]

Dewey was a philosopher, educator, and social activist whose thinking revolutionized American education. He considered himself "first, last, and all the time, engaged in the vocation of philosophy."[4] His philosophy of education transformed education in this country and affected other nations' educational systems as well, so that in the words of one eminent British philosopher "he killed the subject stone dead."[5]

Dewey fits our model of intellectual, political, social, and cultural leader. His educational philosophy has a transforming moral vision; he had followers in education as well as in social and political activism; and he was cultural leader as well, strongly influencing that heroic generation of painters known as Abstract Expressionists. Moreover, his career and thought embodied the element of risk that Howard Gardner noted as characteristic of great leaders.

LIFE

On the surface, John Dewey's life appears ordinary. Indeed, his friend and disciple, Max Eastman, would remark that there was something "divinely *average* in John Dewey's early life and circumstances."[6] Dewey was born in Burlington, Vermont, in 1859 of parents whose Yankee stock placed them among the town's elite. The mother, Lucina, was the more cultivated of the two, coming from a prosperous "old American" family that included a grandfather who was a United States Congressman. The father, Archibald, descended from a line of farmers, but he opted for a grocery store.[7]

John Dewey was painfully shy as a young man. He was not precocious, thus belying his potential genius, and people were "more impressed with his sweet temper and selflessness than with his brains."[8] He loved the outdoors and, with his older brother Jack, took many fishing trips, some as far north as French Canada. In addition to household chores, Dewey obtained spending money by delivering newspapers and working in a lumber yard as a counter. Dewey, then, presented a persona as reserved, unemotional, thrifty, and hardworking—in short, the stereotype of the New England Yankee.

However, upon closer examination, a darker psychological portrait emerges. There was the traumatic experience in the Dewey household of the accidental death of an older brother, age two, by scalding. Dewey became "the replacement child," born almost nine months to the day after the freak accident.[9] Years later, Dewey's eight-year-old son, Gordon, would die while the family was on a European tour and the Deweys would immediately adopt their "replacement child," an Italian boy named Sabino. Both Dewey's mother and wife were severely affected emotionally by the death of their children for the rest of their lives.

In the mother's case, the event reinforced her "intense piety" and "missionary zeal."[10] The effects on the young Dewey were mixed. On the one hand, Lucina's constant probing of her two surviving sons regarding whether they "were right with Jesus" had a negative impact on Dewey. At age seventy, Dewey would regard his mother's "evangelical piety" as an "inward laceration," and that "too much moralistic emotional pressure had been exerted" on him.[11] Alan Ryan was probably correct in assuming that the "mother's continuous attention to (Dewey's) moral and spiritual welfare" was the result of guilt over the older boy's death.[12]

On the other hand, the mother's devotion to her "missionary" work could not but have provided Dewey with a role model for his social activism. She had worked with the poor in Burlington and exerted strong leadership through her church, in her words, to "make Burlington a temperate and moral city."[13] Her church colleagues regarded her as a "mystic visionary" who sought things "as they ought to be."[14]

The mother can be credited with another positive influence in that she encouraged both sons to attend college in an age when only a few pursued higher degrees. Dewey's daughter, Jane, would write (with Dewey's approval) that "it was largely due to (Lucina's) influence that the boys broke with family tradition and obtained a college education."[15] Both of Lucina's brothers had graduated from college, whereas none of Archibald's family had attended college. Indeed, Archibald "had hoped that at least one would become a mechanic."[16]

The Burlington of John Dewey's youth in the late nineteenth century was fast industrializing and not the "typical Vermont village."[17] Burlington boasted some ten thousand inhabitants with a "culturally mixed" society of native Yankees, who constituted the local elite, and Irish and French-Canadian immigrants, who comprised the poor and working class. Dewey's biographer, George Dykhuizen, would proclaim in his 1973 biography that this "cultural mix" imbued the young Dewey with a sense of democracy "that became part of the marrow of his bones."[18] He speculated that Dewey "inevitably had contact with the children" of these immigrants at school and in the playgrounds, thus "undoubtedly providing liberalizing values" despite his family being among "the cultivated society" of the town.[19] This view of the origins of Dewey's democratic impulse is reasserted some forty years later in Robert B. Westbrook's book, *John Dewey and American Democracy*.

However, a revisionist view was argued by Neil Couglan in his 1975 study, *Young John Dewey*. Couglan asserts that "boyhood in Burlington could hardly have been an unambiguously democratic experience" since "the people with whom the Deweys socialized had little to do with . . . the Irish and French-Canadians . . . living apart in inferior neighborhoods."[20] Rather, Couglan maintains "the Yankees seem to have known who 'the better people' were among themselves" and it was to this circle the Deweys belonged.[21]

There is little evidence of Dewey's having negative attitudes toward the Irish and French-Canadian immigrants. What evidence exists favors Dewey. As a scholar of French-Canadian heritage from a town similar to Burlington (Lewiston, Maine), I am sensitive to condescending attitudes toward my ethnic group. We know that the Dewey family was "free of snobbery" but "not naturally egalitarian."[22] More importantly, the Dewey boys made an effort to understand the French-Canadian immigrant. According to Dewey's daughter, on their fishing trips to French-Canada the Dewey boys "added to the French they had picked up in Burlington so that they read French novels before they studied French in school."[23] This effort displayed uncommon sensitivity for the time, much less for the present. Most probably, Dewey empathized with the plight of the ethnic immigrants to a high degree, yet retained the emotional detachment that was to be characteristic of his life and thought.

As noted, Dewey did not immediately excel in his schooling, despite the fact that he was a "happy" bookworm.[24] He abhorred the recitation method in the lower grades. And at college he was a "half-hearted" student his first two years.[25] Indeed, Dewey initially found his intellectual sustenance through most of his school and college years with "outside" reading. It lent to one of his most important educational insights: that the educational process is not confined to what happens in the classroom. According to Dewey, he came to the "realization that the most important parts of his own education until he entered college were obtained outside the classroom."[26] Again, in his words this insight "played a large role in his educational theories" so that he was to propose "occupational activities . . . (in class as) . . . the most effective approaches to genuine learning."[27]

And in college, "outside" reading was the initial key to Dewey's intellectual development. His "first awakening" came reading the philosopher Auguste Comte, then Herbert Spencer and the novels of George Eliot.[28] His "favorite reading" was the British intellectual periodicals.[29] By his junior year he was more enthused by his classwork and graduated second in his class and Phi Beta Kappa.

His defining moment was intellectual. While reading the Darwinian T. H. Huxley's *Elements of Physiology* in college, he perceived an underlying and immutable truth system. It made him decide on philosophy as an all-consuming life interest. According to Dewey, he:

> derived from that study a sense of interdependence and interrelated unity that gave form to intellectual stirrings that had previously been inchoate, and created a type of model of a view of things to which material in any field ought to conform. Subconsciously, at least, I was led to desire a world and a life that would have the same properties as had the human organism in the picture of it derived from the

study of Huxley's treatment. . . . I date from this time the awakening
of a distinctive philosophic interest.[30]

This intellectual defining point was reinforced a few years later with a
mystical experience. Upon graduating from college, Dewey's first job was
as a teacher and assistant principal in a high school in Oil City,
Pennsylvania. His teaching record both in public school and in his long
distinguished career at elite universities—Michigan, University of
Chicago, and Columbia—was poor by most accounts. His biographer concedes that Dewey "seemed to lack all the essentials of a good teacher" and
that students found his college classes a "boring experience."[31] In the latter
he taught seated, gazing sideways into the windows and talking "very
slowly and with little emphasis and long pauses" in between.[32] Yet there
were the devoted few, such as Max Eastman, who could discern the genius
mind underneath. Eastman observed that Dewey was "thinking rather
than lecturing" and that "his personal dignity" and "moral force" was
"very impressive in the classroom."[33]

The nineteenth century was characterized by neurasthenia and mystical
experiences, denoting among men and women a seriousness of purpose.
Like his friends, William James and Jane Addams, Dewey claimed such a
mystical experience, albeit not as famed in the literature and much different in kind. Whereas their dark nights of the soul were full of angst and
turmoil, Dewey's was a "supremely blissful feeling" one evening, most
probably in the winter of 1880 in Oil City, after reading the pantheists Walt
Whitman and William Wordsworth.

Dewey's mystical experience was first told by Max Eastman in 1940 as
follows:

> One evening while he sat reading he had what he calls a 'mystic ex-
> perience'. It was an answer to the question which still worried him:
> whether he really meant business when he prayed. It was not a very
> dramatic mystic experience. There was no vision, not even a defin-
> able emotion—just a supremely blissful feeling that his worries were
> over. . . . 'I've never had any doubts since then' he adds, 'nor any be-
> liefs. To me faith means not worrying' . . . Dewey likens it to the po-
> etic pantheism of Wordsworth, whom he was reading at the time,
> and to Walt Whitman's sense of oneness with the universe.[34]

Most scholars accept Eastman's story at face value, although Alan Ryan
holds the story suspect since he questions Eastman as a reliable source

because of Eastman's reversal in politics from socialism to conservatism. Nonetheless, Dewey never recanted the story, and the consensus among scholars is that it did occur. It happened at a tender age and before he was to fully develop as an individual. The calmness of the incident befits a New England Yankee. Most important, it was an *emotional* confirmation to the *intellectual* insight that had occurred when reading Huxley. Again, it was the product of reading, in this case, poetry.

Compare Dewey's mystical experience with that of William James' dark night of the soul sometime in the spring of 1870. James's is one of the more celebrated incidents partly because it is included, anonymously, in his classic study of religious experience, *The Varieties of Religious Experience.* Again, James's experience formed a defining moment in his life.

> Whilst in this state of philosophical pessimism and general depression of spirits about my prospects, I went one evening into a dressing-room in the twilight to procure some article that was there: when suddenly there fell upon me without any warning, just as if it came out of the darkness, a horrible fear of my own existence. Simultaneously, there arose in my mind the image of an epileptic patient whom I had seen in the asylum . . . entirely idiotic . . . moving nothing but his black eyes and looking absolutely non-human . . . *That shape am I*, I felt, potentially . . . I became a mass of quivering fear . . . After this the universe was changed for me altogether . . . the fear was so invasive and powerful that if I had not clung to scripture-texts . . . I think I should have grown insane.[35]

Addams's experience was not far removed from that of James's, but certainly in tone and feeling of greater turmoil than Dewey's. Watching a bullfight in Madrid, fresh from college on a grand tour of Europe, she had "not thought much about the bloodshed."[36] However, the "inevitable reaction came" that evening and she felt herself "tried and condemned, not only by this disgusting experience but by the entire moral situation it revealed."[37] She wrote in her autobiography, *Twenty Years at Hull House*, that "nothing less than the moral reaction following the experience at a bullfight had been able to reveal to me that so far from following in the wake of philanthropic fire, I had been tied to the tail of the veriest ox-cart of self-seeking."[38] She then returned to Chicago and founded the first settlement house for the poor, Hull House.

Once more at first glance Dewey's long academic life at elite universities—some forty years—appears placid and as befits a reigning American philosopher. In this setting Dewey was to produce 40 books and over 700 articles. Yet, Dewey continually took risks, both intellectual and in terms of his career. For example, the very act of becoming a philosopher was a major career risk. Dewey left public school teaching to attend Johns Hopkins University to pursue the study of philosophy at a time when there was not a career track for philosophers at most American universities. Westbrook concluded that Dewey's decision was "somewhat risky" since there were but a "handful of institutions" with enough philosophy courses to warrant a job line.[39]

Dewey's philosophy of instrumentalism and his educational philosophy came under severe attack from conservatives. Most important, through his social activism Dewey was involved with the major controversies of his long life; he was a model for the *philosophe éngagé*, or today's *public intellectual*. In short, Dewey was constantly testing the limits of American democracy.

His list of public activities reads like an abbreviated social history of his times. He was a founding member of the American Federation of Teachers while also belonging to the parent organization, the National Education Association. He helped found the New School for Social Research and lobbied for the pardoning of Sacco and Vanzetti. He was instrumental in the expulsion of communist locals from the American Federation of Teachers, was a major player in the American commission that investigated Stalin's charges of treason against Trotsky, and in the 1920s he founded an independent politically liberal party, albeit short-lived, that was ideologically between the socialists and the mainline parties. According to one admirer, Dewey was on "the advanced edge of social change."[40]

Given the nature of his message and his activism, it was inevitable that he would be considered a security risk by J. Edgar Hoover and his Federal Bureau of Investigation. The initial reason for FBI surveillance was a trip Dewey made to the Soviet Union in 1928 to examine the Soviet schools. Dewey's favorable reaction to Soviet education made him a target of Matthew Wald, a vice president of the American Federation of Labor who accused him of being a supporter of Soviet communism. The FBI file was opened in 1930, and it was only a decade later in 1943 that Dewey received a "conditional clearance because of the subject's advanced age and the fact that there is no indication that he is presently engaged in any activity which would be considered inimical to the best interests of the internal security of this country."[41] Yet in 1957—at the height of the cold war and the launching of the Soviet space satellite *Sputnik* that triggered national hysteria in the United States—Hoover requested "a summary on John Dewey, the educator who fathered the idea of progressive education"—four years after Dewey's death.[42] Critics, such as President Dwight D. Eisenhower and Admiral Hyman Rickover had laid blame for America's losing advantage in the space race with the Soviets to progressive education. (Parenthetically, one FBI agent's reports on Dewey noted that his speech was a "monotonous drawl" and that his "writings are numerous, involved, and complicated" and that "reading him is a task."[43]

Westbrook places Dewey's activism "in the radical wing of progressivism" and Dewey as "the most thoroughly democratic" of the progressive intellectuals.[44] Although Dewey "flirted with socialism," Westbrook maintains that Dewey was "wary of identifying himself with it."[45] Westbrook concludes that Dewey's radicalism was "limited" since he eschewed "anything resembling a *political* strategy for the redistribution of power Dewey proposed."[46] Rather, Westbrook argues Dewey "remains wedded to moral exhortation as the sole means to ends that required democratic politics."[47]

DEWEY AND EDUCATION

John Dewey has been the most important figure in the history of American education. He redefined what constitutes intelligence and how we think and give a holistic purpose to education. Much of what is best in American education comes from Dewey.

Although he regarded himself primarily as a philosopher, one could argue that his contribution to education ranks as high as that of his influence in philosophy. Indeed, his influence in education has been so deep and wide that, since Dewey, no single scholar has been able to synthesize a comprehensive philosophy of education. Yet, many have followed in Dewey's path: Howard Gardner on intelligence; Lawrence Kohlberg and Carol Gilligan on moral development; Amy Gutman on democratic education; and Henry Giroux on the social charge of education—to name but a few. A thorough reassessment of Dewey's contribution in education awaits a definitive postmodern review.

Dewey's approach to education was renaissance in scope. Dewey's philosophy of education encompassed what he considered the "whole child," that is, the development of intellectual, moral, social, and artistic abilities of the child. Learning was not a genetically fixed operation but was essentially process oriented and significantly responsive to schooling. Learning is developmental. This was the mantra of progressive education. For our purpose, we shall examine four key aspects to the Dewey canon: (1) his redefinition of intelligence and how we think; (2) his contribution to moral development; (3) his emphasis on the social; and (4) and his cultural contribution, with a case study of Dewey's influence on the Abstract Expressionist painters who established American art as a dominant world force. Dewey becomes an intellectual, moral, social, and cultural leader.

For Dewey, the true test of ideas was their grounding in experience. Like William James, this proposition seemed to answer the age old epistemological conundrum of what is knowledge. It was part and parcel of the pragmatist/instrumental dogma. Dewey would apply this concept to how we think and how we learn. Dewey defined thinking as essentially problem-solving. Only by confronting a real life situation and solving it could one be said to actually be thinking—and correspondingly be learning.

Dewey argued that "the origin of thinking is some perplexity, confusion, or doubt . . . given a difficulty, the next step is suggestions of a way out . . . the consideration of some solution for the problem.[48]

For Dewey, "thinking begins in what may fairly enough be called a forked-road situation."[49] In his classic statement on thinking, *How We Think*, Dewey proposed a process that occurs when thinking: (1) a "suggestion . . . to a possible solution"; (2) "an intellectualization of the difficulty that has been *felt* (directly experienced) into a *problem* to be solved"; a "*hypothesis,* to initiate and guide observation and other operations in collection of factual material"; and "testing the hypothesis by overt or imaginative action."[50] Dewey's definition of thinking has lasted beyond his years. Howard Gardner, whose theory of multiple intelligences currently dominates much of educational thought, defined intelligence, seventy-four years after *How We Think*, as "the ability to solve problems, or to create products, that are valued with one or more cultural settings."[51]

Dewey wrote *How We Think* as a prescription for teachers. In his 1933 revision of the book, he acknowledges his purpose to be to "restate all ideas that were found by teachers to give undue trouble in understanding . . . [since] . . . large changes that have taken place in the schools, especially in the management of teaching."[52] Indeed, in the greatly expanded revision, Dewey entitled one section "The Problem of Training Thought," and another "Why Reflective Thinking Must Be an Educational Aim."

Undergirding Dewey's philosophy of education was a strong moral component. After nurturing intellectual abilities, Dewey argued "the development of character is the end of all school work."[53] In a small treatise, *Moral Principles in Education* (1909), Dewey perceived "the child" as "an organic whole, intellectually, socially and morally, as well as physically."[54] The first order of business "was the immediate attention of teachers and pupils . . . upon intellectual matters."[55]

But the school had a task to inculcate moral values. Dewey wanted teachers to see that "moral ideals . . . be realized in persons."[56] He proposed a "moral trinity of the school . . . of social intelligence, social power, and social interests."[57] In short, Dewey equated moral values with a social consciousness aimed at restructuring society. In this sense, the "moral responsibility of the school . . . is to society . . . (since) . . . the school has the power to modify the social order."[58]

And for Dewey the school was the key institution in society to restructure the social order—not the churches, business, or the military. One critic perceptively observed that Dewey "made a religion out of education."[59] Moreover, Dewey was aware that schools taught a "hidden curriculum" of majoritarian values. He spoke of an "indirect" curriculum whereby teachers "teach morals . . . every moment of the day, five days in the week" but "the school has no moral end nor aim."[60] Dewey argued that: "The social work of the school is often limited to training for citizenship, and citizenship is then interpreted in a narrow sense as meaning capacity to vote intelligently, disposition to obey laws, etc."[61]

In short, schooling aimed at adjustment to a society that maintains the status quo and great inequality. It was a cruel irony that progressive education would devolve into life adjustment despite Dewey's challenge to build a new society. Yet, one of Dewey's most sympathetic scholars, Lawrence Cremin, believed that in the vagueness of Dewey's writings "however torturous the intellectual line from *Democracy and Education* to the pronouncements of the Commission on Life Adjustment Education, that line can be drawn."[62]

Dewey's most severe critics came from the Roman Catholic right. Set off by Dewey's atheism, they misunderstood his message and so accused him of promoting a "pagan philosophy of secular education."[63] In our time, Joseph Campbell presents a more sober analysis. He interpreted Dewey's "philosophy as essentially religious."[64] With hindsight Campbell contends that:

His is a religious philosophy not in the sense that it is concerned with things unseen or supernatural, nor in the sense that it emphasizes such topics as guilt or grace or redemption. Dewey's philosophy is religious rather in the sense that it attempts to focus human concern up on the overarching ideal of cooperation and community, and to foster "the miracle of shared life and shared experience." . . . The religious spirit thus serves as the driving force of Dewey's philosophy.[65]

From the left, postmodern critics scored Dewey for not presenting a "grand strategy for transforming American schools into institutions working on behalf of radical change."[66] Westbrook presents a more balanced view noting that Dewey was cognizant of the "limits of school reform" in the face of what Dewey termed the "opposition of those entrenched in the command of the industrial machinery."[67]

Dewey's *Democracy and Education*

John Dewey's magnus opus in the philosophy of education was his seminal work *Democracy and Education* published in 1916. The book has been translated into several languages and is still in print, being the all-time bestseller of his forty books. Dewey himself considered it the favorite of his books, and the one that, in his words, "most fully expounded" his philosophy of education.[68] *Democracy and Education* became the "bible of the Columbia's Teachers College, which was to be the central headquarters of progressive educators."[69]

Intended as a text for teachers complete with concise summaries at the end of each chapter, *Democracy and Education* fully explores the terrain of the political world of a democratic state based on education. Dewey was clear about the necessity for democracy and its symbiotic relation to education. "The devotion of democracy to education is a familiar fact," he wrote. "The superficial explanation is that a government resting upon popular suffrage cannot be successful unless those who elect and who obey their governors are educated."[70]

Moreover, Dewey's democracy was to be open to social mobility and avoid rigid class stratification. He perceived such stratification as "fatal" to democracy and argued for "intellectual opportunities [that would be] accessible to all on equitable and easy terms" as a counterpoint.[71] The role of the schools, then, is to insure that the democratic state be open and just to all elements of its society. Westbrook would conclude that for Dewey "the principal obstacle to democratic education was the powerful alliance of class privilege."[72]

In this sense, Dewey argued, the school must emphasize the social. Alan Ryan would observe there exists a "pious quality to [Dewey's] constant invocation of the social."[73] And he would equate the social with the moral. "The moral and the social quality of conduct," Dewey argued, "are . . . identical with each other."[74]

And Dewey strongly posited that "education is development," "education as growth" of mind and character.[75] It is a "cultivating *process*."

(emphasis added)[76] For Dewey, the key words are *development* and *process*. "The word education," he wrote, "means just a *process* of leading or bringing up" (emphasis added).[77]

And the main end of schooling is teaching students to *think* through experience, and, as Westbrook observed, *scientific* thinking. "All which the school can or need do for pupils, so far as their *minds* are concerned," Dewey maintained, "is to develop their ability to think."[78] For Dewey, thinking, which is problem solving, is "creative, an incursion into the novel . . . inventiveness."[79]

Yet the schools are not the sole means of the education process. Dewey emphasized that the "schools are, indeed one important method of the transmission [of knowledge] . . . but it is only one means, and, compared with other agencies, a relatively superficial means."[80] The wide world of experience was a teacher. But, as Dewey pointed out, the schools offer guidance and coherence when properly structured and raise the education process to a higher level.

NOTES

1. Max Eastman, "John Dewey," *Atlantic*, December 1941, p. 671.

2. Alan Ryan, *John Dewey and the High Tide of American Liberalism* (New York: W. W. Norton and Co., 1995), p. 47.

3. Ibid., p. 23.

4. George Dykhuizen, *The Life and Mind of John Dewey* (Carbondale: Southern Illinois University Press, 1973), p. xiv.

5. Phillip S. Riner, "Dewey's Legacy to Education," *The Educational Forum* (Winter 1989): 186.

6. Eastman, "John Dewey," p. 672.

7. Jane Dewey, "Biography of John Dewey," in *The Philosophy of John Dewey*, edited by Paul Arthur Schlipp (New York: Tudor Publishing Co., 1951), p. 6.

8. Eastman, "John Dewey," p. 672.

9. Ryan, *John Dewey and the High Tide of American Liberalism*, p. 42.

10. Jane Dewey, "Biography of John Dewey," p. 6.

11. Ryan, *John Dewey and the High Tide of American Liberalism*, p. 46; Jane Dewey, "Biography of John Dewey," p. 7.

12. Ryan, *John Dewey and the High Tide of American Liberalism*, p. 46.

13. Robert B. Westbrook, *John Dewey and American Democracy* (Ithaca, N.Y.: Cornell University Press, 1991), p. 4.

14. Ibid.

15. Jane Dewey, "Biography of John Dewey," p. 6.

16. Ibid.

17. Dykhuizen, *The Life and Mind of John Dewey*, p. 3.

18. Ibid., p. 2.

19. Ibid.

20. Neil Coughlan, *Young John Dewey* (Chicago: University of Chicago Press, 1975), p. 91.

21. Ibid.

22. Ryan, *John Dewey and the High Tide of American Liberalism*, p. 44.

23. Jane Dewey, "Biography of John Dewey," p. 8.

24. Dykhuizen, *The Life and Mind of John Dewey*, p. 5.

25. Jane Dewey, "Biography of John Dewey," p. 5.

26. Ibid., p. 9.

27. Ibid.

28. Ibid., p. 12.

29. Ibid., p. 5.

30. Ryan, *John Dewey and the High Tide of American Liberalism*, p. 54.

31. Dykhuizen, *The Life and Mind of John Dewey*, pp. 249, 97.

32. Eastman, "John Dewey," p. 682.

33. Ibid.

34. Ibid., p. 673.

35. William James, *The Varieties of Religious Experience* (New York: Longman, Green & Co., 1902), pp. 157–58.

36. Jane Addams, *Twenty Years at Hull House* (New York: Macmillan Co., 1945), p. 86.

37. Ibid.

38. Ibid.

39. Westbrook, *John Dewey and American Democracy*, p. 8.

40. Dykhuizen, *The Life and Mind of John Dewey*, p. xxiii.

41. John A. Beinecke, "The Investigation of John Dewey by the FBI," *Educational Theory* (winter 1987): 49.

42. Ibid., p. 51.

43. Ibid., pp. 47, 48.

44. Westbrook, *John Dewey and American Democracy*, p. 189.

45. Ibid.

46. Ibid., p. 179.

47. Ibid.

48. John Dewey, *How We Think* (Boston: D. C. Heath, 1910), p. 15.

49. Ibid., p. 236.

50. Ibid., p. 107.

51. Howard Gardner, *Frames of Mind: The Theory of Multiple Intelligences* (New York: Basic Books), p. x.

52. Dewey, *How We Think*, pp. iii–iv.

53. John Dewey, *Moral Principles in Education* (Cambridge, Mass.: The Riverside Press, 1909), p. 49.

54. Ibid., p. 8.

55. Ibid., p. 2.

56. Ibid., p. 60.

57. Ibid., p. 43.

58. Ibid., p. 7.

59. Neil G. McCluskey, *Public Schools and Moral Education* (New York: Columbia University Press, 1958), p. 253.

60. Dewey, *Moral Principles in Education*, p. 3.

61. Ibid., p. 8.

62. Lawrence Cremin, *The Transformation of the School: Progressivism in American Education 1876–1957* (New York: Vintage, 1961), p. 239.

63. *The Tablet*, December 2, 1939, p. 15.

64. James Campbell, *Understanding John Dewey* (Chicago: Open Court, 1995), p. 268.

65. Ibid.

66. Richard Pratte, "Reconsiderations," *Educational Studies* (summer 1992): 139.

67. Westbrook, *John Dewey and American Democracy*, p. 192.

68. Ryan, *John Dewey and the High Tide of American Liberalism*, p. 181.

69. Ibid., p. 186.

70. John Dewey, *Democracy and Education* (New York: The Free Press, 1916), p. 87.

71. Ibid., p. 88.

72. Westbrook, *John Dewey and American Democracy*, p. 172.

73. Ryan, *John Dewey and the High Tide of American Liberalism*, p. 187.

74. Dewey, *Democracy and Education*, p. 358.

75. Ibid., pp. 49, 41.

76. Ibid. p. 10.

77. Ibid.

78. Ibid., p. 152.

79. Ibid., p. 158.

80. Ibid., p. 4.

3

John Dewey and the Abstract Expressionists

I owe Dewey part of my sense of process.

—Robert Motherwell

By midtwentieth century, American art had made a giant breakthrough to international recognition. That tiny band of Abstract Expressionist painters located in Greenwich Village, New York, brought modern art to its logical abstract conclusion. In the process, these "heroic" artists closed out high modernism and established American painting as a dominant world force. A key influence in this generation of American artists was the quintessential American philosopher, John Dewey. In 1934, John Dewey extended his pragmatism/instrumentalism philosophy to art in his book *Art as Experience*. The book influenced the development of modern American art.

In this chapter I shall make a number of key points regarding *Art as Experience* and the Abstract Expressionists. First, I shall summarize Dewey's theory of art; second, I shall review the debate by art scholars as to Dewey's influence on Abstract Expressionism; third, I shall compare the statements of these artists (and their contemporary art critics) to their work with some of Dewey's main ideas in *Art as Experience*; fourth, I shall cite the accumulating historical evidence that Dewey was *one* crucial source in the development of these artists; and fifth, I shall summarize Dewey's influence on the development of art education in the schools, which coincided to some degree with the impact of the Abstract Expressionists.

DEWEY'S THEORY OF ART

Dewey's aim in *Art as Experience* was to define the nature of the aesthetic experience. He also wanted to bring art out of the museums and into the general life of the American public. For Dewey, the "'museum' attitude to-ward art has infected aesthetic theory."[1] Dewey was uncomfortable with an "institutional theory of art" since he believed that "there is no work of art apart from the human experience."[2]

Consequently, Dewey sought to define the nature of the artistic experi-ence. In his excellent analysis of Dewey's art theory, *John Dewey's Theory of Art, Experience and Nature: The Horizons of Feeling*, Thomas Alexander con-cludes that "the most significant idea in Dewey's aesthetics [is] having *an* experience."[3] For Dewey, there was the "art product" displayed in muse-ums, and then there was *an* experience of art. That experience entailed the entire process of the art endeavor from original concept to art product. One cannot separate the art product from the developmental process. Dewey states that "such an experience is a whole" that has a "unity."[4] In short, "It is *an* experience" as opposed to mere experience.[5] Alexander re-states Dewey's theory of an experience in art as "an affair of *temporal* de-velopment . . . [with] . . . progressive integration . . . interacting . . . [in a] . . . dramatic unity so that there is a cumulative sense of an overall event being accomplished or brought to completion."[6]

What is an experience then? An experience is a dynamic interaction be-tween artists and environment involving an emotional struggle to resolve the tension between inspiration and creation. It is a coherent, organic, and unified whole—a developmental process, and it requires a high degree of intelligence. Indeed, Dewey felt that "genuine art probably demands more intelligence than the so-called thinking that goes among those who pride themselves on being 'intellectuals' "[7] An experience is also highly emo-tional. As Alexander explains, "the continuity of interaction creates a dy-namic, growing experience in which the relationship between parts is perceived."[8] He gives as a case in point that "a Jackson Pollock may at first seem entirely random, but gradually there emerges a sense of basic rhythms and richness of texture."[9]

Alexander argues that Dewey was not simply "rounding" out his philos-ophy by writing *Art as Experience* but producing a "central and crucial text" in the Dewey canon.[10] According to Alexander, art was for Dewey "the most successful effort to have *an* experience."[11] An experience, then, means a total involvement of mind and spirit resulting in the deepest meaning and fulfill-ment of the human condition. Most experience is *not* "*an* experience." Alexander remarks that "Dewey finds this the human tragedy."[12]

Dewey posited a theory of expression that contained emotion. "Emotion," Dewey wrote, "is essential to that act of expression which pro-duces a work of art."[13] Alexander would call Dewey's theory of expression one of his "central concepts" in *Art as Experience*, whereby "the nature of aesthetic experience be expressive" and based on "the articulation of emotion."[14] For Dewey, "the objects of art are expressive, they communicate."[15] The process of art, then, involves not only emotion on the part of the artist but also expressive and emotional response in the viewer. "Every art communicates because it expresses," Dewey wrote, "it enables us to share vividly and deeply in meanings to which we had been dumb."[16]

Furthermore, Dewey's art theory was grounded in his moral sense. In *Art as Experience* he wrote that true art was essentially moral, that "the imagination is the chief instrument of the good" and that "art is more moral than the moralities."[17] Alexander maintains that "in writing a book on art, Dewey is presenting a radical theory of human life and conduct; the artistic use of experience marks a principle for ethics and social theory which cannot be ignored."[18]

TWO VIEWS ON DEWEY'S INFLUENCE

There has been a dispute among art scholars as to Dewey's influence on the Abstract Expressionists. Writing in *The Journal of Aesthetics and Art Criticism* in 1960, the art scholar Leon Jacobsen dismissed such an influence, stating that it was "*as if* the majority" of these artists "having read carefully *Art as Experience*, had decided to see how far they could depart from its central art recipe in their own creations" (emphasis added).[19] A diametrically opposite view was offered by the art scholar Stewart Buettner in the same journal fifteen years later. Buettner contended that "*even if* these artists never had contact with Dewey's theories, they worked with the same presuppositions in mind" (emphasis added).[20] However, neither scholar had benefit of the historical evidence that has been accumulating in the past decade or so, strongly indicating that Dewey's *Art as Experience* not only was read by many of the Abstract Expressionists but also that some of these artists attributed Dewey as an influence.

Jacobsen based his argument on Dewey's alleged preference for representational art. He then compared that interpretation with the "evidence of the non-objective character of American visual art practice between 1946 and 1952," the seminal years of Abstract Expressionism, and concluded in his reading of Dewey "how little the real world of American art today accords with Dewey's life-long objective art views as expressed in *Art as Experience.*"[21] He maintains that, in Dewey's words, the philosopher preferred "objects and scenes of ordinary experience" rather than abstraction, which dealt with the relationship of line to color.[22] He interprets Dewey's examples of such painters as Degas, Cezanne, and Renoir as indicating that Dewey was concerned mainly with representational art. In one instance,

Jacobsen cites Dewey's use of the word *object* in one paragraph "seven times in as many lines" to bolster his case.[23]

Jacobsen does not feel kindly toward Dewey. In proposing a creative experience for the masses depicting scene painting, Dewey, according to Jacobsen, was close to advocating agitprop art. "The problem which Dewey poses in *Art as Experience*," he writes, "namely, the separation of art from the experience of the masses (occurs) the less objectively real does it appear."[24] Consequently, Jacobsen contends that *Art as Experience* "never gets beyond objective reality" and was "fated to be a prescription for the making and enjoyment of illustration, perhaps just as such exists in the 'people's democracies' of our time."[25]

Jacobsen is wrong, however, to assume that Dewey had no interest in abstraction. Although it is true that many of Dewey's examples are from the representational art of the Impressionist and post-Impressionist period, Dewey did not box himself into a rigid formula that rejected abstraction. On the contrary, he saw essentially that, in the art process, abstraction, whether in Cezanne or Picasso, had no limits: "Every work of art abstracts in some degree from the particular traits of objects expressed. Otherwise, it would only, by means of exact imitation, create an illusion of the presence of things themselves . . . There is not *a priori* rule to decide how far abstraction may be carried."[26] Still, the paradox remains that Dewey's *Art as Experience* did influence a regionalist scenic painter, such as Thomas Hart Benton, on the one hand, and the Abstract Expressionist, Robert Motherwell, on the other. It is clear, then, that it was possible for Dewey's theories to affect representational and abstract artists alike.

In his 1975 essay, Stewart Buettner argued that "the heart of Dewey's aesthetics resides in his formulations of experience" and that Jackson Pollock's "total emotional involvement in the act of painting could have provided Dewey with no better illustration of an artist completely engaged in having 'an experience' while engaged in the act of painting."[27]

The strength of Buettner's article is that it suggests for the first time a link between Dewey and the Abstract Expressionists. Moreover, he raises a most interesting speculation that "the great American philosopher's marked divergence from the tradition of continental aesthetics" freed the Abstract Expressionists; otherwise, they "might have remained nothing more than a highly unorthodox interpretation of Surrealist doctrine."[28]

The weakness of Buettner's essay is the lack of hard historical data to support his thesis. He is unsure whether any of these artists either read Dewey or discussed him. Lacking these data, he acknowledges that his "intention is not to make a direct causal link between Dewey's *Art as Experience* and subsequent events in the development of painting and sculpture in the United States."[29] Rather, using only the example of Pollock, he bases his interpretation on the nature of their work and the similarity to ideas expressed in *Art as Experience*. Buettner argues that Pollock illustrated Dewey's notions that the experience of art unleashed its own dialectic and gave expression to the attendant emotion involved. He cites the influence of Dewey's ideas as promulgated in the Works Project Administration Fine Arts Program (1935–1943) by its director, Holger Cahill, where many of these artists apprenticed their craft. However, he is unable to cite direct attribution to Dewey by these artists.

Undoubtedly Pollock personified Dewey's spirit of experience, action, and emotion. But in Buettner's essay no direct link is made. Instead, Buettner discusses Pollock's relationship with the regionalist painter, Thomas Hart Benton, who was "highly influenced by Dewey's ideas" and "borrowed at times heavily from Dewey's key phrases and ideas."[30]

There is no evidence that Pollock read *Art as Experience*. There is evidence, however, that Pollock was acquainted with some of Dewey's writings. An inventory of the painter's bookshelves at the time of his death in 1956 revealed that Pollock kept a number of copies of the socialist journal, *Modern Monthly*, dated 1933–1934, which featured contributions from John Dewey.[31]

But, as Buettner first noted, it is Pollock's close relationship with the regionalist painter, Thomas Hart Benton, who was Pollock's first major teacher—and surrogate father—that indicates strongly that Pollock was exposed to Deweyan ideas on art. From 1931 to 1937, Pollock was Benton's "favorite" student and also became part of the Benton household where Pollock had "created a new, more affectionate family than the one he had left behind."[32] Also, Benton was a disciple of Dewey's philosophy. According to the most recent biography of Pollock, Benton had "met the philosopher John Dewey and adopted Dewey's" ideas.[33] Moreover, although he abhorred abstract art, Benton borrowed heavily from *Art as Experience*, emphasizing in his art and teaching "emotions, direct experience, and living art."[34] Given Benton's strong personality and Pollock's close relation to him, it is inconceivable that Pollock would not be familiar, in some form, with the ideas embedded in *Art as Experience*.

ART AS EXPERIENCE AND THE ABSTRACT EXPRESSIONISTS

When one deconstructs *Art as Experience* and compares the book to the published writings of the Abstract Expressionists (and their contemporary critics), one notes an amazing similarity of concept. Dewey's art education was received from a former student, Albert C. Barnes. Barnes had first accumulated a large fortune and then an impressive collection of the modern art of his day—wholly European and Paris-based. Indeed, Dewey was exposed to the European tradition and, when writing *Art as Experience*, discussed art theories for a modern art movement that was yet to appear, but which finally did appear as Abstract Expressionism.

Barnes reversed the role of student and teacher by "tutoring" Dewey on modern art. With his collection of European masters from Cezanne to Picasso in his own museum, Barnes exposed Dewey to the cutting edge of modern art. He also sponsored and subsidized Dewey's tour in 1926 of the major museums in Paris, Vienna, and Madrid. Theirs was a lifelong friendship that ended with Barnes's death a year before that of Dewey in 1952.

Dewey dedicated *Art as Experience* to Barnes and cited his "greatest indebtness" to Barnes who "inspired the work of which this book is a part."[35] He noted "in gratitude" that he had "the benefit of conversations" with Barnes "in the presence of the unrivaled collection of pictures he has assembled" and acknowledged that "the influence of these conversations" was "a chief factor in shaping my own thinking about the philosophy of aesthetics."[36]

Dewey's ideas in *Art as Experience* and the statements of the Abstract Expressionists are remarkably similar. Dewey's concept of art as "*an* experience" became a major feature of Abstract Expressionism. Willem de Kooning would comment that the "texture of experience is prior to everything else."[37] Indeed, the following statements by the artists read as if they were uttered by the same person.

Jackson Pollock described his method of painting in the following terms: "On the floor, I am more at ease. I feel nearer, more a part of the painting, since this way I can walk around it, work from the four sides and literally be *in* the painting. When I am *in* my painting, I'm not aware of what I'm doing. It's only after a sort of 'get acquainted' period that I see what I have been about."[38]

And Willem de Kooning would say that: "I am always in the picture somewhere. The amount of space I use I am always in, I seem to move around in it, and there seems to be a time when I lose sight of what I wanted to do, and then I am out of it."[39]

And Mark Rothko: "I paint very large pictures. . . . The reason I paint them . . . is precisely because I want to be very intimate and human. To paint a small picture is to place yourself outside your experience, to look upon an experience as a stereopticon view with a reducing glass. However, you paint the larger pictures, you are in it."[40]

Echoing Dewey's emphasis on process, Robert Motherwell remarked that "what I know how to do is paint the experience of trying to make a picture."[41] And Ad Reinhardt wrote that "it is more difficult to write about abstract painting than any other painting because the content is not in a subject matter or story, but in the actual painting activity."[42] In 1952, art critic Harold Rosenberg perceptively captured this spirit in his classic essay, "The American Action Painters," in terms that might as well have been found in Dewey's *Art as Experience*. "If a painting is an action, the sketch is one action, the painting that follows it is another," he wrote, "call this painting 'abstract' or 'expressionist' or 'Abstract Expressionist'. . . . What matters always is the revelation in the act."[43]

Most estheticians interpret Dewey's theory of expression to mean that the creative act not only must have emotion but also that the art product must embody emotion as well. This is a hallmark of Abstract Expressionist painting and sculpture in which the art product was uniquely emotional. In their painting, we have violent strokes and expressive colors. It was an art that was regarded as "hot," compared to its successor art movement, Pop Art, which was a revolt against the previous masters and regarded as "cool." The emotionality of the New York School art was one reason for the appellation "Expressionism."

Dewey did not hedge on declaring that "the role of emotion in the act of expression" was a dominating characteristic of great art.[44] His language is full of "hot" words. "To be set on fire by a thought or scene," he wrote, "is to be inspired."[45] He goes on to describe the creative act as "the interaction of the fuel with material already afire"; "an impulsion . . . thrown into commotion, turmoil"; "to generate the indispensable excitement"; "materials undergoing combustion because of intimate contacts."[46] Indeed, Dewey concluded that "without emotion, there may be craftsmanship, but not art."[47]

The Abstract Expressionists echoed Dewey's sentiments. Jackson Pollock informed his radio host in the early 1950s that he formulated his famed pouring technique to fit his emotions. "A method of painting is a natural growth out of a need," he declared. "I want to express my feelings rather than illustrate them . . . [because] . . . the modern artist expresses his feelings rather than imitating [nature]."[48] And in delineating the difference between his paintings and those of his friend, de Kooning, he made his classic remark to de Kooning that "you know more, but I feel more."[49] The reference was to the paintings, the art product.

Not to be outdone in the feeling department, de Kooning told an interviewer some years later that "I paint the way I do because I can keep putting more and more things in—like drama, pain, anger, love, a figure, a horse, my ideas of space . . . [since] . . . through your eyes it becomes an emotion or an idea."[50] On another occasion, he described his urban landscapes that followed his highly emotional first *Women* series as "emotions, most of them."[51]

Robert Motherwell observed that "the School of New York is not intellectual, but intensely emotional, though its members include the most cultivated among the painters that I know of."[52] For example, The Club, a discussion group formed by the artists, featured a lecture titled "Emotional Architecture."[53] Describing Abstract Expressionism in 1991, art critic Jack Flam concluded that it was "an art in which strong feeling is directed and focused by a powerful intellect, without apology for either the strength of the feeling or for the focus of the intellect."[54]

Dewey also believed that in having *an* experience there is a degree of spontaneity. "Works of art often present to us an air of spontaneity," Dewey observed, "the spontaneous in art is complete absorption in subject matter that is fresh."[55] Abstract Expressionist painter James Brooks said that "my work is improvisation to start with . . . if I can manage to keep a balance with improvisation, my work gets more meaning, it reaches a certain fullness."[56] De Kooning would tell filmmaker Robert Snyder that "I paint fast, to keep that glimpse, which is my way of doing it."[57] The personification of spontaneity, of course, was Jackson Pollock with his pouring technique forever captured in Hans Namuth's short film. An art critic who was a major advocate for the Abstract Expressionists (especially Pollock) was Clement Greenberg, who defined the "label 'Abstract Expressionism,'" as among other things, "painterliness: loose, rapid handling, or the look of it."[58]

Another similarity between *Art as Experience* and the Abstract Expressionists is the belief that great art had to be moral in content. Dewey's concern with the moral in art is uniquely American. In France, a recent philosophical essay question asked of all senior lycée students was: Does art have to be moral? For Dewey and the Abstract Expressionists, the question would have sounded redundant.

However, just as there is a lack of precision in Dewey's definition of the moral in art, there existed a degree of confusion among the Abstract Expressionists as to what they meant by the moral in art, which is perhaps why the subject was constantly discussed among them. In his interview with de Kooning, William C. Seitz gives us a good example of this confusion. On the one hand, de Kooning informed Seitz that he was "disinterested in the cosmic voids" yet, on the other hand, in his words, "painting

... is a way of living, a style of living."[59] For the Abstract Expressionist, the moral and the spiritual were often interchangeable.

But there is a consensus among art historians that the work of the Abstract Expressionists was essentially moral and spiritual. In his 1997 documentary, *American Visions*, art critic Robert Hughes concluded that "Abstract Expressionism had its theological side, a yearning for transcendent experience that would go beyond the things of this world."[60] As a case in point, Hughes cited Mark Rothko, whom he felt "was obsessed with the idea of an abstract art that would carry the full weight of religious meaning."[61] Indeed, Rothko's mysticism was legendary among his fellow artists, and he acknowledged himself that "when a person is a mystic he must always strive to make everything concrete."[62] Seitz would note as two of his ten summative characteristics of Abstract Expressionism "the transcendental reality which begins to approach a mystical dissolution of the ego" and "the ultimate focus of their work being a search for 'the Reality of Realities.' "[63]

Other critics have echoed the spiritual theme, and they have defined this search for the transcendent as "high modernism" in contrast to the preoccupation with popular culture, or "low art" in postmodernism. In his seminal essay "The American Action Painters," Rosenberg observed that the "new movement is, with the majority of painters, essentially a religious movement . . . [which however] . . . has been experienced in secular terms."[64] And a generation later, Jack Flam would reinforce that insight by declaring that Abstract Expressionism was "rooted in the philosophical idealism, mythopedia, and secular spirituality of high modernism."[65]

For some of the artists the moral question implied not only spirituality but some form of ethical artistic conduct. Reinhardt noted that "ethics and morality come up now more and more frequently in artists' discussions."[66] Reinhardt himself was continually making lists as guides in his "search for a code of ethics."[67] Motherwell's course syllabus for his 1955 art class at Hunter College revealed a preoccupation with the moral. Two of his seven lectures dealt with "the distinction between 'moral' (social) and 'ethical' " and "the artist as ethical individual."[68] And The Club would sponsor a panel discussion entitled "Morality and Art" as late as 1962.[69]

THE HISTORICAL EVIDENCE

What clearly emerges from the historical data is that Dewey's ideas on art formed one source of influence in the formative years of the New York School (who were also called the "Action Painters"). *Art as Experience* was published at a time when these young artists were struggling to achieve a distinctive voice that would gain them world renown. They had declared for themselves no less a task than to make American art the equal of Europe's.

There were many artistic influences on the Abstract Expressionists: the school of Surrealism that emphasized psychic automatism; the Mexican muralists such as Siquerios and Orozco, with whom many of the fledgling Abstract Expressionists worked in the WPA/FAP in the 1930s; and the three great modernists of the 20th century—Cezanne, Matisse and Picasso. But Dewey provided the most American influence to a group that was heavily represented by European emigrés (de Kooning, Arshile Gorky, Hans Hoffman, Milton Resnick, and Mark Rothko are but a few examples).

The clearest testimony concerning Dewey's influence comes from Robert Motherwell, the most eloquent and formally educated of the Abstract Expressionists. This testimony came to light in 1986 in a dissertation by Robert Saltonstall Mattison who interviewed Motherwell (published as *Robert Motherwell: The Formative Years*). Motherwell had studied philosophy at Stanford and Harvard and later art history at Columbia with Meyer Schapiro, an important link between Dewey and the New York School. As an undergraduate at Stanford in the mid-thirties, Motherwell had read *Art as Experience* and considered it "one of my early bibles."[70] Motherwell had found in Dewey the sense of process and a sanctioning of abstraction to reveal one's inner self. He told Mattison that: "I owe Dewey part of my sense of process. He demonstrated philosophically that abstract rhythms, immediately felt could be an expression of the inner self. . . . Everyone knows that modern art is experimental . . . and . . . John Dewey's whole philosophy, 'radical empiricism' is just another name for experimentalism."[71]

Mattison would observe that "even the rough, unfinished character of many of (Motherwell's) early paintings can be related to Dewey's experimentalism."[72] Consequently, Mattison concluded that "Dewey thus became one source for Motherwell's early understanding of art as a process of abstract relationships which communicates emotions."[73] Moreover, Motherwell shared his enthusiasm for Dewey with his fellow artists. He informed Mattison that he introduced the surrealist Wolfgang Paalen to the philosophy of John Dewey.[74] Art historian Dore Ashton observed that Paalen had "begun to question his allegiance to surrealism" after his "discovery of the philosophy of John Dewey."[75]

Another key document that spaced in 1983 was the belated publication of William Seitz's 1955 dissertation at Princeton, *Abstract Expressionist*

Painting in America. Seitz was an intimate of the Abstract Expressionists and was able to interview six artists in depth in relation to their work: Motherwell, de Kooning, Mark Rothko, Hans Hoffman, Arshile Gorky, and Mark Tobey. In his foreword to the book, Motherwell called Seitz's evaluation of the work of the Abstract Expressionists a "stunning effort to clarify the actual nature of Abstract Expressionism" with an "analysis not only what we artists were saying, but more importantly, were *painting*."[76] He concluded that "Seitz's book remains unsurpassed."[77] In Seitz's study, Dewey figured prominently. Indeed, Seitz was to conclude that "the idea of the creative process" as practiced by the Abstract Expressionists was "an aesthetic close to John Dewey's *Art as Experience*."[78]

Seitz's dissertation profited by his unique relationship to the Abstract Expressionist painters. In Motherwell's words, Seitz was "not only a skilled scholar" but also a "talented, practicing painter."[79] He had taken the same route as many of the Abstract Expressionists, being a "very young employee" at the WPA/FAP. He was a habitué of the two key Greenwich Village haunts of the Abstract Expressionists: The Cedar St. Tavern, the legendary watering hole of the Abstract Expressionists, and The Club, a discussion group formed in 1949 by these painters where art and other intellectual subjects were analyzed, and which Dore Ashton was to call "a significant force in the making of a movement."[80] Indeed, Seitz's changes of address for 1951–1954 at Princeton were listed three times in the records of sculptor Philip Pavia who managed The Club.[81]

In her introduction to Seitz's book, Ashton observed that Seitz was a "creative witness to the period" who was "an alert chronicler of the animated exchanges that occurred informally at the Cedar Bar, but also at the gatherings of The Club."[82] Ashton herself was part of the scene as a young art critic for the *New York Times*; she was married to a painter, patronized the Cedar Bar, and was an occasional speaker at The Club. She also was friendly with Seitz, having visited him at Princeton while he was researching his study.

Ashton, too, noted the Dewey influence. "Whereas in subsequent years the influence of John Dewey waned and later scholars tended to overlook him as a source," she wrote, "Seitz was working at a time when Dewey's *Art as Experience* could be found in many studios."[83] Ashton described Seitz's process as follows:

> In selecting a passage to present his artists in relation to Dewey's thought he retrieved an important element. His quotation of Dewey is to the point: "If the artist does not perfect a new vision in his

process of doing, he acts mechanically and repeats some old model fixed like a blueprint in his mind . . . the real work of an artist is to build up an experience that is coherent in perception while moving with constant change in its development."[84]

Seitz interwove his interviews with the artists with his analysis of their work. He noted early on that Motherwell "was first attracted to the theory of art as a student of philosophy at Stanford and Harvard Universities, then to John Dewey's concept of 'art as experience.'"[85] He perceived that Dewey's influence seemed to be strongest in the formative period of the creative process. Seitz observed that a characteristic of these painters was an "emphasis on process rather than completion" and that this was "closely related in spirit to Henri Bergson's élan vital, John Dewey's 'art as experience,' A. N. Whitehead's 'process,' and Paul Klee's naturalism."[86]

Although influenced by some of the Surrealists with their automatic art, the Abstract Expressionists went beyond pure automatism. They revised considerably from an initial idea or emotion or in Dewey's terms, a "blueprint," which "has to be moving with constant change in its development."[87] Indeed, the classic revisionist was de Kooning who painted his work over a number of times, most notably the first *Woman* series. In discussing the creative process of the Abstract Expressionists, Seitz noted that "the importance of revising a conception during its growth is stressed by John Dewey" and that Dewey "would not have condoned automatic beginnings."[88]

Moreover, Seitz described the content of the paintings of the Abstract Expressionists as essentially emotions. "The emotional qualities in the works of these people have been translated into the terms of their medium" so that "in John Dewey's sense, the emotion is aesthetic."[89] In short, the Abstract Expressionists emphasis on the emotional content of their painting led them to be accused of, in Seitz's words, "'emptying their guts in public', of reducing painting to a form of indiscreet catharsis."[90]

My own investigations corroborate that Dewey's *Art as Experience* was read and discussed by a number of Abstract Expressionists.[91] In response to my written inquiry, Dore Ashton recalled that the Surrealist and friend of Motherwell, Matta, was "'influenced' by Dewey and probably engaged Gorky's interest as well" and that "at least several" of the Abstract Expressionists "did refer to Dewey."[92]

I also contacted surviving members of the first generation of Abstract Expressionists, who confirmed that Dewey was discussed by the artists. One key figure was Philip Pavia, sculptor and manager of The Club. In response to my written inquiry, Pavia recalled, regarding Dewey's *Art as Experience* and the Abstract Expressionists, that:

> Some artists I knew read him, but not many. But when I was a student in Paris in the 1930s . . . all the expatriates knew Dewey well. . . . One of the first lectures we had in our Club was on Dewey's *Art as Experience* . . . (the lecturer's) . . . name was Rifkin. He explained some very important parts of Dewey. Especially about the Primitive arts.[93]

Another surviving member of this generation was the painter Milton Resnick, a close friend of Jackson Pollock and de Kooning. In answer to my written inquiry, Resnick replied (through his painter wife, Pat Passlof) that he had "never read Dewey" but that most of his "artist friends were self-taught but pretty well read" and "remembered that Dewey was discussed" although for some he was "disliked . . . since it's very difficult to mix educational theory and art."[94] And one of the second generation of Abstract Expressionists painters, Norman Bluhm, also a friend of Pollock's and de Kooning's among others, wrote to me saying that he had read *Art as Experience*.[95]

Fielding Dawson, a Black Mountain writer/painter on the scene and a surrogate son to Franz Kline (writing a homage to him entitled *An Emotional Memoir of Franz Kline*, 1967), recalled that some of these painters were familiar with Dewey. In his response to my inquiry, Dawson was "sure that De Kooning read *Art as Experience*, he read a lot" and that other New York School painters read Dewey such as "Jack Tworkov, Elaine De Kooning, Motherwell for sure, and maybe (Philip) Guston."[96] Moreover, Dawson stated that he was "sure *Art as Experience* was discussed at The Club."[97]

Another Abstract Expressionist exposed to Dewey's ideas was Mark Rothko. For nearly twenty years (1929–1946), Rothko taught painting to children at the Brooklyn Jewish Center Academy, which was modeled on the progressive settlement house, albeit for the affluent, and the progressive school. The Brooklyn Jewish Center Academy was based on Dewey's progressive education theories. "The staff believed that Dewey was God," one former student observed, "and came down from heaven to reveal his theory of education."[98] Rothko was thoroughly at home with Dewey's ideas. In the journal he kept sometime in the late 1930s, *The Scribble Book*, Rothko observed that "The progressive school is a symbol of liberalism" and that "progressive education is the expression of liberalism."[99]

Rothko's biographer, James E. B. Breslin concluded that Rothko was a "liberal who shared the academy's commitment to progressive methods in education."[100]

Moreover, Rothko's art classes reflected the idea of emotion in art that Dewey proposed in *Art as Experience*. According to another of his pupils, Rothko's art classes were "very freewheeling" where Rothko perceived his function to be to "stimulate . . . the emotional excitement" of his pupils.[101] Indeed, in *The Scribble Book*, Rothko would mull over the idea in his painting of "an emotional expressionist objective tendency."[102]

An important link between Dewey and the Abstract Expressionists was the art historian, Meyer Schapiro. Schapiro was a child of the progressive era, a colleague of Dewey's at Columbia, and a friend to the Abstract Expressionists. He provided a bridge between Dewey's ideas and the artists of the New York School. Schapiro attended the Hebrew Settlement House in Brownsville, New York, where he was the only art student of the painter John Sloan of the Ashcan School. While completing his doctoral work at Columbia, the university hired him to teach art history in the late 1920s. John Dewey invited his junior colleague to review a draft of *Art as Experience*. Schapiro read two of the last chapters on art philosophy and criticism. Dewey acknowledged Schapiro's contribution stating that he had asked Schapiro "to make suggestions which I have freely adopted."[103] And as art historian Udo Kultermann pointed out, Meyer Schapiro "was under the spell of the great philosopher (and) while not directly referring to Dewey, Schapiro nevertheless emphasized 'experience' in his analysis of a work of art's quality."[104] Describing Abstract Expressionism in 1957, Schapiro was to employ Deweyan terms. "The artist came to believe that what was essential in art," Schapiro wrote, "were two universal requirements . . . (an) . . . order or coherence, a quality of unity . . . (and) . . . that the forms and colors chosen have a decided expressive physiognomy, that they speak to us in a feeling-charged whole."[105] Again, Schapiro noted that the purpose of this art is "the occasion of spontaneity or intense feeling."[106]

Schapiro was familiar to the emerging Abstract Expressionists. Two of his students at Columbia were Ad Reinhardt and Robert Motherwell. Motherwell considered his relation to Schapiro "the single most decisive factor in my development."[107] Schapiro also introduced Motherwell to the emigré Surrealists in New York, which Motherwell ranked "as the second most important factor in my orientation."[108] And, Ad Reinhardt included Dewey in his lectures at Brooklyn College. In his survey course on art history, Reinhardt listed Dewey in his class notes under the "post-impressionistic aesthetic."[109]

Moreover, Schapiro was a regular speaker at the panel discussions of The Club. Also, his lectures at the New School on modern art from 1936–1952 "had a particular importance for artists . . . in that they coincided with the development of a New York school of painting that was to win widespread international acclaim," according to the *New York Times* art critic John Russell.[110] One such painter was Barnett Newman who would recall the insight Schapiro had for him in developing his art. "The issue for me and I think it existed for all the fellows, for Pollock, for Gottlieb," he recalled, "(was) what are we going to paint?"[111] He credited Schapiro with making the distinction between "a subject in painting" and "the objects of a work" so that even though Newman's abstractions "did not have any of the (representational) objects, that it did not necessarily mean, therefore, that there was no subject matter."[112] And Schapiro encouraged de Kooning in his development by proclaiming that the artist's *Woman 1* was a masterpiece and not a failure, as the painter had thought, and that it was the beginning "from which other successes would surely come."[113]

One other key influence of Dewey was in the Work Projects Administration in the Federal Arts Projects that Franklin D. Roosevelt instituted at the height of the Depression in the 1930s. The Federal Arts Program was imbued with the Dewey aesthetic by its administrator, Holger Cahill. A significant number of future Abstract Expressionists worked in the Federal Arts Projects. Among them were Pollock, de Kooning, Rothko, Barnett Newman, Adolph Gottlieb, Clyfford Still, Phillip Guston, James Brooks, and Arshile Gorky. Cahill credited "John Dewey and his pupils and followers . . . (with) . . . the greatest importance in developing American resources in the arts" through their influence among teachers in schools (such as Rothko).[114] Therefore, he was determined to shape the FAP with the Deweyan vision of art "as a mode of interaction between man and his environment."[115]

Reflecting on the WPA/FAP in 1939 at Dewey's eightieth birthday celebration, Cahill summarized the results of the government program in the arts: "At its very beginning it received the impetus of two powerful forces which helped to establish its character. One of these is the Mexican mural program. . . . The other is the philosopher John Dewey. . . . the ideas of John Dewey had influenced teachers in every section of the country, and had become part of the thought patterns of hundreds of American artists."[116]

Cahill had studied with Dewey at Columbia University. He came away from his very first lecture with Dewey in the summer of 1914 with a seminal idea that he would try to operationalize when he created the WPA/

FAP in 1935. He recalled that Dewey was "speaking of the fact that philosophical ideas have a way of getting translated into programs of action."[117]
Years later he would conclude that "it seems to me that the ideas of John
Dewey . . . have been taken as plans of action . . . this is due partly to the
fact that they are sound, workable ideas, but is also due to the fact that
they are very much in the American grain."[118]

From Dewey's *Art as Experience* Cahill culled the grand idea that art was
primarily a process—an experience—and secondarily a product. Francis V.
O'Conner of the Smithsonian Institute, who discovered and finally pub-
lished Cahill's report some thirty years after it was written, concluded that
Cahill "saw the Project he created and administered as a translation of
(Dewey's) philosophic ideas into a program of action."[119]

DEWEY AND ART EDUCATION

John Dewey also exerted a great influence over the development of art
education in the nation's schools and universities for over a half century.
His ideas on the teaching of art, which began with his Laboratory School
in 1896, influenced the development of art education in some form until the
1970s. It is reasonable to speculate that the work of the Abstract Expressionists, in turn, if it did not directly influence the teaching of art in the
schools, at least reinforced Deweyan ideas. Indeed, as recently as 1997, a
cartoon in the academic journal for schoolteachers and administrators, *Phi
Delta Kappan*, illustrated this point. A kindergartner has just finished a
painting in the manner of Abstract Expressionism with blobs of paint seem-
ingly in an unfinished canvas and informs his teacher: "What do you mean,
'What is it?' It's the spontaneous, unfettered expression of a young mind
not yet bound by the restraints of narrative or pictorial representation."[120]

In his study, *A History of Art Education: Intellectual and Social Currents in
Teaching Visual Arts*, Arthur D. Elfand charts the course of Deweyan ideas
in the formation of art education in the United States. In his account of the
Laboratory School experiment, Dewey enunciated the principle that art be
a major part of the curriculum, and be rooted in a child's experience as
he/she develops naturally out of a Rousseauian conception of the inner
grace of childhood. For Dewey, art education should develop "first-hand
experience . . . [that] . . . will enable (the student) to express himself in a variety of artistic forms."[121] Dewey saw the arts as an integral part of the curriculum and taught in a related manner with other subjects. He perceived
the nature of the artistic experience as an opportunity to develop personally as well as communally.

Dewey's ideas on art education were assimilated in various degrees by other movements in American art education. Some progressive educators in the 1920s, such as Harold Rugg and Ann Shumaker, claimed Dewey as an antecedent of their child-centered school, but departed from the great philosopher by emphasizing only personal growth in a child's artistic development, ignoring Dewey's emphasis on community. For Rugg and Shumaker, the idea was to mainly encourage creative self-expression.

Elfands's *A History of Art Education* describes two other art education movements that had some roots in Dewey's thought—The Expressionist Stream in the 1930s and 1940s, which continued the emphasis on creative self-expression, and the Arts-in-Education movement of the late 1960s and 1970s, which advocated art as "'an experience' to be had by participating in the artistic process."[122]

Holger Cahill had pointed out that the art teachers in the schools in his generation of the 1920s and 1930s were imbued with Deweyan ideas. Indeed, Mark Rothko taught in such a progressive school where Deweyan ideas were paramount. In turn, a significant number of Abstract Expressionists taught art in colleges and universities either on a part-time or full-time basis. After Pollock's death in 1956 their work became popular and sold well.

CONCLUSION

Did John Dewey approve of the Abstract Expressionists? Although there was overlap between their signature breakthroughs and the last years of Dewey's life, there is no evidence to suggest that Dewey either favored or disliked their art. The Deweyan philosopher Richard Rorty speculates that "it's possible that Dewey might have been taken to a relevant gallery by Meyer Schapiro or Clement Greenberg."[123] If so, there is no written record of his reaction to his experience of Abstract Expressionism. Dore Ashton does not recall "Dewey commenting on the Abstract Expressionist artists."[124] Moreover, Professor Larry Hickman, Director of the Center for Dewey Studies, conducted a search (at my request) of Dewey's "correspondence database as well as the complete text of the *Later Works* and found no mention either of Abstract Expressionism or Jackson Pollock," the most famous of New York School painters in Dewey's last years.[125] Indeed, British philosopher Alan Ryan concluded in his study of Dewey that *Art as Experience* was a "curious work" since "Dewey never analyzed a painting or poem at length" leaving the reader of the book to have "little sense of exactly how he would have set about it."[126]

Yet, it is inconceivable that Dewey would have been unaware of the emergence of the New York School. The most popular magazine of the day, *Life*, had profiled Pollock in August of 1949 with the provocative title: "Is He the Greatest Living Painter?" A short three months later, Dewey was profiled in the same pages on his 90th birthday: "*LIFE* Congratulates Dewey." And in January 1951, *Life* had featured a classic picture of the eighteen "Irascibles"—Abstract Expressionists who had protested the Metropolitan Museum of Art's discrimination against modern American artists. Dewey contributed an article to the *Journal of Aesthetics and Art Criticism* in 1950, the pivotal year that the art historian April Kingsley called "the turning point" when "Abstract Expressionism finally took shape."[127] Yet, Dewey's article merely restated his art theories. Perhaps Dewey was more comfortable with art theory than with art itself.

Whatever Dewey's personal response to Abstract Expressionism may have been, however, the evidence suggests that John Dewey provided a distinctive American voice to the development of one of the major world art movements of the twentieth century.

NOTES

1. Thomas M. Alexander, *John Dewey's Theory of Art, Experience and Nature: The Horizons of Feeling* (Albany: State University of New York Press, 1987), p. 191.

2. Ibid., p. 187.

3. Ibid., p. 185.

4. John Dewey, *Art as Experience* (New York: Capricorn Books, 1934), pp. 35, 202.

5. Ibid., p. 35.

6. Alexander, *John Dewey's Theory of Art, Experience and Nature*, p. 201.

7. Dewey, *Art as Experience*, pp. 45–46.

8. Alexander, *John Dewey's Theory of Art, Experience and Nature*, p. 208.

9. Ibid.

10. Ibid., p. 184.

11. Dewey, *Art as Experience*, p. 35.

12. Alexander, *John Dewey's Theory of Art, Experience and Nature*, p. 198.

13. Dewey, *Art as Experience*, p. 69.

14. Alexander, *John Dewey's Theory of Art, Experience and Nature*, pp. 185, 213.

15. Dewey, *Art as Experience*, p. 104.

16. Ibid., p. 244.

17. Ibid., p. 348.

18. Alexander, *John Dewey's Theory of Art, Experience and Nature*, pp. 195–96.

19. Leon Jacobson, "*Art as Experience* and American Visual Art Today," *Journal of Aesthetics and Art Criticism* (winter 1960): 117.

20. Stewart Buettner, "John Dewey and the Visual Arts in America," *Journal of Aesthetics and Art Criticism* (summer 1975): 388.

21. Jacobsen, "*Art as Experience* and American Visual Art Today," p. 117.

22. Ibid.

23. Ibid., p. 120.

24. Ibid., p. 145.

25. Ibid., p. 125.

26. Dewey, *Art as Experience*, p. 94.

27. Buettner, "John Dewey and the Visual Arts in America," pp. 387, 388.

28. Ibid., p. 383.

29. Ibid.

30. Ibid., p. 390.

31. Jackson Pollock, "The Papers of Jackson Pollock," Archives of American Art, Smithsonian, Washington, D. C., 1975.

32. Steven Naifeh and Gregory White Smith, *Jackson Pollock: An American Saga* (New York: Clarkson N. Potter, 1989), p. 192.

33. Ibid., p. 383.

34. Ibid., p. 389.

35. Dewey, *Art as Experience*, p. xviii.

36. Ibid.

37. William C. Seitz, *Abstract Expressionist Painting in America* (Cambridge, Mass.: Harvard University Press, 1983), p. xviii.

38. Jackson Pollock, "My Painting," in *Possibilities 1: An Occasional Review, Problems of Contemporary Art*, No. 4 (New York: Wittenborn, Schultz, 1947), p. 79.

39. Robert Motherwell and Ad Reinhardt, eds., *Modern Artists in America* (New York: Wittenborn, Schultz, 1951), p. 12.

40. Mark Rothko, "A Symposium on How to Combine Architecture, Painting and Sculpture," *Interiors* No. 10 (May 1951): 104.

41. Public Broadcasting System, *Robert Motherwell and The New York School: Storming The Citadel*, (television) New York, 1991.

42. Ad Reinhardt, *Art-as-Art: The Selected Writings of Ad Reinhardt* (New York: The Viking Press, 1975), p. 49.

43. Harold Rosenberg, *The Tradition of the New* (London, Eng.: Thames and Hudson, 1962), pp. 26–27.

44. Dewey, *Art as Experience*, p. 67.

45. Ibid., p. 65.

46. Ibid., pp. 65–66.

47. Ibid., p. 70.

48. Melvyn Bragg, ed., *Portrait of an Artist: Jackson Pollock* (Film) (London: South Bank Show, 1987).

49. Willem de Kooning, *The Collected Writings of Willem de Kooning* (New York: Hanuman Books, 1988), p. 112.

50. Ibid., pp. 167–68.

51. Ibid., p. 87.

52. Robert Motherwell, *The Collected Writings of Robert Motherwell* (New York: Oxford University Press, 1992), p. 77.

53. Philip Pavia, "The Records of The Club," Archives of American Art. Smithsonian, Washington, D. C., 1965.

54. Jack Flam, *Motherwell* (New York: Rizzoli International Publishing, 1991), p. 7.

55. Dewey, *Art as Experience*, p. 70.

56. Motherwell and Reinhardt, *Modern Artists in America*, p. 18.

57. Robert Snyder, *Willem de Kooning: Artist* (Film) (Pacific Palisades, Calif.: Masters & Masterworks, 1994).

58. Clement Greenberg, *The Collected Essays and Criticism of Clement Greenberg 1957–1969*, Vol. 4 (Chicago: University of Chicago Press, 1993), p. 123.

59. Seitz, *Abstract Expressionist Painting in America*, p. 134.

60. Robert Hughes, *American Visions: The Empire of Signs* (Episode 7), Public Broadcasting System, (television) 1997.

61. Ibid.

62. James E. B. Breslin, *Mark Rothko: A Biography* (Chicago: University of Chicago Press, 1993), p. 276.

63. Seitz, *Abstract Expressionist Painting in America*, p. 152.

64. Rosenberg, *The Tradition of the New*, p. 31.

65. Flam, *Motherwell*, p. 7.

66. Reinhardt, *Art-as-Art*, p. 151.

67. Ibid., p. 160.

68. Motherwell, *The Collected Writings of Robert Motherwell*, p. 268.

69. Pavia, "The Records of The Club."

70. Robert Saltonstall Mattison, *Robert Motherwell: The Formative Years* (Ann Arbor, Mich.: UMI Research Press, 1986), p. 6.

71. Ibid., pp. 6–7.

72. Ibid., p. 7.

73. Ibid.

74. Ibid., p. 36.

75. Dore Ashton, *The New York School: A Cultural Reckoning* (New York: Penguin Books, 1992), p. 125.

76. Seitz, *Abstract Expressionist Painting in America*, p. xii.

77. Ibid.

78. Ibid., pp. 98–99.

79. Ibid., p. xii.

80. Ibid., p. xvii.

81. Pavia, "The Records of The Club."

82. Seitz, *Abstract Expressionist Painting in America*, p. xvii.

83. Ibid.

84. Ibid.

85. Ibid., p. 7.

86. Ibid., p. 152.

87. Ibid., p. 96.

88. Ibid.

89. Ibid., p. 92.

90. Ibid.

91. I was a young graduate student at New York University in 1956 living on 10th Street off University Place studying Dewey among others. One early name for

the Abstract Expressionists was the Tenth Street School because that was where many of the artists' studios were located. I patronized the Cedar Tavern until its close in 1963 and had a passing acquaintance with a number of the artists.

92. Dore Ashton to Maurice R. Berube, May 23, 1996.

93. Philip Pavia to Maurice R. Berube, October 17, 1996.

94. Pat Passlof (wife of Milton Resnick) to Maurice R. Berube, November 18, 1996.

95. Norman Bluhm to Maurice R. Berube, July 14, 1997.

96. Fielding Dawson to Maurice R. Berube, July 28, 1997.

97. Ibid.

98. Breslin, *Mark Rothko*, p. 113.

99. Mark Rothko, "The Scribble Book," Archives of American Art, Smithsonian, Washington, D.C. (circa: late 1930s).

100. Breslin, *Mark Rothko*, p. 114.

101. Ibid., p. 113.

102. Rothko, "The Scribble Book."

103. Dewey, *Art as Experience*, p. vii.

104. Udo Kultermann, "John Dewey's 'Art as Experience': A Reevaluation of Aesthetic Pragmatism," *Art Criticism* (1990): 23.

105. Meyer Schapiro, *Modern Art: Selected Papers—19th and 20th Centuries* (New York: George Braziller, 1979), p. 215.

106. Ibid., p. 218.

107. *New York Times*, March 4, 1996, p. D10.

108. Ibid.

109. Ad Reinhardt, "The Papers of Ad Reinhardt," Archives of American Art, Smithsonian, Washington, D.C., 1940s.

110. *New York Times*, March 4, 1996, p. D10.

111. Emile de Antonio, *Painters Painting* (Film) (New York: *New Video*, 1972).

112. Ibid.

113. *New York Times*, March 4, 1996, p. D10.

114. Holger Cahill, "American Resources in the Arts," in *Art for the Millions*, edited by Francis V. O'Conner (Boston: New York Graphic Society, 1973), p. 37.

115. Ibid.

116. Ibid., p. 39.

117. Ibid., p. 33.

118. Ibid.

119. Francis V. O'Conner, ed., *Art for the Millions* (Boston: New York Graphic Society, 1973), p. 17.

120. *Phi Delta Kappan*, January 1997, p. 353.

121. As quoted in Arthur D. Elfand, *A History of Art Education: Intellectual and Social Currents in Teaching Visual Arts* (New York: Teachers College Press, 1990), p. 169.

122. Ibid., pp. 244–45.

123. Richard Rorty to Maurice R. Berube, May 10, 1996.

124. Dore Ashton to Maurice R. Berube, May 23, 1996.

125. Larry Hickman, Director, The Center for Dewey Studies, to Maurice R. Berube, June 24, 1996.

126. Alan Ryan, *John Dewey and the High Tide of American Liberalism* (New York: W. W. Norton & Co., 1995), pp. 264–65.

127. April Kingsley, *The Turning Point: Abstract Expressionists and the Transformation of American Art* (New York: Simon and Schuster, 1992).

— 4 —

Howard Gardner and the Theory of Multiple Intelligences

My universe was framed by Dewey and Piaget on one axis, by Joyce and Picasso on the other.

—Howard Gardner

Howard Gardner is an educational industry. He is available on video cassette explaining his theory of multiple intelligence in a set of three videos. Nearly two dozen groups and individuals offer workshops on applying multiple intelligence theory to classroom settings, including the prestigious educational administrator organization, Phi Delta Kappa, which offers workshops to teachers throughout the country entitled "Teaching for Multiple Intelligences: Seven Ways of Knowing," through its Center for Professional Development. There is a bimonthly magazine entitled *Provoking Thoughts* devoted to multiple intelligence theory (MI). Also there are three newsletters on MI as well. There is even a card game with exercises in which one can develop each of one's intelligences called Provoking Thoughts Game.

Gardner has achieved God-like status among educators, being a fixture at educational conferences and a member of national reform commissions. He responded to this adulation in the pages of *Phi Delta Kappan*, the bible of educational administrators, by saying that he "was unprepared for the large and mostly positive reaction to the theory among educators . . . taking pleasure from—and was occasionally moved by—the many attempts to institute an MI approach to education in the schools and classrooms."[1]

Moreover, Gardner is a crossover intellectual. He is easily recognized by both worlds of his own academic discipline of psychology and the literate public at large—much like his intellectual subjects in *Leading Minds*,

Margaret Mead, J. Robert Oppenheimer, and Robert Maynard Hutchins. The radical journal, *Mother Jones*, in its twentieth anniversary issue, selected him as one of twenty public intellectuals to comment on the future of America along with other culture heroes such as William F. Buckley, Betty Friedan, Camille Paglia, and Maya Angelou. He was the first of a half dozen intellectuals to christen the *New York Times* "Think Tank" series; Gardner's contribution was on intelligence testing.[2] He debated Charles Murray on his book, *The Bell Curve*, on National Public Radio. Gardner is a regular contributor to educational and general intellectual publications.

Like Dewey, Gardner has been both prolific and anointed as a "genius." He has published 18 books and over 400 articles. He is chiefly known for his monumental work, *Frames of Mind: The Theory of Multiple Intelligences* (1983), which caused a major paradigm shift in the thinking on what constitutes intelligence. In short, Gardner proposed that there exists seven (perhaps more) distinct intelligences, only two of which have been traditionally measured by IQ and other standardized tests. He has been labeled a genius in the popular press; "a world renowned authority on intelligence," one reporter wrote, "he is as close to a certified genius as most Americans get."[3] He has received the "genius grant" from the MacArthur Foundation, the Louisville Grawemeyer Award in Education, and the American Psychological Association's William James Award, among other honors. "He has become the guru of what enthusiasts regard as the most profound new idea in education," one newspaper reporter wrote, "since John Dewey espoused 'learning by doing' in the early part of the century."[4]

LIFE

Born in 1943 in Scranton, Pennsylvania, Gardner had essentially two "crystallizing" experiences in his young life. The first was the more positive one. In the autobiographical portion of his book, *To Open Minds* (roughly a third of the book entitled "An American Education—At Midcentury"), he begins his story with his apprenticeship to classical piano at the age of seven with his mother seated beside him. He was "not enjoying the experience particularly but neither did I dislike it."[5] He informs us that he was expected to practice and he did not "want to disappoint my mother."[6] It was the beginning of a lifelong love of art and artistic development.

By the age of twelve, he was a serious student of music, serious enough to gain a local reputation and be considered as embarking on a professional career as pianist or composer. However, when his teacher told him that he needed to raise his level of play by practicing three hours each day,

Gardner quit the piano. But the seeds of artistic interest with its creative element were planted in him forever and would surface later in his work as a developmental psychologist.

The second "crystallizing" experience was familial and of a darker nature. Gardner's parents were middle-class German Jews who were prescient enough to escape the Nazi Holocaust by leaving Germany in 1938. Five years after their exodus, they lost their first born eight-year-old son, Eric, in a freak sleigh riding accident with Gardner's mother "looking on helplessly."[7] She was pregnant with Howard at the time. The parents decided to shield the young Howard (and perhaps themselves) from the tragedy by denial. When young Howard would ask who the boy was in the pictures displayed in the household, his mother would reply that "he is just a little boy from the neighborhood."[8] It was not until he was ten years of age that Howard was told the truth.

Like Dewey, Gardner, then, was a replacement child. And like Dewey, he felt the burden acutely. "My parents had had great expectations of their first son," he writes. "Could I, in any way, replace or equal him?" Moreover, his parents added to his sense of guilt by telling him that "if my mother had not been pregnant with me, they would have killed themselves after Eric's death."[9] For Gardner, this declaration "increased the already sizeable burden I unconsciously felt" since [I was not] "expected to make my—and my family's—mark in the New World."[10]

But from the beginning the young Gardner did not recoil from the task that his family had set before him. The "growing youngster" seeking to "ultimately compose his identity," drew on his German-Jewish heritage "representing the height of civilization" with such "Jewish heroes as Freud, Marx, Einstein and Mahler."[11] It was with pride that he could declare that "I came from the same group as they."[12]

There is none of the angst in these remarks of either William James, Jane Addams, or, to a lesser extent, John Dewey. These are the thoughts of a confident, focused young man who has discovered a usable past. Yet, Gardner still felt that, because his refugee family was of Jewish heritage, he was "a marginal person."[13] The feeling of being an outsider was to remain with him throughout his career.

Gardner did not lay great stress on his early education. He regarded his schooling as having "played a much smaller role in my earlier life."[14] Although his mother and father were not college educated, had few books at home, and were unable to guide him or his younger sister, Marion, about "scholastic choices to make," he regarded the greatest influence on his "growth" to be his "extended family [and its] values [the stress on education]."[15]

His parents recognized his precocity. He had taught himself to read at an early age before his schooling. By the time he was 13, his parents had him tested for his intellectual abilities—a five-day ordeal, at the end of which the psychologist concluded that young Howard was "very gifted . . . [and] . . . could probably do anything he wanted."[16]

He "found little to say" of his elementary public school years except that the "teachers were well meaning . . . but limited."[17] At Scranton Central High School in Pennsylvania, he was "learning remarkably little from the well-meaning but largely ignorant faculty."[18] Transferring to Wyoming Seminary in Pennsylvania, he was to find the beginnings of his "identity," although, at first, he had "totally forgotten the importance" of the school in his personal development (which would last for twenty-five years).[19]

At Wyoming Seminary, Gardner made enormous social strides. Not suited to athletics, but immersed in music and words, he became the newspaper editor and leader of the key high school clique. "For the first time," he would reflect, "I felt somewhat less marginal. I had an identity now as a young scholar and as a leader of the school."[20] He regarded the teachers more positively, noting that these teachers had "attended first-rate universities" and, although not scholars, "cared about intellectual pursuits."[21]

Yet, despite his scholarly proclivities Gardner's choice of college was haphazard. He had been attracted to Notre Dame and Georgia Tech because of its attendant football publicity and "catchy 'fight' songs."[22] Yet he learned of Harvard, his ultimate choice, by reading the back of an issue of *Classic Comics*. Harvard was to prove the turning point where he "soon realized that things would never be the same again."[23]

Harvard was a moveable intellectual feast. For the provincial from Scranton, who had been "cast into an uninteresting, intellectually stagnant, and economically depressed Pennsylvania valley," Harvard was the realization of his dreams.[24] Gardner would taste "at least a morsel of the many things a great university had to offer" from a star-studded faculty.[25] He cited a list of "influences" among professors and readings, and he would have a "special craving for intellectual mentors," two of whom would change the course of his life—Erik Erikson and Jerome Bruner. "Erikson was the perfect initial guide," he tells us, and "Bruner, the ideal career model."[26] He would switch interests from history and political science, along with his intention to becoming either a lawyer or physician, to the "hard sciences" and a life as a psychologist.

He found the work of the psychologist Jean Piaget and the cultural anthropologist Claude Levi-Strauss to "powerfully influence my thinking."[27]

Piaget's ideas on the nature of a child's mind proved to be "exciting."[28] Levi-Strauss's work was "equally imposing."[29] Indeed, on his honeymoon he attended a lecture by Piaget in London since he "wanted the master of our chosen field "to bless our union.'"[30] But his was to be a running battle with Piaget, "a three decade-long quarrel with the Piagetian legacy."[31] He would also absorb Dewey and eventually distance himself somewhat from Dewey's ideas on school reform.

While completing a postgraduate year at the London School of Economics, Gardner was confirmed as a cultural modernist with strong roots in the Eurocentric tradition. He acknowledged that he "became a full—and perhaps uncritical—devotee of a modernist sensibility" who was more comfortable with "Picasso, Stravinsky, Eliot and Woolf" than the postmodern culture stars of his era.[32] He tried his hand at writing fiction, completing a "thousand-page novel" that was a "thinly disguised autobiographical account" in three weeks.[33] He followed this literary endeavor with essays and reviews on a variety of topics from culture criticism to movie reviews. These offerings were submitted to public intellectual journals such as *Commentary* and *Harper's*. None of this work was accepted for publication. Yet, it was a fruitful apprenticeship that would eventually lead to an extremely prolific number of books and articles.

Harvard Graduate School was not such a moveable feast. Gardner found the "professional" atmosphere uncongenial, and his mentors, Erikson and Bruner, with whom he "had been friendly began to treat him differently."[34] He was expected to become expert in a traditional field of psychology and conduct experimental research. These expectations left him depressed so that "after a decade of relatively free-ranging intellectual growth, I was back upon the piano bench, playing someone else's music."[35] After six months, he "considered quitting."[36]

His emerging direction as a psychologist cut against the grain of traditional psychology. His professors worried that he "was apparently not involved in research."[37] He was interested in artistic development and a wide range of psychological and philosophical thought. He had apprenticed to the philosopher Nelson Goodman working with Goodman's newly formed Project Zero at the Graduate School of Education examining artistic knowledge. After passing his doctoral written examinations, he nearly flunked his orals because one of the examining professors did not consider "the topic of artistic development" a psychological "field."[38] He had wanted to elongate an article he had written noting the similarities between Piaget and Levi-Strauss into his dissertation, but was dissuaded by his advisor who recommended an experimental study. Consequently, his dissertation was on artistic sensitivity in children; it took three months for him to accumulate his data. After receiving his doctorate he mused that he had become an outsider within his chosen discipline: "I was distinctly an odd bird. . . . I did not have an area . . . my 'skills' were appropriate only for a field that might not exist; and my writing flowed completely outside the mainstream. . . . What had happened to me?"[39]

Gardner was able to nurture his two "long-term interests," art and creativity, into a series of studies, mostly qualitative in nature.[40] These interests led him to the study of intelligence. At least eight of his book titles have the word *mind* in them. After graduate school, Gardner worked at a Boston Veteran's Administration hospital where he had hoped to find "artists who have suffered a stroke" so that he could study "the fate of creativity following the ravages of brain damage" but none of the patients had been artists.[41] He redirected his study so that he "*could* assess artistic abilities" among the patients.[42] These early studies prepared him for the huge task of examining what constitutes intelligence. He recalled that "as early as 1976, I had outlined a book called 'Kinds of Minds' . . . [and that] . . . by the middle 1970s, I had already arrived at the central methodological insight that undergirds my research."[43]

In 1979, Gardner, by now a research associate at Harvard, was asked by the dean of the graduate school of education, Paul Yvislaker, to head a team of Harvard scholars to study "what 'human potential' really is."[44] The project was underwritten by the Bernard Van Leer Foundation in the Netherlands for a four year period with a budget of one and a half million dollars. It was to prove a defining moment for Gardner. Having had a strong apprenticeship and having published a number of books in the field, he was at age 36 poised for a major breakthrough. "I had early decided on my plan," he writes, "I had elected to define various human capacities as different 'intelligences' and to present my case as an attack on unitary concepts of intellect."[45] The result was his signature study, *Frames of Mind: The Theory of Multiple Intelligences*. The outsider was to turn the psychological establishment upside down. But the psychological community initially was skeptical although the educational community embraced him wholeheartedly and the general public was "largely positive."[46]

FRAMES OF MIND

Howard Gardner had published five respected books on the relationship of art, creativity and the brain before publishing *Frames of Mind: The Theory of Multiple Intelligences* in 1983. Gardner was forty at the time and had no idea that the book would have such an enormous impact. Ten years later he would reflect that he had viewed the work "principally as a contribution to my own discipline of development psychology" and that he "did not anticipate that the book would find a receptive audience in so many circles across so many lands."[47] Gardner had become—in the words he was to use to describe Margaret Mead—"virtually a household name in literate America."[48]

Frames of Mind is a sophisticated review of largely qualitative research and some quantitative data. Scholarship can be of two sorts; one, original data with a significant interpretation; or two, a significant reinterpretation of existing data; *Frames of Mind* is the latter. Gardner acknowledges that *Frames of Mind* is largely descriptive using case studies to exemplify his "candidate" list of seven separate intelligences and that, moreover, one can find traces of the idea of multiple intelligences in history. But his aim in the book is to "establish that 'multiple intelligences' is an idea whose time has come."[49]

His method was to review "evidence from a large and hitherto unrelated group of sources" that included "studies of prodigies, gifted individuals, brain damaged patients, *idiots savants*, individuals from different cultures," and compare them to "normal children, normal adults."[50]

From this review he had distilled seven "candidate" intelligences (there possibly could be more). He would then anchor a subsequent work, *Creating Minds* in a case study approach of "six men and one woman who early in this century were instrumental in formulating modern consciousness in the West . . . Sigmund Freud, Albert Einstein, Igor Stravinsky, Pablo Picasso, T. S. Eliot, Martha Graham, and Mahatma Gandhi . . . [whereby each] . . . exemplifies one of the seven intelligences."[51]

Frames of Mind is a brilliant, provocative, and gracefully written book. Gardner gives a straightforward account of his theory of multiple intelligences. Instead of one general intelligence, "g"—as posited by psychometricians a century ago, he contends that there are at least seven separate intelligences, each correlating to the other, with the possibility of more to be discovered. The psychometrician's "g" became the standard interpretation partly because it was easily measurable by IQ and other related standardized tests. But Gardner forcefully argues that the IQ and other standardized tests only measure a small portion of intelligence, to wit, linguistic and logical/mathematical abilities. In "surveying the work of other scholars" on brain research and cognition, Gardner comes up with the major idea that there is more to intelligence than can be measured by the IQ and offers his theory of multiple intelligence, thus "proposing a new orientation."[52]

The seven intelligences, in the order that Gardner presented them, are: (1) linguistic, (2) musical, (3) logical/mathematical, (4) spatial, (5) bodily-kinesthetic, (6) intrapersonal, and (7) interpersonal. The first four are self-evident. Bodily-kinesthetic relates to athletic ability whether it be as a ballet dancer or as an athlete. The latter two "personal" intelligences refer, respectively, to knowledge of oneself (perhaps the most difficult to develop) and the intelligence to deal effectively with others and the outside world. Each person has all seven intelligences in varying degrees. There are other intelligences, perhaps, and Gardner has mused that "some form of 'spiritual intelligence' may well exist."[53] The decision to limit the search of intelligences to available research was "a deliberate one" to contain a "manageable number" useful to the practitioner.[54]

Gardner departs from the psychometricians in another way. Whereas "g" for them is also genetically fixed, Gardner shows his indebtedness to Dewey and Piaget by positing a developmental aspect to intelligence. He believes in a genetic component, but one which can be developed by learning and practice. *Frames of Mind* has sections on "the *development* of linguistic intelligence," "the *development* of musical intelligence," "the *development* of spatial intelligence," "the *development* of bodily-kinesthetic intelligence" (emphasis added).

It is a grand idea that has done much to relegate the concept of IQ to the dustbins of history. Gardner derived this insight from his work in the arts, both as practitioner and scholar, and with the brain-damaged patients he studied in the hospital. His acquaintance with great minds at Harvard has given him a further appreciation of the possibilities of mind. In reading *Frames of Mind*, the examples range from the genius—Da Vinci, Mozart, Einstein, and Picasso—to the *idiots savants*—"more than a few" who have demonstrated "unusual musical *skills*."[55]

However, it is an unproven theory needing experimental verification. But as new research in brain and cognition develop, the evidence weighs in heavily on Gardner's side. Yet Gardner exercises caution by referring to his seven intelligences as "useful fictions" for both experimental verification and as a guide to educational practice.[56] He states that "until now we have supported the fiction that adult roles depend largely on the flowering of a single intelligence."[57] But Gardner warns that "the notion of multiple intelligences is hardly a proven fact."[58] He goes on to note that "controlled experiments could either confirm or disconfirm MI" or that "one or more of the justified" or that "there are candidates that I have not considered."[59] And in an oft-quoted statement, Gardner states that "these intelligences are fictions—at most, useful fictions—for discussing processes and abilities that (like all of life) are continuous with one another."[60]

Frames of Mind was a crossover book from the beginning. It was initially reviewed in the general press as well as in academic journals. Neither venue hailed the birth of a revolutionary idea. Most reviewers damned the book with faint praise. For example, *Harper's* reviewer would call "Gardner's relatively *errant* approach still worthwhile" because the nature of intelligence "is still an open question" (emphasis added).[61]

Gardner's former mentor Jerome Bruner's assessment of *Frames of Mind* in the *New York Review of Books* was not much better. First, the editor of the *Review* did not consider the book of major importance, relegating it to the back pages in a joint review with three lesser, forgettable books on child development. Bruner sought to be kind to his former protégé, but when one deconstructs the essay, one senses a high level of discomfort with MI theory. Bruner cleverly uses (or misuses) Gardner's quotes to undermine him. Asking rhetorically, "How far does he succeed?", he answers: "According to his own critical evaluation (which comprises one of the best chapters in the book), only moderately well, but that is not bad for a beginning."[62] And he concludes that "as Gardner himself says, "These intelligences . . . are at most useful fictions . . . sets of knowhow'. With this conclusion, I find myself in complete agreement."[63] Yet he cloaks his discomfort for MI theory by calling *Frames of Mind* "heroic" and "in many ways a brilliant book" with an "approach . . . so far beyond the data crunching of mental testers that it deserves to be cheered."[64]

The New York Sunday Times gave *Frames of Mind* a more important review, but one that was more severe than Bruner's ambivalent essay. The review was featured on the front page [placed on page 5], a right handed full page review making it the second most important review in the issue. The reviewer, George A. Miller, a Distinguished Professor of Psychology at Princeton, called MI "less a scientific theory than a line on which (Gardner) hangs out his intellectual laundry."[65] For Miller, "the result is good reading . . . but how much of it will pass the critical test of further research is debatable."[66] Moreover, Miller argues, "it is probable, therefore, that Mr. Gardner's catalogue of intelligences is wrong."[67] Yet, Miller gives Gardner credit for "his attempt to integrate diverse approaches" for which he "deserves everyone's gratitude."[68] Since a positive review in the *Sunday Times Book Review* translates into sales, it is a wonder that *Frames of Mind* was not remaindered in bookstores, much less becoming a bestseller. That it survived despite such a poor reception is a testament to the vitality of the idea.

But, *Frames of Mind* was to dramatically change Gardner's life. As he recounts the experience some ten years later, he was to become famous to at least one group—school practitioners:

> Some months after the publication of *FRAMES*, I was invited to address the annual meeting of the National Association of Independent Schools. . . . I expected the typical audience of fifty to seventy-five persons. . . . Instead . . . I encountered a new experience: a much larger hall, entirely filled with people, and humming with excitement. It was almost as if I had walked by mistake into a talk given by someone who was famous . . . this was an unprecedented experience for me, but . . . one with which I was to become increasingly familiar in subsequent years.

> Before that moment, I had concluded that my book was not of much interest to my fellow psychologists . . . [but] . . . there was another audience with a genuine interest in my ideas—the audience of professional educators.[69]

Gardner had made his mark.

It was inevitable that there would be a counterattack from the psychometric community. In 1994, psychologist Richard Herrnstein and political scientist Charles Murray responded with a huge tome entitled *The Bell Curve*. The authors updated the quantitative research that had been assembled by psychologist Arthur Jensen in 1969 ("How Much Can We Boost IQ and Scholastic Achievement?" *Harvard Educational Review*), which purported to show that there was a general intelligence which was largely heritable and that social class was largely determined by this intelligence. (I criticized Jensen in *Commonweal* [October 10, 1969] in my essay *Jensen's Complaint*.) Herrnstein accumulated the psychometric evidence and Murray drew the implications for social policy. As in Jensen's work, *The Bell Curve* had a subtext with racist overtones: African-Americans score lower on IQ and standardized tests; ergo, their intelligence must be of a lower order. In writing *The Bell Curve*, the authors confronted the charges made against Jensen. They peremptorily dismissed Gardner and his theory of multiple intelligences on the basis that Gardner's "work is uniquely devoid of psychometric or other quantitative evidence."[70]

The Bell Curve became a cause celebre, the subject of a media feeding frenzy. Newspapers, newsweeklies, television, and radio were bombarded with opinions and guest interviews with Charles Murray. Murray even took his act on the road with a polite debate with Alvin Poussaint at various colleges. *The Bell Curve* became the subject of conversation at cocktail and dinner parties. It enjoyed Andy Warhol's famous fifteen minutes of fame, and more curious still, in all the fuss and furor over the book, scarcely was there a mention of Howard Gardner's Theory of Multiple Intelligences, although the ten year anniversary edition of *Frames of Mind* was published a short year before *The Bell Curve*.

The Bell Curve became one of the great unread bestsellers of modern times. Opponents, including the President of the United States, denounced the book without so much as cracking the book's binding. As an example, President Bill Clinton, in response to a question from a reporter on *The Bell Curve* at a news conference, would declare: "Well, if you're asking me first of all about Mr. Murray's book, I haven't read it. But as I understand the argument of it, I have to disagree with the proposition that there are inherent racially based differences in the capacity of the American people to reach their full potential. I just don't agree with that. It goes against our entire history and whole tradition."[71]

Newsweek would call *The Bell Curve* an "angry book."[72] *The New Republic* ran seventeen essays from contributors denouncing the book, but none was from Howard Gardner. *New York Times* African American writers, Bob Herbert and Brent Staples, dismissed the book as "bogus" and "pseudo-science" without displaying that they had read the book.[73]

However, the book had its advocates. For the most part, the *New York Times* received the book well in its book review pages and added a handsome front page profile of Charles Murray in their *Sunday Times Magazine* section. Economist Peter Passell reviewed the book in the *Times* daily pages, hailing the book as an "appeal to sweet reason" although "some critics have been inclined to hang the defendants without a trial."[74] The *Sunday Times Book Review* treatment by Malcolm Browne, the newspaper's science reporter, was prominent, extensive, and accepted the argument that "*The Bell Curve* makes a strong case that America's population is becoming dangerously polarized between a smart, rich, educated elite and—a population of unintelligent, poor and uneducated people."[75] The *Sunday Times Magazine* profile of Murray by another *Times* reporter, Jason DeParle, was essentially flattering despite the provocative title that Murray was "the most dangerous conservative."[76] DeParle consulted few critics in the field of psychology, save Robert Sternberg of Yale whose theory of a practical intelligence is somewhat similar to Gardner's personal intelligences.

But it would have been unimaginable for the father of the theory of multiple intelligences to not be called upon to challenge *The Bell Curve*.

Gardner gave a brilliant rebuttal of the book in the magazine, *The American Prospect*, as well as engaging Murray in debate on National Public Radio.

In his essay in *The American Prospect*, Gardner attacked the author's database and policy conclusions in robust language. He labeled *The Bell Curve* a "strange work" based on scientific data that "was questionable when it was proposed a century ago" and that "has now been completely supplanted by the development of the cognitive sciences and neurosciences."[77] He condemned the policy recommendations as "exotic" and grounded on "subliminal messages" of race and class that provide a "frightening . . . innuendo."[78] For Gardner, this was "scholarly brinkmanship" involving "special pleading, based on a biased reading of the data."[79] Moreover, he cautioned that "there is never a direct road from research to policy."[80]

In opposition to the psychometric data, Gardner offered his theory of multiple intelligences, as well as Sternberg's studies on practical intelligence and Claude Steele's work on cultural conditioning and standardized testing, as countervailing arguments against the psychometricians. He notes that African-Americans will be "deeply hurt by the hints that they are genetically inferior."[81] Gardner concludes with the Deweyan insight that intelligence must be coupled with a moral sense. "High intelligence and high creativity are desirable," Gardner argues, "but unless they are linked to some kind of moral compass, their possessors might best be consigned to an island of glass-bead players, with no access to the mainland."[82]

Shortly after the publication of *The Bell Curve*, Murray and Gardner engaged in a spirited debate on National Public Radio. It was a debate in which the psychologist Gardner had the upperhand over the political scientist Murray whose main scholarly area was *not* psychology. Murray's calm and reasonable demeanor contrasted sharply with Gardner's more passionate responses. The hour-long program focused exclusively on *The Bell Curve* with only parenthetic reference to Gardner's theory of multiple intelligences.

Murray staked out his ground by declaring that he and Herrnstein were in the "scientific mainstream" and that Gardner was "on the periphery." He described *The Bell Curve* as an attempt to "air" the dirty secret of IQ and its relation to social class that he alleged is talked about in private conversations. He claimed that *The Bell Curve* was based on "the current state of knowledge which is not so frightening as many people think." He quickly maintained that "the focus on race is not what this book is about." In fact, he argued that the book was in the "scientific middle of the road" and that the prospective reader would discover that its argument is "180 degrees opposite from what the New York *Times* and Howard Gardner . . . has been telling me for years."

Gardner parried Murray's argument and responded with a savage attack. He challenged what he considered the thesis of the book: that "IQ is a smoking gun for our social problems." He criticized the "omission" of large data bases on brain research, where "less than ten percent [of the brain] has been mapped," and studies on the effect of culture on intelligence. Consequently, Gardner considered *The Bell Curve* "scientifically one hundred years out of date." Gardner was most upset by the policy implications of a cognitive elite whereby "IQ is destiny." He called such a diagnosis "a red herring to the things that cause social pathology." And he countered the charge of his marginality. "Even though within the psychometric community, the position I take is not a majority position," he declared, "once you leave that community and look at the rest of psychology, neuroscience, anthropology, then the view of a very small group of people becomes very peripheral instead." He finished by predicting that "by a year or two from now there is going to be very little of this book as far as scientific authenticity." The show's host ended by humorously commenting that Murray was well on the road to being "the least popular man in America."[83]

CASE STUDY: SPATIAL INTELLIGENCE AND THE ARTS

Let us examine one of Gardner's intelligences more closely—that of spatial intelligence and how it relates to the art of painting. Although Gardner was a pianist as a child, we will look at painting to maintain symmetry with Dewey's case study on his influence on the Abstract Expressionists in the previous chapter.

Gardner presents a strong argument for a distinct spatial intelligence in *Frames of Mind*. His examples of a spatial intelligence based on elaborate drawings by *idiots savants* and autistic children is extremely persuasive. Also, Gardner offers cross-cultural examples by making strong points, such as the Kalahari bushmen "who can deduce from the spoor of an antelope, its size, build and mood" attesting to a "keen visual memory."[84] Gardner further reviews studies of the blind with "spatial capacities" and other "unusual forms of spatial ability and disability" to strengthen his case.[85]

But it is in fleshing out his concept of spatial intelligence with artistic geniuses that Gardner excels. Gardner is at his best when employing case studies of geniuses; indeed, he has called himself a "student of geniuses."[86] His portrait of Pablo Picasso in *Creating Minds* is nothing short of brilliant. Here we have a painting genius examined as a case study for the argument that a spatial intelligence exists.

Gardner's first premise is that all of his seven intelligences have a ge-netic base but must be further developed. He is attracted to Picasso as an example for a number of reasons. First, Picasso was a child prodigy, which resonates strongly with Gardner, the child pianist. Second, one of Picasso's dictums was that true art first resides with the child, a "genius of child-hood," in Picasso's words, that "it has taken me a whole lifetime to learn to draw like them."[87] Gardner's studies with young children (ages 2–7) show that these children have "the ability to make fine discriminations of line, color, shape, pitch, and timbre . . . [without] . . . need for formal train-ing . . . [which]. . . constitutes a golden period."[88]

Picasso is a classic example for Gardner's spatial intelligence. He was a painting prodigy, the son of an academic painter. Gardner would argue that a "significant genetic . . . component exists in the prodigy."[89] But as Picasso's biographer John Richardson pointed out, Picasso had to work hard at painting to achieve success. Gardner locates Picasso's strength in "the visual-spatial, bodily-kinesthetic, and interpersonal areas."[90] Picasso "hated school" and "performed poorly," especially in "learning to read and write and [had] even greater difficulty in mastering numbers."[91] Some critics claimed that Picasso "never mastered certain scholastic skills and had trouble with abstract thinking."[92]

Picasso studied art at the academies in Barcelona and Madrid. As a struggling young artist in Paris at the turn of the century (albeit partially supported financially by his family), he made the difficult "transition from youthful prodigy to adult master."[93] By the age of thirty he was successful, painting in a neo-impressionist style of his blue and rose period. Indeed, Gardner is amazed that "Picasso's rise to prominence occurred with sur-prising speed."[94] The blue and rose period, while establishing him com-mercially, was "a distinctive, but not yet truly innovative, style."[95]

Enter risk and immortality. In 1907, the young Picasso painted a shock-ing work, *Les demoiselles d'Avignon*, the precursor to cubism that as Gardner writes, "many see as the most important painting of the cen-tury."[96] A clear and controversial departure, the painting was regarded by even his friends as "monstrous."[97] "Painting is freedom," Picasso declared, "if you jump, you might fall on the wrong side of the rope. But if you are not willing to take the risk of breaking your neck, what good is it?"[98]

Cubism, Gardner wrote, was to cause an "epochal change or 'paradigm shift' " that would revolutionize art.[99] And for Picasso, works of art had to have both emotion and spirituality. He argued that a work of art must make a person "feel strongly" and that he "always believed that artists . . . live and work with spiritual values," sentiments echoed by the Abstract Expressionists.[100]

Gardner has had a lifelong interest in studying art and creativity. His first book, *The Arts and Human Development*, which grew out of his doctoral dissertation at Harvard, opened up a field of inquiry that has fascinated him throughout his career. The book was primarily a work addressed "chiefly to scholars," not like the later "literary" works where he found he "could address a general as well as a scholarly public."[101] In rereading the book two decades later, Gardner was amazed to discover that he "had virtually nothing to say about intelligence."[102] His starting point was Deweyan. "I considered the arts," he writes, "to be an intellectual, cognitive enterprise, one that involves problem solving and problem finding."[103]

Gardner was to write three books specifically correlating art and creativity and a number of other books using case studies of creative geniuses. In studying artistic development in children he observed "the dramatic change in attitude" regarding "the relationship between child and artist."[104] He noted that in the history of art "the denouement of the march toward realism" resulted in a "rapid and near total collapse of the Renaissance style of representational art."[105] "And with the abstract expressionism of the forties and fifties," Gardner declares, "the breakdown was total."[106] The result was that "the kinds of work esteemed now have at least a superficial resemblance to those produced by children [so that] the collection of scribbles [that] would have been ignored in years gone by, a person who values the simple forms . . . as the abstract lines of Jackson Pollock or Franz Kline, cannot be so dismissive."[107]

One can see the clear influence of John Dewey (and to some extent the example of the Abstract Expressionists) in Gardner's attempt to discern the developmental stages of art in children. In his fifth book, *Artful Scribbles: The Significance of Children's Drawing*, published in 1980, Gardner anchors some of his key ideas regarding art in Deweyan thought without directly attributing them to Dewey.

As a developmental psychologist with a deep interest in art and creativity, Gardner's intention is to study the various stages of artistic ability in children. He discovers a golden age, the "magic years" of five through seven, whereby the "flowering of child art is real and powerful."[108] However, such a burst of creativity is "seasonal" and a child's artistic abilities decline in the middle years as his/her education and maturity increase, only to resurface in adolescence for the truly motivated and talented. Gardner concludes that in these "magic years . . . most youngsters in our society achieve notable expressiveness in their drawings" that some argue possess real artistic merit.[109]

In studying this artistic flowering, Gardner describes the endeavor of a child's art in Deweyan terms, as an experience, a process, that is deeply emotional and results in an expressive art product which exhibits "organization and coherence."[110] Gardner writes that "perhaps the child is enmeshed in the *process* of producing components while having scant [or fleeting] interest in the eventual *product*" (emphasis added).[111] These art products may be no more than "happy accidents" that the child has "no intention of creating," yet has "no choice about what he *feels* compelled to produce" (emphasis added).[112]

Gardner finds in this stage of child art, emotion and expressiveness as the key. The child artist in this golden stage is "expressing himself through his drawings," so that he/she "is speaking directly" conveying "inner feelings."[113] For Gardner, *"expressiveness"* in child art is "one sign that he can fashion a work of art."[114] He compares examples of fine child art with the work of the Abstract Expressionists. For example, one young preschooler's "brilliant watercolors" painted in "less than fifteen minutes" calls to Gardner's mind "the work of Jackson Pollock and other abstract expressionists" with its "painterly streaks, vivid primary colors, and fiery explosiveness."[115] On another occasion, he makes the "case for children's drawing as works of art" with some children's drawings as "inescapable parallels with the work of such Abstract Expressionists as "Helen Frankenthaler, Adolph Gottlieb, and Willem de Kooning."[116] Indeed, in the controversy over whether child drawing should be considered art, Gardner leans toward the affirmative. He is fond of quoting Picasso's oft-repeated remark that "once I drew like Raphael, but it has taken me a whole lifetime to draw like children."[117]

And in concluding his study, Gardner describes the artistic journey in terms which would have delighted the Abstract Expressionists:

> We can in fact propose that creative works are the means, the artist's necessary means, of expressing his being and those feelings that are often inarticulate and inexpressible in other media. . . . And it is here we encounter a direct and genuine link to the young child, for he, too, still inarticulate but already harboring many important if ineffable feelings, resorts spontaneously and with deeply felt need to the media at his disposal—most often and most significantly, to drawing[118]

SCHOOL REFORM

Since *Frames of Mind*, Gardner has taken an activist stance as a school reformer. Although he had written in the introduction to the book that "MI theory was devised as a scientific theory and not as an instrument of social policy," he encouraged MI to be implemented as a reform strategy.[119] Indeed, he had also written in *Frames* that he "wished to examine the educational implications of a theory of multiple intelligences" so that MI theory could "prove of genuine utility to those policy makers and practitioners charged with the 'development' of other individuals."[120]

Gardner would now redirect Project Zero toward the implementation and support of MI ideas. Hundred of MI projects were created in American classrooms by enthused teachers and principals at a growth rate of three or four a month. In Norfolk, Virginia, one such project, the Atlas Project, was conceived with school reformers James Comer of Yale University, Ted Sizer of Brown University, and Gardner. By 1993, he would publish a reader, *Multiple Intelligences: The Theory in Practice*. The book was a compilation of essays, some coauthored, that sought to "delineate the general configuration of an educational system based on a multiple intelligences perspective."[121] In addition, Gardner reviewed "projects, based on 'MI' thinking, that run the gamut from preschool through high school" and he discussed "new forms of assessment" to replace IQ tests and similar standardized instruments.[122]

One extensive guide on how to operationalize MI has been made by Thomas Armstrong in his paperback book, *Multiple Intelligences in the Classroom*. Moreover, Armstrong's manual on how to create an MI classroom was published in 1994 by the Association for Supervision and Curriculum Development, giving another testimony to the educational establishment's enthrallment with MI theory. In his brief preface to the book, Gardner declares the book to be a "reliable and readable account of my work."[123] He proclaims that there are "many differences among people . . . [and] . . . the multiple variations in the ways that they learn."[124] His admonition is to "Let 100 MI schools bloom" and that "Thomas Armstrong shares this vision."[125]

According to Armstrong, it took him eight years to apply the "theory of multiple intelligences to the nuts-and-bolts issues of classroom teaching."[126] This teacher's guide describes the theory by relating it to teaching strategies, curriculum development, classroom management, assessment, special education, and cognitive skills. Each chapter describes suggested activities with a checklist to be followed. For example, there is a checklist under the seven intelligences to assess each student's intelligence. To follow the example of spatial intelligence (and art), Armstrong's checklist includes such items as whether the student reports clear visual images, reads maps and charts more easily than the text, enjoys art activities, draws far advanced for his/her age, likes to view films and slides, doodles, and learns best from pictures rather than words.

Regarding the assessment of a student's work, Armstrong proposes the portfolio method whereby a variety of assessment experiences can be combined. These are to include anecdotal records, work samples, audio cassettes, videotapes, photography, journals, interviews, informal texts, and some criterion referenced assessments.

Other efforts are underway to flesh out the theory into practice. Professor Sue Teele developed an assessment for MI theory called the Teele Inventory of Multiple Intelligences (TIMI). As described by Teele, the TIMI for elementary students consists of a pictorial inventory of panda bears representing characteristics of each of the seven intelligences and provides students twenty-eight opportunities to make their selections of two choices.[127] At this writing the TIMI is still being validated, but preliminary indications are that the TIMI has a satisfactory rate of validity and reliability. One of the first uses of the TIMI was by Oscar Scott Jr. who conducted an assessment of giftedness among African American fourth grade students in Virginia Beach, Virginia (which was a dissertation I directed). Scott compared the TIMI with other standardized tests in determining giftedness and concluded that the TIMI was a better instrument to ascertain the abilities of African-American students than the traditional standardized tests.

Although he is gratified by the instantaneous applications of MI theory in school reform projects, Gardner was moved to caution reformers on their overly enthusiastic efforts. Having been "content to let MI theory take on a life of its own" without direction from the master, he finally issued guidelines for future projects.[128] Gardner listed seven myths about MI that he observed in "some problematic applications of MI theory," recommending instead "three more positive ways in which MI theory can be—and has been—used in the schools."[129] He worried that enthusiasts would use MI as a "'position' on tracking, gifted education, the layout of the school day, the length of the school year, or many other 'hot button' educational issues."[130] On the other hand, he has been delighted by some programs incorporating MI ideas such as the "use of a 'multiple intelligences curriculum' to bridge communication gaps between children from different cultures."[131]

Gardner is an active participant in many national reform forums, such as the Pew Forum on Education Reform. The Pew Forum was established in 1990, underwritten by the Pew Charitable Trusts, and monitored by the Stanford University School of Education. Some twenty-eight original members of the forum were selected representing education schools, school practitioners, civil rights organizations, and business. They meet three or four times a year to brainstorm on specific reform issues, such as standards, accountability, and public involvement, publishing the results of their conversations in book form.

For Gardner, "American education is at a turning point."[132] He was uncomfortable with the equity school reform movement of the 1960s, shaped by the Civil Rights Movement, that sought to educate the poor. He believed that "much of the educational program of the 1960s . . . was not well considered."[133] Yet he was also not completely at ease with some excellence reformers of the 1980s and 1990s. He finds that he is "equally convinced that many of the cures suggested by the neoconservative reformers are worse than the disease."[134] One must remember that Gardner's point of orientation was not as a reformer but as a psychologist; he was propelled into school reform to a great extent by the enthusiasm of the education lobby. Moreover, as a theorist his transition to activist is marked by the same vagueness of strategy that was characteristic of Dewey's prescriptions for social change.

Establishing his independence as a school reformer, Gardner sympathizes with some excellence reform ideas but is more a progressive than a conservative. He has championed national standards in education, worrying that without a national body to oversee the standards movement it "may fall apart, like a crumbling Babel, or . . . it may end up by crippling some of the most promising reform efforts underway in our country."[135] He has memorialized Albert Shanker, former president of the American Federation of Teachers (AFL-CIO), a vocal conservative proponent of standards, and a "giant in every sense of the word"—a man many black and white school reformers of the 1960s accused of racism in the community control struggle (including myself).[136]

Gardner published his most complete prescription for school reform in 1991 in a book titled, *The Unschooled Mind*, subtitled *How Children Think & How Schools Should Teach*. In short, Gardner links his theory of intelligence with the latest agenda for school reform. This reform movement, dubbed the "excellence school reform" movement by its advocates, seeks to restructure American public education to serve, essentially, the best and brightest. It is a reform movement that was christened by the U.S. Department of Education's polemic *A Nation at Risk: The Imperative for School Reform* in 1983, which argued that American public school students were lagging in international tests compared with European and Japanese students. It reversed the emphasis on educating the poor, which was a hallmark of school reform from the 1960s and shaped by the civil rights movement.

The Unschooled Mind drew praise in a blurb for the paperback edition from Albert Shanker who called the book "visionary yet practical" and a "stunning achievement." Shanker went so far as to say that "if we closed schools today" and then "could reinvent them" that his "answer would be: 'according to the ideas and models in Howard Gardner's *The Unschooled Mind.*'"[137] Another blurb advertisement came from neoconservative historian and excellence school reformer, Diane Ravitch, who called *The Unschooled Mind* "extraordinarily useful and insightful" that "provides practical, well-grounded advice to school reformers."[138]

And Gardner attacks the advocate for cultural literacy based in a Eurocentric tradition, E. D. Hirsch Jr. Hirsch was urged by Ravitch to write his best-selling book, *Cultural Literacy*, as an answer to the growing trend towards multiculturalism in school curricula. *Cultural Literacy* departs significantly from Dewey's idea of learning by reviving rote memorization of facts, a practice mainly derived from Eurocentric and American culture. Hirsch has stated that "Dewey was deeply mistaken" about education.[139] Indeed, Gardner distances himself somewhat from Dewey by describing progressive education as a "difficult undertaking" that "ultimately defeated Dewey" since "progressive education works best with children who come from richly endowed homes."[140] Yet he has not completely thrown off the Dewey influence suggesting an art portfolio as one of not an assemblage of "best works," but a "process-folio" that includes "initial brainstorming ideas, early drafts, and first critiques"; "journal entries on 'pivotal moments' when ideas jelled" and other such items as peer critiques and outside experts.[141] The developmental psychologist is not about to discard all traces of John Dewey.

Yet in the final analysis Gardner is a full-fledged card-carrying progressive reformer. He supports national standards, national testing, and a national curriculum that will establish cultural literacy. Gardner's contribution to excellence reform is the joining of his ideas on intelligence to the national current of educational thinking. He adds to this list his concept of "education for understanding" which he defines as a "sufficient grasp of concepts, principles, or skills."[142]

CONCLUSION

There are some troubling concerns about MI theory, as there are with any revolutionary idea. These are acknowledged by Gardner as well as by his sympathetic critics. MI theory lacks experimental quantitative verification. Also, Gardner's interest in geniuses as case studies has aroused concern with one sympathizer of MI theory. Elliot W. Eisner notes that "exemplars that Gardner uses . . . are virtually 'pure cases' . . . [whereas] . . . most individuals are nowhere as clean."[143] And Gardner limits himself to modernist geniuses, stating that his "sentiments are closer to those of the modern era than to those of the postmodern era."[144]

Moreover, another sympathizer with MI theory, Robert J. Sternberg, argues that MI "does not provide the royal road to school reform" and that it will "prove another distraction to our confronting the real issues that face us if we want to improve schools."[145] Certainly, portfolios intended to replace standardized assessment in the classroom also bring with them dangers of possible misuse. One can foresee some teachers labeling African-American students, for example, with primarily musical or athletic intelligences.

Equally important, Gardner lacks a holistic approach to school reform. Absent are both a moral and social aspect to his MI theory—characteristics of Dewey's thought. Yet, our educational history suggests that an innovative idea may need instant application rather than waiting to be incorporated into a grand strategy for school reform.

In the final analysis, Gardner has brought Dewey's main ideas on thinking a step further. And, like Dewey, his academic career has been predicated on risk. Further scholarship on intelligence must begin with MI theory. "Intelligence testing," Gardner wrote, "was a lofty idea that is losing altitude; the biological, psychological and anthropological evidence is strongly against this unitary notion of intelligence."[146] Howard Gardner is responsible for a major paradigm shift on the thinking on intelligence.

NOTES

1. Howard Gardner, "Reflections on Multiple Intelligences: Myths and Messages," *Phi Delta Kappan*, November 1995, pp. 201–2.

2. "Ways We've Changed," *Mother Jones*, February 1996, p. 43.

3. Maureen Dezell, "Studying with a 'Student of Genius,'" *Boston Globe*, August 20, 1995, p. B24.

4. Richard A. Knox, "Brainchild," *Boston Globe Magazine*, November 5, 1995, p. 38.

5. Howard Gardner, *To Open Minds* (New York: Basic Books, 1989), p. 19.

6. Ibid.

7. Ibid., p. 22.

8. Ibid.

9. Ibid., p. 24.

10. Ibid.

11. Ibid.

12. Ibid., p. 12.

13. Ibid.

14. Ibid., p. 22.

15. Ibid., p. 36.

16. Ibid., pp. 27, 36.

17. Ibid., p. 29.

18. Ibid., p. 25.

19. Ibid., p. 33.

20. Ibid.

21. Ibid.

22. Ibid.

23. Ibid., p. 38.

24. Ibid.

25. Ibid., p. 43.

26. Ibid.

27. Ibid., p. 56.

28. Ibid.

29. Ibid.

30. Ibid., p. 58.

31. Ibid., p. 54.

32. Howard Gardner, *The Arts and Human Development* (New York: Basic Books, 1994), p. xxii.

33. Gardner, *To Open Minds*, p. 57.

34. Ibid., p. 59.

35. Ibid., pp. 62–63.

36. Ibid., p. 63.

37. Ibid., p. 62.

38. Ibid., p. 76.

39. Ibid., p. 86.

40. Ibid., p. 111.

41. Ibid., p. 90.

42. Ibid., p. 92.

43. Ibid., p. 97.

44. Ibid., p. 107.

45. Ibid., p. 110.

46. Ibid., p. 111.

47. Howard Gardner, *Frames of Mind: The Theory of Multiple Intelligences* (New York: Basic Books, 1993), p. ix.

48. Howard Gardner, *Leading Minds: An Anatomy of Leadership* (New York: Basic Books, 1995), p. 72.

49. Gardner, *Frames of Mind*, p. 11.

50. Ibid., p. 9.

51. Howard Gardner, *Creating Minds* (New York: Basic Books, 1993), p. xvii.

52. Gardner, *Frames of Mind*, p. 10.

53. Ibid., p. xviii.

54. Gardner, *Multiple Intelligences: The Theory in Practice* (New York: Basic Books, 1993), p. 45.

55. Gardner, *Frames of Mind*, p. 120.

56. Ibid., p. 70.

57. Gardner, *Multiple Intelligences*, p. 26.

58. Gardner, *Frames of Mind*, p. 70.

59. Gardner, *Multiple Intelligences*, p. 38.

60. Gardner, *Frames of Mind*, p. 70.

61. Benjamin Singer, "Review of *Frames of Mind*," *Harper's*, December 1983, p. 267.

62. Jerome Bruner, "State of the Child," *New York Review of Books*, October 27, 1983, p. 86.

63. Ibid.

64. Ibid.

65. George A. Miller, "Varieties of Intelligence," *New York Times Book Review*, December 25, 1983, p. 5.

66. Ibid., p. 20.

67. Ibid., p. 5.

68. Ibid.

69. Gardner, *Multiple Intelligences: The Theory in Practice*, pp. xii–xiii.

70. Richard J. Herrnstein and Charles Murray, *The Bell Curve: Intelligence and Class Structure in American Life* (New York: The Free Press, 1994), p. 18.

71. *New York Times*, October 22, 1994, p. 6.

72. *Newsweek*, October 24, 1994, p. 53.

73. *New York Times*, October 26, 28, 1994.

74. Peter Passell, "Review of *The Bell Curve*," *New York Times*, October 27, 1994, p. C19.

75. Malcolm Browne, "Review of *The Bell Curve*," *New York Times, Sunday Book Review*, October 16, 1994, p. 3.

76. Jason DeParle, "The Most Dangerous Conservative," *New York Times Magazine*, October 9, 1994.

77. Howard Gardner, "Cracking Open the IQ Box," in *The Bell Curve Wars*, edited by Stephen Fraser (New York: Basic Books, 1995), p. 23.

78. Ibid.

79. Ibid., pp. 25, 24.

80. Ibid., p. 25.

81. Ibid., p. 35.

82. Ibid.

83. *Talk of the Nation*, National Public Radio, October 26, 1994.

84. Gardner, *Frames of Mind*, pp. 200–201.

85. Ibid., p. 185.

86. Dezell, "Studying with a 'Student of Genius,'" p. B24.

87. Gardner, *Creating Minds*, p. 145.

88. Gardner, *To Open Minds*, pp. 100–101.

89. Gardner, *Creating Minds*, p. 138.

90. Ibid., p. 141.

91. Ibid.

92. Ibid.

93. Ibid., p. 140.

94. Ibid., p. 148.

95. Ibid., p. 149.

96. Ibid., p. 159.

97. Ibid.

98. Ibid., p. 163.

99. Ibid.

100. Ibid., pp. 178–79.

101. Howard Gardner, *The Arts and Human Development* (New York: Basic Books, 1973) p. xxiii.

102. Ibid., p. xxii.

103. Ibid., p. xxi.

104. Howard Gardner, *Art, Mind and Brain* (New York: Basic Books, 1982), p. 92.

105. Ibid., p. 65.

106. Ibid., pp. 68–69.

107. Ibid., p. 100.

108. Howard Gardner, *Artful Scribbles* (New York: Basic Books, 1980), p. 142.

109. Ibid., p. 94.

110. Ibid., p. 261.

111. Ibid., p. 100.

112. Ibid.

113. Ibid., p. 107.

114. Ibid.

115. Ibid., p. 3.

116. Ibid., p. 129.

117. Ibid., p. 110.

118. Ibid., p. 111.

119. Gardner, *Frames of Mind,* p. xxii.

120. Ibid., p. 10.

121. Gardner, *Multiple Intelligences: The Theory in Practice*, p. xv.

122. Ibid.

123. Thomas Armstrong, *Multiple Intelligences in the Classroom* (Alexandria, Va.: Association for Supervision and Curriculum Development, 1994), p. vii.

124. Ibid., pp. vii–viii.

125. Ibid.

126. Oscar Scott Jr., "Multiple Intelligences and the Gifted: Identification of African-American Students" (Ph.D. diss., Old Dominion University, Norfolk, Va., 1996).

127. Gardner, "Reflections on Multiple Intelligences: Myths and Messages," p. 207.

128. Ibid., p. 206.

129. Ibid.

130. Gardner, *Multiple Intelligences: The Theory in Practice*, p. 68.

131. Ibid., p. 69.

132. Ibid.

133. Ibid.

134. Howard Gardner, "The Need for Anti-Babel Standards," *Education Week*, September 7, 1994, p. 44.

135. Howard Gardner, "Remembering AL," *Education Week*, May 14, 1997, p. 37.

136. Howard Gardner, *The Unschooled Mind* (New York: Basic Books, 1991).

137. Ibid.

138. Ibid.

139. E. D. Hirsch Jr., *Cultural Literacy: What Every American Needs to Know* (New York: Houghton Mifflin, 1987), p. xvii.

140. Gardner, *The Unschooled Mind*, pp. 196–98.

141. Ibid., p. 240.

142. Ibid., p. 18.

143. Elliot W. Eisner, "A Symposium on *Multiple Intelligences: The Theory in Practice*," *Teachers College Record* (summer 1994): 569.

144. Gardner, *Creating Minds*, p. 403.

145. Robert J. Sternberg, "A Symposium on *Multiple Intelligences: The Theory in Practice*," *Teachers College Record* (summer 1994): 562.

146. Howard Gardner, "Lofty Ideas That May Be Losing Altitude," *New York Times*, November 1, 1997, p. A23.

5

Carol Gilligan and Moral Development

with CLAIR T. NEWBOLD

> We have come more recently to notice not only the silence of women
> but the difficulty in hearing what they say when they speak.
>
> —Carol Gilligan

Carol Gilligan is the first feminist culture star to have had substantial impact on American education. Her contribution has been twofold: on adolescent girls and moral development, and how young women form distinctive feminist identities. In her studies of adolescent girls she was able to "notice the silence of women."[1] She discovered that girls and women have a different voice on moral issues than Lawrence Kohlberg's studies showed about boys. Whereas Kohlberg perceived an "ethic of justice," Gilligan discovered an "ethic of care."[2] She found the inner voice of women that, in her words, resulted in a "major paradigm shift in psychology."[3]

Like Howard Gardner, she received the accolades of literate society. Her signature book, *In a Different Voice*, was chosen for the Outstanding Book Award in 1983 by the American Educational Research Association and has been translated into a dozen languages. In 1984, the feminist magazine Ms. anointed her as their Woman of the Year. She was accorded the prestigious Grawemeyer Award in Education in 1992, as had been Howard Gardner in an earlier year. *Time* magazine made her one of their twenty-five "most influential people" in 1996. *Time* described Gilligan's book as a "landmark study" that has changed the voice of psychology.[4] *Time* asked rhetorically: "How likely is it that a single book could change the rules of psychology, change the assumptions of medical research, change the conversation among parents and teachers and developmental professionals about the distinction between men and women, boys and girls?"[5]

The next year Harvard created its first Center for Gender Studies and made her chair with a half million dollar budget. In 1997, she was one of five recipients to receive an award from the Heinz Family Foundation as one who "define[s] the American spirit" for introducing "the previously disregarded voice of women into the study of human development."[6] She has been the recipient of many honorary degrees from American universities.

Gilligan's key work, published in 1982, was fully titled *In a Different Voice: Psychological Theory and Women's Development*. As of 1998, over 600,000 copies have been sold worldwide. The book consists of original research (and not a sophisticated review of the literature as was Howard Gardner's *Frames of Mind*) employing a qualitative methodology with interviews of women. The methodology is the most appropriate given the "silence" of women. The book consists of two main studies: a college survey of students in a moral and ethics class at an elite university, and a study of women involved in the most personal and most feminine decision—whether to have an abortion. Her research pointed to a difference in "that men and women may speak different languages."[7]

At Harvard Graduate School, Gilligan was inspired by two men: Erik Erikson and Lawrence Kohlberg. She was to acknowledge that her interest in adolescence and identity formation was "spurred by Erikson's attention to the relationship between life history and history."[8] She was influenced "by two insights in the work of Kohlberg: first, that following the Nazi holocaust, psychologists must address the problem of moral relativism, and second, that adolescents are passionately interested in moral questions."[9] The final touch to her own identity formation as a feminist came as the feminist movement gained ascendancy as the result of the Civil Rights movement of the 1960s. She recalled that she "began writing *In a Different Voice* in the early 1970s, at a time of resurgence in the Women's Movement."[10] It was a case of the feminist movement creating a feminist who, in turn, moved the feminist movement in a new direction.

LIFE

Carol Gilligan was born in 1936 in New York City, an only child to first-generation children of Jewish immigrants. She was raised on the West Side of New York and went to progressive education schools: nursery school at Walden, Hunter Model School for elementary students (a public school), and Walden for high school. These were elite schools and she was "in the middle of progressive education."[11] It was her mother's decision to send her to Walden because "she valued the central place of the arts in education at Walden" and because she was "very pro-progressive education."[12] Gilligan was "influenced by Dewey's schools, not by Dewey as a philosopher."[13]

Her father was born in the back of a dairy store. He personified the "Irving Howe story" of successful immigrant Jews in America.[14] He received a Regents scholarship and went to Cornell to be a chemist. He entered the business world during the Depression and quickly redefined himself by going to law school and becoming "a successful and beloved Wall Street lawyer."[15] During World War II he was an air raid warden for his block and "was one of those who was loved by everyone."[16]

Her mother also redefined herself. Initially, she did a "bunch of things" such as "working with an oriental rug person with fabrics and decoration" since "she was artistic."[17] She also worked for the Menhorah Journal. Later, she went to the Bank Street School of Education, received a degree, and became a special object relations therapist at Bank Street's Child Development Center.

Gilligan was precocious. She did well in school and "was very involved in the arts," especially modern dance (which she still does today), the piano and choral singing which, she says is a clue to "understanding my work in voice" of the silence in women.[18] She spoke three languages including Hebrew and French, which she learned in school. She "loved books as a child" and her mother used to "read to me and sing."[19] She would say that "she loved words."[20]

Her literary bent was established early. And it was reinforced at Swarthmore College by a professor of English, Sam Hines, "who influenced me profoundly."[21] She was an English major at college. Since her work is replete with literary allusions and a narrative style befitting a fiction writer, she was asked in our interview whether she ever desired to write novels. She replied jokingly that it "is what I am doing now."[22] She modified that statement by saying that she was "never consciously aware of wanting to do it until fairly recently."[23] Furthermore, in a 1998 essay reminiscing about her friendship with Lawrence Kohlberg, she declared that she considered herself a "writer who happened to wander through psychology."[24]

One of the major themes in Gilligan's research is the "disconnect" age of eleven or twelve when young girls go from being self-confident and doing well academically to a slide into low-self-esteem and doing poorly in school (to be more fully discussed later in this chapter). Gilligan argues that the key relationship at that age—in addition to teachers and other community figures—is that of mothers and daughters. She was careful to answer our question in the interview. She admitted that, at that age, she and her mother also were struggling with developing an "authentic relationship,"[25] and that her mother was "remarkable in the sense of hanging in there."[26]

This struggle gave Gilligan insight into "what was at stake for women teachers, mothers and therapists" dealing with adolescent girls going through this turmoil.[27]

But Gilligan framed the relationship between mother and daughter in a larger cultural and historical matrix, "three millennia of patriarchy."[28] Indeed, it is that patriarchical society, she felt, that was most responsible for encouraging a "break in relationships between mothers and daughters."[29] She cited the work of women novelists such as Charlotte Brontë, Toni Morrison, and Jamaica Kincaid as examples of those who have written eloquently about that "break point." Her own work "shows what the break is among girls."[30] It is a moment in their lives "where girls feel pressed to not know what they know" undermining "authentic relationships between women and girls."[31] She concludes that if there is to be "anything resembling an authentic relationship between mothers and daughters it means having to challenge the perpetuation of the patriarchical order."[32]

Gilligan came to psychology through literature. She intended to be a clinical psychologist pursuing her doctorate at Howard. But she found the "clinical language abrasive"; it was "flat" and "simplistic" and "reduced in a way that I didn't associate with gender at all."[33] After completing her Ph.D. she intended "to leave psychology" because she "could see no way of connecting my voice to the voice of the field."[34] But she was eventually "drawn back into psychology by two men whose voices had the ring of truth: Erik Erikson, who showed that you cannot take a life out of history," and Lawrence Kohlberg, who argued that "philosophy was a moral science."[35]

She came to feminism as an activist in the civil rights and antiwar movements of the 1960s. She recalled that as a young faculty member at the University of Chicago she "sat in at the administration" as a "protest against the university's policy of using grades to decide who would be drafted and sent to Vietnam."[37] Using a key question that she would later employ in her studies on herself—How would you describe yourself to yourself?—she would have replied at the time that she "was a mother of three young children, and deeply involved in politics and the arts."[38]

From this activist background, she co-taught a class with Erik Erikson and Lawrence Kohlberg at Harvard on moral and political choice. She noticed that the male students were reluctant to discuss the draft. She intended to conduct a study of their responses to "how people make actual (moral) decisions."[39] She recalled that "gender was not salient for me" at the time.[40] But, with the end of the draft and the *Roe v. Wade* Supreme Court decision legitimizing abortion for women, her project changed dramatically. She regarded the Supreme Court decision as "total serendipity" that "produced at that moment in history an all female sample which was the last thing I thought about."[41] She realized that "this historical moment raised the question of relationship" that women asked: "Why is it selfish to speak in my own voice?"[42] Her new focus gave her an opportunity to study "real life decision making" to "show how the self appears in moments of conflict and choice" that determines "how the personal pronoun I comes in."[43] Most important, she could determine whether "moral language guides that choice."[44]

Sixteen years after the publication of *In a Different Voice*, Gilligan would recall the impetus for her work:

> It was listening to women talk about this decision and hear the dissonance between what was the oral problem for women, (since) that decision was embedded in a whole network of relationships including how do women get pregnant in the first place and then the decision about whether to continue or abort a relationship. It was completely at odds with the right to life/right to choice conversations. So when I wrote *In a Different Voice* it was about changing the voice of the public conversation that was the conversation about psychology, the conversation about morality, the conversation about development, the conversation about what it meant to have a sense of self was to bring in women's voices meant changing the theme of conversation so you heard everybody differently. So it was this moment in history that happened, and I think it is no accident that the abortion decision was so interesting because what had been seen as goodness for women was helplessness. To be responsible to others and to sort of put yourself last. But here what happened in that turning point the Supreme Court legitimatized women's voices where suddenly women said wait a minute it's not responsible to be selfless it's irresponsible. Because if you're selfless, you are not there and if you're not there how can you take care of the child. So, it suddenly turned around the understanding of what responsibility means, what morality means, what it means to be a mother, a good mother, what it means to be in a relationship. This notion that relationship means being selfless the women (in my study) were saying that's not relationship. So it was a real paradigm shift.[45]

FEMINISM AND EDUCATION

The resurgence of the feminist movement in the 1960s and 1970s resulted in some startling research on the education of girls. First, the feminist movement was reborn as a result of the civil rights movement of the

1950s and 1960s. When the civil rights movement underwent a transformation in 1966 from seeking equal opportunity and integration to a new
emphasis on black power and group cohesiveness, a new concept
emerged, the question of identity: Who Am I? That idea of black power redefined African American identity and was quickly absorbed into the new
feminist movement.

There were key events in the rise of the new feminism. Betty Freidan
published an influential best-selling book in 1963, *The Feminine Mystique*,
that updated French existentialist philosopher Simone de Beauvoir's 1949
tome, *The Second Sex*. Mainstream feminist organizations such as the
National Organization of Women grew and developed a clear feminist
agenda. There were also publications that gave women a distinct feminist
voice: *Ms.* magazine became the popular bible of the new feminism, and
Signs became the first feminist academic journal. Women's Studies programs, some with departmental status, sprung up in academe. On the political front, there was a move for a constitutional amendment that failed
for an Equal Rights Amendment. And in the historic 1973 U.S. Supreme
Court decision of *Roe v. Wade*, women were given the right to choose to
have an abortion should they so wish.

So it was no surprise that a corps of feminist scholars would examine
the role of the schools in the education of girls and women. As the report of the Association of University Women pointed out, "girls and
boys enter school roughly equal in measurable ability" but girls get behind on all standardized tests the further they progress.[46] The greatest
gender gap is in the crucial areas of science and math—areas traditionally considered "male" provinces. Patricia B. Campbell's studies
showed that girls do better than boys in math in elementary school and
junior high school but trail seriously behind by the time of high school.
She also concluded that "there is no evidence that the differences in
math and science have a genetic or biological basis."[47] Moreover, the research of David and Myra Sadker discovered that teachers—both male
and female—teach to the boys, whether consciously or unconsciously.[48]
The Sadker study was a three year long longitudinal investigation of
one hundred classrooms in the fourth, sixth, and eighth grades. The
Sadkers found that teachers favored boys in four types of teacher com-
ments: praise, acceptance, remediation, and criticism. Moreover, teachers favored boys in the crucial realm of the developing of problem
solving skills.[49] This favoritism toward boys continued through college
and graduate school where they were more apt to enjoy a mentoring relationship with a professor.

Most important, there is a "self-esteem slide" for adolescent girls at the beginning of their teenage years (this is a major subtext of Gilligan's research and will be discussed more fully later in this chapter). The Sadkers found that over 67 percent of boys in elementary school were happy with themselves compared with 60 percent of the girls. By the Gilligan disconnect age of eleven and the beginning of middle school, only 37 percent of girls felt content about themselves and that figure dropped to 29 percent in high school.[50] Girls begin to experience depression, eating disorders, sexual harassment, teenage pregnancy, and become extremely conscious about their body image and weight.

Yet despite the rise of the new feminism in the 1970s and the attention given to gender by scholars, there is no mention of girls and women in the excellence reform movement of the 1980s and 1990s. Neither did the polemical treatise of the excellence reform movement in 1983 that launched reform, the federal government's publication, *A Nation at Risk: The Imperative for Educational Reform*, President George Bush's *America 2000*, nor President Bill Clinton's *America 2000*, mention gender. Nevertheless, feminist scholars and activists have called for an educational agenda to redress the balance between the sexes in education.

Relationship to Kohlberg

Contrary to popular myth, Gilligan was neither Lawrence Kohlberg's student nor his post-doctoral assistant. She had met Kohlberg at a party in the spring of 1969. A few days later he asked her to run a study of adolescents. And the following year she taught a section of Kohlberg's course on moral and political choice. She became influenced to a degree with Kohlberg's belief on morality that after the Holocaust there could be no value-free social science. Consequently, she would recall in 1998 that "my work flowed through the area of moral development for a period of time."[51]

According to Gilligan, Kohlberg "came to psychology through philosophy."[52] They co-authored a paper on adolescence that was "mostly written by Larry" and that if she were "to rewrite the paper" would "bring in girls voices and give it a new title."[53]

The relationship with Kohlberg remained close with a long conversation between different perspectives. Kohlberg held on to a "universal, objective moral truth" despite the fact that the Holocaust occurred in a highly developed European civilization. For Gilligan, this paradox translated into a viewpoint that held that "education, social class, culture and civilization were not necessarily associated with higher stages of moral reasoning."[54]

Consequently, she would recall that "our two roads diverged in a way that stressed our conversation, our relationship and our friendship."[55] She felt that she was "not being heard."[56]

Kohlberg and Moral Development

Lawrence Kohlberg became interested in the psychology of morality while teaching at Harvard. He founded the Center for Moral Development and conducted his famous fifteen-year longitudinal study of moral development with a group of 75 boys, which constituted a major paradigm shift in thinking about morality. Kohlberg's beginning premise was that after the Holocaust cultural relativism could no longer be a tenable position. Kohlberg criticized the "fallacy of value neutrality."[57] He began his study in 1957 and was heavily influenced by the work of Piaget on moral development among children and John Dewey's key concept of education as part moral development.

Kohlberg discovered that his subjects could be grouped into six hierarchical stages, with three main levels: preconventional, conventional, postconventional. Each stage is a whole and represents a gradual movement from being self-centered to a higher level of abstract ideas of justice. Stage one involves doing right to avoid punishment; stage two, following rules when it is in one's interest; stage three, responding to family and peers; stage four, meeting one's moral obligations to avoid the breakdown of society; stage five, a sense of obligation to law for the greatest good for the greatest number; and stage six, having universal principles. Kohlberg's discoveries deeply influenced the psychology of morality and education. He spawned the values clarification movement and character education in the 1970s. However, his experiments in operationalizing his findings into programs in the schools resulted in only having students move to the third stage where moral sense relates to family and peer groups.

Gilligan acknowledged her debt to Kohlberg in *In a Different Voice* while also declaring her intellectual independence. She noted that "in the early 1970's, when I was working with Lawrence Kohlberg as a research assistant, I found his argument very powerful."[58] And she acknowledged him first in her intellectual debts in the book, stating that Kohlberg "illuminated for me the study of morality and who has been, over many years, a good teacher and friend."[59] Yet, she points out that "in the research from which Kohlberg derives his theory, females simply do not exist."[60] She goes on to contrast her finding about girls with Kohlberg's findings about boys. One example suffices to show the different perspectives. Kohlberg viewed Mahatma Gandhi as "exemplifying the sixth stage of moral judgment"—Kohlberg's highest stage—because of Gandhi's involvement in social revolution. Gilligan looks upon Gandhi's harsh treatment of his wife (Gandhi admitted to being a "cruelly kind husband") as a moral failure.[61]

Kohlberg was deeply influenced by John Dewey. He saw in Dewey's idea of development a theme that was consonant with his own work. He taught Dewey's *Democracy and Education* as one of four books in his graduate seminar at Harvard entitled "Moral Development and Moral Education." Indeed, Phillip Eddy was to conclude that Kohlberg "often expressed his intellectual indebtedness to John Dewey . . . [and] . . . Kohlberg's writings are sprinkled with favorable references to the philosopher."[62]

Kohlberg revealed the Dewey influence most strongly in what Eddy called "one of his major essays" in the *Harvard Educational Review*—essentially a "paean to a peculiarly Deweyan form of educational Progressivism."[63] The essay was entitled "Development as the Aim of Education" and was co-authored with Rochelle Mayer in 1972. Kohlberg argued for a Deweyan approach to revitalize American education. "The present paper," he wrote, "recapitulates the progressive position first formulated by John Dewey . . . that the aims of education may be identified with development, both intellectual and moral."[64] Kohlberg linked the joining of these two aims by Dewey and he emphasized that "the progressive educator stresses the essential links between cognitive and moral development."[65] He argued that "the developmental-philosophic strategy for defining educational objectives, which emerges from the work of Dewey and Piaget . . . is consistent with, if not 'proved' by, current research findings."[66]

So it comes as no surprise that in the essay he co-authored with Carol Gilligan in *Daedalus* in 1971, "The Adolescent as a Philosopher: The Discovery of the Self in a Postconventional World," he would invoke Dewey. The authors seek to redefine adolescence for the Vietnam/civil rights period and also grasp "the implications of these changes for education."[67] Kohlberg and Gilligan found in disaffected youth a crisis of meaning whereby adolescents "reject not only the *content* of adult society but its *forms*."[68] In seeking to identify this new adolescence they revise the psychological findings of Piaget and others and offer Kohlberg's six stages of moral development. In terms of education the authors conclude that "the problem of meaning . . . is the problem of whether the high school has meaning to the adolescent."[69]

And for the educational solution the authors declare that "we return to the thought of John Dewey which is at the heart of a democratic educational philosophy."[70] They interpreted Dewey to mean that "education was the stimulation of development."[71] Moreover, Kohlberg and Gilligan argue that "Dewey's educational thought needs revival" so that "development rather than achievement . . . be the aim of education."[72]

The second and last collaboration between Kohlberg and Gilligan was a paper presented to the Jean Piaget Society and printed in a collection of essays as late as 1977. Of interest is that Gilligan is first author and she mentions co-teaching Kohlberg's course "on moral and political choice" and conducting a study on moral development with these college students.[73] For the most part, the paper restates Kohlberg's six stage research but there is mention of a study by another psychologist on sex differences and moral development. There is indication of what is to come in Gilligan's research where the authors mention that some of the college students studied evidenced "a considerable struggle to reconcile principles with experience" and that the authors will "have to wait until we have among our subjects people further in life."[74]

Gilligan and Moral Development

Gilligan's 1963 doctoral dissertation, "Responses to Temptation: An Analysis of Motives," was a precursor to her interest in moral development in girls. She established her focus thus: "Consequently, resistance to temptation has been used as the dependent variable in research attempting to compare the effects of different child-rearing practices or different social environments on the development of *conscience*."[75] (emphasis added)

This dissertation came at a time of much social unrest in the nation when the civil rights movement was in full bloom. Yet the concept of feminism was hardly a byword, and morality and ethics was just beginning to be researched by Kohlberg. Gilligan's later work with girls was foreshadowed by this early study, although her dissertation was with boys. The subjects of the study included 127 sixth grade boys of upper middle-class status. Gilligan stated that she chose this socioeconomic group to eliminate any confounding variables that higher or lower social status may present. The chair for her dissertation was David C. McClelland, a leading name in the field of psychology.

The design included presenting conflict situations to the boys whereby they had to deal with the conflicting desires to cheat or not, and the guilt that ensued. The situations were simulated, not unlike in her later work with boys and girls and the famous "Heinz dilemma" that also involved a response to a speculative rather than a real situation. She looked at two main variables: achievement (obtained through the cheating) and guilt. It was a quantitative study employing a chi square inferential statistic.

Gilligan found that attempting to suppress cheating by arousing guilt or pride in honesty was not effective. However, she also found that although it was not effective as means of a deterrent, it was an influence on behavior. Gilligan's data showed that resistance to temptation may be motivated by the need to maintain a certain self-concept which includes honesty as an important attribute. She confirmed temptation situations as ones of motive conflict and discovered two types of guilt—temptation-produced guilt, such as the anxiety arising from the conflict created by the temptation itself, and deviation-produced guilt, generated from giving in to the temptation. Gilligan concluded that more research needed to be done on the conflicting drives by controlling for one and studying the other.

The dissertation is of interest in that one can see the connections between this work and her later work with girls and moral development. Gilligan has studied how girls face moral situations differently than boys, which is something that historically has been believed to be similar in nature. Whereas boys view moral conflict in terms of "justice" issues, girls tend to see it in terms of "webs" and relationships.

In Gilligan's dissertation, the theme of situational ethics emerges and is repeated throughout. She found that most children will cheat in certain situations but not in others. "The response to temptation is a response to a conflict," Gilligan stated, "resistance or yielding to temptation is conceptualized as a function of the relative strengths of both the drive for the prohibited gratification and the need to act in accordance with internalized moral standards."[76] Gilligan plumbs moral development by using conflict situations and moral dilemmas, either speculative (like this study and the Heinz problem) or real (such as the abortion study).

This situational theme is carried over into her future research when she did the abortion study in her book, *In a Different Voice*. Her interest in moral dilemmas is precisely because of the situationality of the problems of life. In short, Gilligan pioneered research dealing with such topics as guilt and moral development from her first work as a doctoral student.

IN A DIFFERENT VOICE

In a Different Voice was published one year before Howard Gardner's *Frames of Mind*. Whereas Gardner had provided a sophisticated reinterpretation of existing studies, Gilligan offered fresh data also with a fresh interpretation. The first part of *In a Different Voice* involved twenty-five college seniors who as sophomores were enrolled in a course on moral choice. The seniors were interviewed and followed up five years later. The second part of the study involved twenty-nine women, ages fifteen to thirty-three, diverse in ethnic background and class, some single, others married, who were contemplating an abortion.

Gilligan had few women scholarly models to emulate. Research on moral development had been the province of Freud, Piaget, and Kohlberg. She found herself a pioneer. She had discovered in Kohlberg's work that "females do not exist" and that "the very traits that traditionally have defined the 'goodness' of others are those that mark them deficient in moral development."[77]

Another key part of the study was a replication of Kohlberg's "Heinz dilemma." In this hypothetical scenario, the participants are questioned whether a man named Heinz should steal a very expensive drug he cannot afford to buy in order to save his wife's life. Since the druggist refuses to lower the price of the drug, the question is: Should Heinz steal the drug?

Gilligan questioned two eleven year olds, one a boy and one a girl. The boy answered that he would steal the drug whereas the girl thought another solution would be some form of negotiation with the druggist. Moreover, the girl perceived the problem in larger terms: the husband could be imprisoned for stealing and of no help to a sick wife in the future. Gilligan deconstructed their different responses and concluded that the boy thought in linear terms as he said "sort of a math problem with humans," whereas the girl perceived it as a narrative or relationships which extend over time.[78] The girl understands the connectedness of each player. Gilligan observed that the girl actually is answering a "different question" in that she "is considering not *whether* Heinz should act . . . but rather *how*."[79] One feminist critic has scored Gilligan's use of the "Heinz dilemma" as a "major obstacle" because its hypothetical nature tells us little about "how they reason in real life situations or, most important, how they act."[80] Although this hypothetical character of all survey research is a serious limitation, Gilligan is able to unearth an important insight in how boys and girls of a certain age view life and morality differently.

The crux of *In a Different Voice* is the abortion part of the study. Here Gilligan is able to have her subjects confront a *real* life situation and not just a hypothetical problem such as the Heinz question. For Gilligan, "the abortion dilemma" is one in which for a woman "there is no way of acting without consequences to other and self."[81] Gilligan argues that abortion is the quintessential feminine moral *decision* a woman can make. Thus a woman's sense of self collides with her ethic of care and responsibility.

Gilligan asks: "How much do you owe yourself?" and "How much do you owe other people?"[82] She finds her women repeatedly using the terms *"selfish* and *responsible* in talking about moral conflict and choice" when considering an abortion.[83] She concludes that "in its simplest construction, the abortion decision centers on the self" and that for a woman "the issue is survival."[84] For a woman to choose an abortion means that "she feels that she is all alone."[85]

The participants in the abortion study were followed up. Gilligan had hoped to find in the abortion crisis "possibilities for growth."[86] For some women, this was the case. One woman moved from, in her words, "deciding who is going to lose the least and who is going to get hurt the least" to, in Gilligan's words, a "compassion . . . that leads to caring and respecting her own and other people's needs."[87] They were able to reconsider "the opposition between selfishness and responsibility" and include themselves in a morality of care.[88] Others found a "moral nihilism" where the women would rather "cut off their feelings and not care."[89] In those cases it was "their abandonment by others" which made them "abandon themselves."[90] Gilligan concluded her study by staying that "changes in woman's rights change women's moral judgments, seasoning mercy with justice by enabling women to consider it moral to care not only for others but for themselves."[91]

Gilligan attempted to resolve the age-old problem of reconciling the concept of self and others in women. Whether she succeeds or not is debatable. But her very definition of the problem in women in their development of identity and morality is significant. In this respect, she echoes the dualism inherent in Dewey. Dewey sought to reconcile democracy and education, school and society. Gilligan speaks of "two moral voices"—one male, one female where a morality or rights is posited against a morality of care. And within the morality of care exists another duality between self and others. Her main aim is to meld the two within the feminine mind, for women to have a developing healthy regard of self and the traditional ethic of care. She writes of a woman's "right to include oneself in a morality of care."[92]

Consider the dualism of such Gilligan statements as:

—"The conflict between self and other thus constitutes the central moral problem for women"

—"selfishness" as the opposite of responsibility"

—"the experience of women caught in the opposition between selfishness and responsibility"

In a Different Voice bespeaks the cultural literacy of the author. Gilligan cites examples from the literature of Tolstoy, Dostoevsky, Shakespeare, Joyce, Virginia Woolf, Ibsen, and George Eliot as well as the films of Ingmar Bergman. She mines insights from a large body of literature.

One of the key concepts in Gilligan's books is that girls/women perceive morality and even identity through the prism of relationships. Whereas men can define themselves almost in abstract terms, women perceive themselves in terms of others. As the feminist literature has argued, the tendency is for women—in their roles as wives and mothers—to define themselves in relationship to men so that, in Gilligan's words, "women have traditionally deferred to the judgment of men."[93] Therefore, when Gilligan interviews her subjects in terms of their "concepts of self and morality," she is confronted by responses which are full of what she sees as an "ethic of care."[94] These women are most concerned in trying to establish an independent self without "hurting others."[95] According to Gilligan this is "a major theme," indeed "the common thread" being "the wish not to hurt others and the hope that in morality lies a way of solving conflicts so that no one will be hurt."[96]

Yet Gilligan defines moral reasoning as "the exercise of choice" and she finds that "women perceive themselves as having no choice."[97] For Gilligan, women's "wish to please" is bartered so that they may "expect to be loved and cared for."[98] Yet Gilligan sees in these changing feminist times that, for women, this ethic of care is "an 'altruism' always at risk."[99]

As with many great works of genius, *In a Different Voice* was not received with all its due worth initially in the mainstream press. The book was assigned to women reviewers who rendered opinions ranging from faint to ecstatic praise. But the reviews were not many and some missed the point of the book altogether.

As a case in point, the premier reviewing journal (in terms of sales and widespread recognition), *The New York Times Sunday Book Review*, did not locate *In a Different Voice* among its prime books to be reviewed. The book was discussed in the less prestigious middle of the magazine at the bottom of page 14 underneath a review (ostensibly to the editors more important) of a journalistic account of a woman in a New York mental hospital.

Gilligan's reviewer, Carol Tarvis, a well-known social psychologist who wrote frequently for the popular journal *Psychology Today*, was ambivalent about *In a Different Voice*. On the one hand she declared that "Carol Gilligan's book is important" and that it "is consistently provocative and imaginative."[100] On the other hand, she devoted most of her analysis to questioning whether the psychology of women should be "the primary basis of moral analysis" in that "what people say about their moral views tells us only what they think" rather than what they do.[101]

Other reviewers were more positive. In a lead review in *The Christian Century*, Sally Cunneen also found *In a Different Voice* "important."[102] She hailed the book as a sign that America is "coming of age culturally when such corrective research can be done under the powerful auspices of Harvard."[103]

Both Tarvis and Cunneen were quick to point out that Gilligan, in Cunneen's words, "does not idealize women's moral reasoning."[104] Tarvis observed that "Gilligan does *not* argue that women's morality is better than men's."[105] Not so Betty Reardon of Teachers College, Columbia University who claimed in the pages of *The Teachers College Record* that "no other work provides so cogent an explanation for the failure of public policy."[106] Moreover, Reardon hails *In a Different Voice* as "the most significant recent work on impediments to disarmament" since it is "a rich source of instruction on possibilities for peacemaking."[107] She concludes that "Gilligan has helped us all, men and women, to understand a fundamental cause of the crisis of human survival."[108] Reardon has made a mighty leap to the superiority of women's moral reasoning.

Turning Point in Girls' Development

The other main thesis of Gilligan's studies is that, until age eleven, girls are relatively secure and confident in themselves as individual human beings. Somewhere between ages eleven and twelve, girls somehow lose their bearings, stifling their voices in order to be included in a world that threatens to disconnect and dismiss them if they speak their minds. What is it that happens to girls at age eleven that threatens to undermine their individuality and ability to vocalize their opinions on their place in the world?

Gilligan more fully explores these changes in her 1990 study *Making Connections: The Relational Worlds of Adolescent Girls at Emma Willard School*, along with Nona Lyons of the Harvard Graduate School of Education, and Trudy J. Hanmer, associate principal of the Emma Willard School, the site of what was to collectively become known as "the Dodge Study." The book is a collection of articles detailing a series of studies co-edited by the three women. The object of the study was to listen to girls of middle school age and their opinions on the topics of the meanings of self, relationship, and morality. The girls involved in the study were pupils at the Emma Willard School, an elite, private boarding school for girls. The school population is racially mixed, with the majority of the students being white, middle, upper-middle, and upper class girls. The school was founded 183 years ago by a woman who was interested in girls' education.

Gilligan and her colleagues suggested that girls between the ages of eleven and sixteen progress through a critical time, experiencing a crisis in terms of relationships. The study sought to discover the connection between feminine psychology and feminine voices in a way that clarifies why girls think the way they do. Gilligan also wondered about the role of education during this crisis of self-discovery. Gilligan had proposed that girls have different moral perspectives than boys and that this moral compass drives the decisions and opinions of adolescent girls in profoundly different ways than boys.

One particular study was conducted with a sample size of twenty-three young women at Emma Willard. An analysis of responses given after asking the question "How would you describe yourself to yourself?" was done to determine the meaning of the girls' descriptions of themselves. The question was asked of the same girls each year for three years.

The struggle to remain confident after the age of eleven is at the crux of a discussion Gilligan had with a young girl named Amy, who steadfastly defended her opinion that a man should not steal even though it would save his dying wife's life, or Tanya, who stated that "people are more important than rules" when told that a homesick seven year old cannot call home to talk to a parent. As girls approach adolescence, their self-assured answers become more ambiguous and disconnected. When Beth, a high school freshman, is asked by her mother to come home from school to babysit her sister, she considers both sides of the situation before responding that either choice she makes will hurt someone, even though she does not want to baby-sit and it would interfere with her plans.

Gilligan restates her main theme: in order to realize one's full potential, girls have to come to terms with the biggest challenge of feminine adolescence—that is, to resolve the conflict between caring for self and caring for others. The losing of one's self in order to care for others, and the fulfilling of one's self at the expense of others, is at the crux of adolescent feminine psychology, and how the girls respond to the questions posed by Gilligan's works bears this out.

Again, this study had a major emotional impact in the public media. In an article in *Ms.* entitled "The Importance of Being Eleven," which reviewed the Willard Study, Lindsy VanGelder states that at age ten or eleven girls have a self-assured, bossy disposition and are not afraid of conflict or care about "being nice."[109] By the seventh grade, the term "I don't know" becomes a regular part of a girl's vocabulary in response to questions of a substantive nature, and they begin to view relational aspects in terms of how self-sacrificial they can be towards others.

In "Confident At 11, Confused at 16" in the *New York Times Magazine,* Rose discussed the Willard School study stating that "around the age of 11, girls go through a moment of resistance—a sharp and particular clarity of vision, an almost perfect confidence in what they know and see, a belief in their integrity and in their highly complex responsibilities toward the world. 'Eleven year olds are not for sale'."[110]

What is it about the age of eleven that changes the way girls view themselves in relation to the world? Gilligan and her colleagues cite the work of Wooley and Wooley, 1980, "Eating Disorders, Obesity and Anorexia," and found that girls are more influenced by body image than boys.[111] Also, Clausen, in "The Social Meaning of Differential Physical and Sexual Maturation," found that boys are given social approval for academic success and achievement, whereas girls are most rewarded for being slim.[112]

One question is the role of body image. Could this conflict explain why girls after age eleven experience difficulty in finding words to describe themselves when asked the question "How would you describe yourself to yourself?" In the prologue to "Making Connections," Gilligan poses this question, along with others, to the girls at the Willard School. Until age eleven, girls have no difficulty answering this question confidently. After age eleven, somehow the girls lose their ability to clearly describe themselves to others. Do girls view the new way that boys look at them as a threat to being taken seriously? According to Gilligan, "women illuminate life as a web rather than a succession of relationships, women portray anatomy rather than attachment as the illusory and dangerous quest."[113] Gilligan mentioned the Persephone myth, whereby the female self mysteriously disappears in adolescence because her thoughts and desires are suddenly viewed as selfish and wrong.

Gilligan and Lyn Mikel Brown further explored the crossroads of adolescence, the "land between childhood and adolescence" that had been "hitherto uncharted territory."[114] Their 1992 five-year study was at another elite, private school with some representation of working class and minority parents among the "fortunate and privileged."[115] One would have expected that "the girls would be flourishing."[116] But at the crossroads of ages eleven, twelve, and thirteen, a major disconnection occurred in their psychological development.

One cause is the shifting perceptions of body image among the girls, "a time of visual change" where they are "disconnected from the world of childhood."[117] Two-thirds of girls experience menstruation and, for many, their physical appearance is caught somewhere between childhood and womanhood—with some being gangly while others are attractive. Consequently, there is a shift in a young girl's mentality from being independent and assertive to being other directed where "they listen to what people say about them."[118] The result is that girls disconnect and lose their voice.

Case Study

As co-author of this chapter, I (Clair T. Newbold) tested out Gilligan's "eleven" hypothesis on my own family in the spring of 1998. I asked my eleven-year-old daughter, Cristin Newbold, the same set of questions asked of the girls at Willard in *Making Connections*. My fourteen-year-old son, Donnie, was also asked the same questions, and the results were compared. This small scale replication in essence further documented Gilligan's insights and research.

I looked forward to hearing Cristin's answers for several reasons. First, she is a wild tomboy born between two boys and is the best athlete in the neighborhood. She is always outside from dawn till dusk when not in school, collecting a variety of bruises and scrapes that defy Band-Aid adhesion. Also her mother (myself) is an outspoken woman who is pursuing a doctorate and tries to be a role model for her. I had a feeling before the interview started that she may be an outlier, answering many of the questions as a boy or very confident girl would.

When Cristin was asked "How would you describe yourself to yourself?" she replied that she was nice, loveable, and sensitive. Her answer was unsure, and the qualities all very affective. She was somewhat hesitant on many of her answers, almost as if she were trying to give me the answers I wanted to hear instead of her own.

One question that I found particularly interesting was when I asked her what morals were. She replied that they are what's right and wrong "in a situation." She also said that this varies as circumstances suggest. In other words, Cristin was explaining situational ethics to me in her own way. This is a feminine way of thinking, with girls seeing people and relationships as being more important than rules. She did say later that she would break a rule to help a friend, which is a more masculine way of thinking, although she confounded her answer by saying that she would also break a rule to prevent a girlfriend from being angry at her.

I was interested to hear what her response would be to the Heinz dilemma. Cristin replied that she would steal the drug to keep her wife alive, a very masculine answer. Her explanation was that life is more important than money or stealing, a much more cut-and-dry answer than most girls would give. The standard girl answer would have involved bartering or talking the druggist into lowering the drug price.

Cristin's ethic of care came out in her response to what society value in women. Included in her answer was to be sensitive, caring, and generous. This care ethic also became apparent when she said she would take care of her brothers because boys are goofy and can't take care of themselves. When asked what society's image of the perfect woman was, she mentioned beauty, kindness, and "big boobs." Now Cristin has a very good image of her body but even she mentions breast size as being important. If a very confident girl is intimidated by the so-called perfect body, then how are other girls handling puberty?

At the end of her interview, I asked her what she would want people to know about her. She said that she really didn't care what other people felt about her, but she wanted them to know that she is nice—a confident, independent, but feminine answer.[119]

As a comparison, I interviewed my fourteen-year-old son, Donnie, using the same questions as I did for Cristin. Donnie was extremely confident and sure of every one of his answers, almost as if he knew ahead of time what they were so he could be prepared. He defined morality in terms of personal beliefs and standards that may or may not agree with anyone else's, indeed a very masculine answer. Not once did he hesitate or seem to wonder what I wanted to hear before he spoke.[120]

Thinking back on my own adolescent experience, I was not nearly as confident as my daughter, although just as good an athlete and just as much a tomboy; I was more hesitant to voice my own opinions and looked more to others for approval. My heroes were my mother and a young famous female gymnast, Olga Korbut (which led me to becoming a gymnast).[121]

It appears that when girls possess physical confidence, whether through participation in athletic activities or not, they seem to have more confidence in other areas of their lives, even in answering questions about themselves and their feelings. My small study confirms Gilligan's main text where girls' attitudes about themselves change with the physical transformations taking place in their own bodies. Before boys and girls reach adolescence and their bodies look alike, girls show much more confidence and self-assuredness than after adolescence. There is some evidence that a girl who is comfortable within her body is more likely to also be comfortable with her responses in her relationship to the world.

I also interviewed a friend of Cristin's, named Brandi. She is a highly intelligent twelve-year-old girl who is also involved in several different sports. I expected her to answer the questions in a very confident way, and she did, although she was very thoughtful and would wait several moments before answering. My hypothesis on this topic is that if a girl is confident with her body, such as an athlete or dancer, she may have an easier time answering her questions confidently and might even make better grades in school. It has been my own experience as a mother and teacher that this is the case.

The point of the interview was to pose several questions, mostly of a moral or "right or wrong" vein, to try to obtain information as to the ethical matrix of the girl.

As the interview began, Brandi was very shy and hesitant, even though I knew her to be outgoing. I attributed this to the novelty of the situation. She was very hesitant to answer the first question and had to be prompted, but after I reassured her, she relaxed and became more open with her answers. She was thoughtful, wanting to make sure she expressed herself in an intelligent manner, so she would wait several moments before answering each question.

Several themes emerged and reappeared during the interview. One was the theme of her athleticism of which she is extremely proud. I find that girls who are accomplished athletes are more confident in other areas of their lives, such as in school and social situations. She mentioned being athletic as one of the most desirable traits a woman can possess and included it in her answer as to what the perfect woman would be like. The athletic theme reappeared nine other times throughout the interview, stressing its importance to the subject.

Another theme that emerged was that of relationships. This theme is very common among girls as they value webs and interpersonal aspects as probably the most important area of life. This idea appeared eight times, including two times where the maintaining or preserving of the relationship was highly important. It was very important to the subject that she have friends and that she also be a friend to them.

A third theme that appeared was that of justice, or as Gilligan calls it, "the ethic of justice." This is traditionally held to be a masculine way of viewing the world, but I expected it to surface in this interview because of the athleticism and confidence level of this girl. A fourth and related theme was that of "the ethic of care" that she also displayed, and that I also expected because, even though she possessed "tom-boy" qualities, she is also feminine.

The next theme was that of trust, which appeared three times. At the base of my subject's relationship model, trust seems to be the main ingredient or the most important factor in defining relationships. Finally, a factor kept reappearing that spoke about the girl's high intelligence level. Brandi asked for verification several times. She wanted to make an intelligent statement, so she wanted to know exactly what I meant by a question so as not to misunderstand and come up with an invalid answer. In general, Brandi responded as I expected her to and supported my hypothesis as to how she would answer the questions. The only surprise was at the beginning when she hesitated to respond out of shyness, which is not a usual trait for her to display.[122]

These personal case studies confirmed Carol Gilligan's theses.

CRITICISM

Critics of Gilligan's work have crossed the spectrum—from anti-feminist to those who are strongly feminist. These critics, some scholarly, others of a journalistic bent, view Gilligan's research as not fitting their particular ideology. Whatever limitations there are to Gilligan's work (as there are to all research studies), the fact remains that there has not been a sufficiently large body of countervailing research to disprove her main theses.

Let us consider initially the range of criticism. The "debunker" of feminist "myths," Christina Hoff Sommers, characterized Gilligan's work as wanting "empirical evidence" and that Gilligan's "standing is generally higher among gender feminists intellectuals than among scholars at large."[123] On the other end of the spectrum, poet and journalist Katha Pollitt characterized Gilligan's research as reinforcing patriarchical stereotypes of "women as earth mothers" who function as the "guardian of all the small rituals that knit together a family and community."[124] She asks rhetorically, "Haven't we been there before?"[125]

The core of the scholarly attacks on Gilligan's research is a meta-analysis of small studies of gender, moral development, and adolescence by Lawrence Walker in 1984. Walker argued that in these studies he could not detect sex difference in moral development. Walker's article was the basis of the Sommers attack, as it was for a round table of female scholars examining Gilligan's work that the feminist academic journal *Signs* sponsored in 1986. In that journal, Gilligan replied that the Walker article did not really pertain to her work since she is interested "in the way people *define* moral problems" and that "Walker's conclusions and use of statistics" in turn, were "seriously challenged by two of the researchers on whose findings he most heavily relies."[126]

The other main charge against Gilligan is her methodology. Most psychologists are well trained in psychometric statistical analysis and are uncomfortable with qualitative research (witness Gardner's critics in the preceding chapter). Sommers "want of empirical evidence" equates to statistical evidence. Two women psychologists in the *Signs* debate were also uncomfortable with Gilligan's methodology. They felt that *In a Different Voice* "demands quantitative as well as qualitative research."[127] Another woman psychologist in that same journal criticized the small samples. On that basis alone, she argued that Gilligan "oversimplified the case and over-interpreted the data."[128]

Yet the *Signs* scholars were arguing on Gilligan's turf. *Signs* had created this "interdisciplinary forum" consisting of one historian, one policy analyst, and three psychologists—all women scholars—with a rejoinder from Gilligan. These scholars were quick to realize that *In a Different Voice* had become a "part of a major feminist redefinition of a social vocabulary."[129] They commended Gilligan for "seeking to right a wrong" and that her book "had a predictably wide audience among women."[130] Further she was praised for "the elegance of her style and by the historical, philosophical depth of what she has to say."[131]

The historian was dismayed that Gilligan "makes only a single, brief reference to women's history."[132] But her main complaint (like Katha Pollitt's) was that "we have heard this argument before, vested in different language" and that this research "bordered on a familiar variety of feminist self-righteousness" that "claimed women were different from—and usually, better than—men."[133]

This latter charge was also the basis of Pollitt's critique. Pollitt scores *In a Different Voice* for being "the mantra of difference feminism" through this "immensely influential book."[134] For Pollitt, Gilligan has become one of the "toasts of feminist social science, endlessly cited and discussed in academia, and out of it."[135] But her message remains the same. It is "what people want to hear: Women are really different."[136]

In her reply to the *Signs* contributors, Gilligan invoked a quote from William James. She noted that "when a new idea is introduced, the first response is to say that it is so obviously false, it is hard to say how anyone could believe it; the second is to say that it is not original, and everyone has always known it to be true."[137] She pointed out that the title of her book was "deliberate" that "it reads in a *different* voice not "in a *woman's* voice."[138]

One of the aspects of Gilligan's work that has brought intense criticism is the implication that women possess a higher moral nature than men, that the disposition for caring transcends male abstract ideals of justice. This is what some feminists define as "difference feminism."[139] Some of Gilligan's disciples have claimed as much, although Gilligan herself has shied away from that implication.

Furthermore, in a 1993 preface to *In a Different Voice*, Gilligan made clear that her work was *not* a part of "difference feminism" or that she thought women were more moral than men. "When I hear my work being cast in terms of whether women and men are really (essentially) different or who is better than whom, I know that I have lost my voice, because these are not my questions. Instead, my questions are about our perceptions of reality and truth: how we know, how we hear, how we see, how we speak. My questions are about voice and relationship."[140]

Although her ideas on that subject have altered slightly through the years, they have remained essentially the same. Gilligan argued that women have the potential to become major agents for social and political change. In a *Ms.* interview in 1981 with the provocative title "Are Women More Moral Than Men?", she staked out her position: "If women have access to another way of thinking about relationships that is more cooperative and less hierarchical, then they know something is very important for everybody. If they bring such knowledge into positions of social power, they may bring about important social change."[141] Note that Gilligan speaks of *knowledge* and *psyche*. Her emphasis is on different *ways of thinking*, changing the hearts and minds of girls/women.

By 1990, she had strengthened her position on the subject. In an essay with the equally provocative title "Joining the Resistance: Psychology, Girls and Women," she goes beyond her initial position of self-knowledge. She made three key points. First, she noted that it was Freud who originally observed the drastic change in adolescent girls, what Gilligan located as "the intersection between political resistance and psychological resistance, at the times of adolescence . . . [in] . . . girls' psychological development."[142] Second, she considered education as "the time-honored, non-violent means of social change, the alternative to revolution" that is "largely in the hands of women (as) mothers, teachers and therapists."[143] And third, she argued that the key is the mother-daughter relationship.

One of the most severe attacks on Gilligan has come from the pen of the feminist poet, Katha Pollitt. The crucial concept for Pollitt is one of power. She argues the major task facing women is changing the patriarchical power structure to eliminate class, racial, and gender discrimination. For Pollitt,

Gilligan neglects issues of class and race in favor of an identity politics based on a feminine mystique. According to Pollitt, Gilligan ignores the fact that "the differences between men and women are the result of their relative economic positions."[144] To Gilligan's credit she does occasionally speak directly about power, about how women avoid "controversial issues" because of a sense of vulnerability which "stems from a lack of power."[145] But unlike Pollitt and other active feminists, Gilligan (like Dewey) is not a strategist. She is, after all, a psychologist conducting research.

IMPACT ON EDUCATION

Gilligan influenced not only society at large but, more specifically, American education. Even her critics acknowledge how her work has found a large audience among women. Four years after *In a Different Voice*, a quartet of women psychologists applied Gilligan's insights to education. They published their work entitled *Women's Ways of Knowing: The Development of Self, Voice and Mind*, which became a popular success. The book was modeled after Gilligan's research. One reason was that its first author, Mary Field Belenky, had studied at Harvard and worked initially with Kohlberg and later was involved with "research on women's development with Carol Gilligan."[146] The authors pay tribute to Gilligan by acknowledging that "from the first, the work of Carol Gilligan and William Perry inspired us and informed us" and that "our work could never have been accomplished without their bold new constructions of human development."[147] In turn, Gilligan called *Woman's Ways of Knowing* "an important book."[148]

Another key study which has had enormous influence was the review of the literature on sex bias in schooling. Commissioned by the Association of American University Women, prepared by the Wellesley College Center for Research on Women, and published in 1995, the book was titled *How Schools Shortchange Girls: A Study of Major Findings on Girls and Education*. Christina Hoff Sommers would claim that the AAUW report "had its own scholar and philosopher in Carol Gilligan" who also served as "an adviser on the development of questions asked in the survey."[149] Moreover, one of the authors was a student at Harvard and Gilligan was her dissertation adviser.[150] The authors acknowledge Gilligan's work as part of a "strong line of feminist research and thinking" that "addresses strengths girls and women can bring to communities through a sense of connection."[151]

The AAUW report goes beyond summarizing research on gender bias in schooling by prescribing recommendations. These include a program for awareness of sex bias in teaching, curricula which values women as well as men, new tests "to reflect the abilities of both girls and boys," and a call for women to "play a central role in educational reform."[152]

CONCLUSION

The evidence supporting Carol Gilligan's theses on women and moral development has proven overwhelming. She has opened a crack in the consciousness of a patriarchical society. Along with other researchers on sex bias, Gilligan deeply influenced administrators, teachers, parents, and students. Her work has significance for a society that strives to be just and needs to eliminate gender bias and reconceptualize itself.

And she has not ceased to seek understanding of adolescence. She has returned to her first foray in moral development to study the turning point in young boys' development. Her question is whether more caring—indeed, feminine—leanings in boys might not be suppressed as they make the transition into adolescence. In short, Carol Gilligan has created, like Gardner, a paradigm shift in how we view women and what that implies for American education.

NOTES

Clair T. Newbold is a graduate teaching assistant and a doctoral student in urban education at Old Dominion University. She is currently writing a dissertation on gender and education.

1. Carol Gilligan, *In a Different Voice: Psychological Theory and Women's Development* (Cambridge Mass.: Harvard University Press, 1982, 1993), p. 173.

2. Ibid., p. 74.

3. Carol Gilligan and Annie Rogers, "Reframing Daughtering and Mothering: A Paradigm Shift in Psychology," in *Daughtering and Mothering*, edited by Janneke Van Mens-Verhulst et al. (London: Routledge, 1993), p. 126.

4. "Twenty-Five Most Influential Americans," *Time*, June 17, 1996, p. 66.

5. Ibid.

6. *New York Times*, April 10, 1998, p. 23.

7. Gilligan, *In a Different Voice*, p. 173.

8. Carol Gilligan et al., eds., *Mapping the Moral Domain* (Cambridge, Mass.: Harvard University Press), 1988, p. xvi.

9. Ibid.

10. Gilligan, *In a Different Voice*, p. ix.

11. Interview with Carol Gilligan, October 14, 1998, Harvard University.

12. Ibid.

13. Ibid.

14. Ibid.

15. Ibid.

16. Ibid.

17. Ibid.

18. Ibid.

19. Ibid.

20. Ibid.

21. Ibid.

22. Ibid.

23. Ibid.

24. Carol Gilligan, "Remembering Larry," *Journal of Moral Education* 27, no. 2 (1998): 128.

25. Interview with Carol Gilligan.

26. Ibid.

27. Ibid.

28. Ibid.

29. Ibid.

30. Ibid.

31. Ibid.

32. Ibid.

33. Gilligan, "Remembering Larry," p. 126.

34. Ibid.

35. Ibid., p. 127.

36. Ibid.

37. Ibid., p. 120.

38. Ibid.

39. Interview with Carol Gilligan.

40. Ibid.

41. Ibid.

42. Gilligan, "Remembering Larry," p. 131.

43. Interview with Carol Gilligan.

44. Ibid.

45. Ibid.

46. The AAUW Report, *How Schools Shortchange Girls* (New York: Marlowe & Company, 1995), p. 3.

47. Patricia B. Campbell, "What's a Nice Girl Like You Doing in a Math Class," *Phi Delta Kappan*, March 1996, p. 517.

48. David Sadker and Myra Sadker, *Failing at Fairness: How America's Schools Cheat Girls* (New York: Charles Scribner's Sons, 1994), p. 44.

49. The AAUW Report, *How Schools Shortchange Girls*.

50. Sadker and Sadker, *Failing at Fairness*, p. 78.

51. Gilligan, "Remembering Larry," p. 125.

52. Ibid., p. 128.

53. Ibid., pp. 128, 137.

54. Ibid., p. 134.

55. Ibid.

56. Ibid.

57. Lawrence Kohlberg, *The Philosophy of Moral Development*, Vol. 1 (New York: Harper & Row, 1981), p. 64.

58. Gilligan, *In a Different Voice*, p. xix.

59. Ibid., p. xxx.

60. Ibid., p. 18.

61. Ibid., p. 104.

62. Phillip Eddy, "Kohlberg and Dewey," *Educational Theory* 38, no. 4 (fall 1988): 405.

63. Ibid.

64. Lawrence Kohlberg and Rochelle Mayer, "Development as the Aim of Education," *Harvard Educational Review* 42, no. 4 (November 1972): 493.

65. Ibid. p. 493.

66. Ibid., p. 450.

67. Lawrence Kohlberg and Carol Gilligan, "The Adolescent as a Philosopher: The Discovery of the Self in a Postconventional World," *Daedalus* 100, no. 4 (1971): 1051.

68. Ibid., p. 1054.

69. Ibid., p. 1055.

70. Ibid., p. 1083.

71. Ibid.

72. Ibid.

73. Carol Gilligan and Lawrence Kohlberg, "From Adolescence to Adulthood: The Rediscovery of Reality in a Postconventional World," in B. Presseisen et al., eds., *Topics in Cognitive Development*, Vol. 2 (New York: Plenum Press, 1977), p. 133.

74. Ibid.

75. Carol Gilligan, "Responses to Temptation: An Analysis of Motives" (doctoral diss., Harvard University, Cambridge, Mass., 1963), p. 1.

76. Ibid., p. 50.

77. Gilligan, *In a Different Voice*, p. 18.

78. Ibid., p. 26.

79. Ibid., p. 31.

80. Katha Pollitt, "Marooned on Gilligan's Island: Are Women Morally Superior to Men?" in *Reasonable Creatures: Essays on Women and Feminism* (New York: Knopf, 1994), p. 48.

81. Gilligan, *In a Different Voice*, p. 108.

82. Ibid., p. 136.

83. Ibid., p. 73.

84. Ibid., pp. 74–75.

85. Ibid., p. 75.

86. Ibid., p. 109.

87. Ibid., pp. 122–23.

88. Ibid., p. 118.

89. Ibid., p. 124.

90. Ibid., p. 149.

91. Ibid., p. 136.

92. Ibid., p. 69.

93. Ibid., p. 74.

94. Ibid., p. 65.

95. Ibid., p. 66.

96. Ibid., p. 67.

97. Ibid.

98. Ibid.

99. *New York Times, Sunday Book Review,* May 2, 1982, p. 32.

100. Ibid., p. 14.

101. *The Christian Century,* December 22–29, 1982, p. 1315.

102. Ibid.

103. Ibid.

104. Ibid.

105. *New York Times, Sunday Book Review,* May 1, 1982, Section 7, p. 32.

106. *Teachers College Record* (summer 1983): 966.

107. Ibid., p. 968.

108. Ibid., p. 969.

109. Lindsy VanGelder, "The Importance of Being Eleven," *Ms.,* July / August 1990, p. 77.

110. Frances Rose, "Confident, Composed at 16," *New York Times Magazine,* January 7, 1990, p. 33.

111. Carol Gilligan et al., eds., *Making Connections: The Relational Worlds of Adolescent Girls at Emma Willard School* (Cambridge, Mass.: Harvard University Press, 1990), p. 167.

112. Ibid., p. 168.

113. Gilligan, *In a Different Voice,* p. 48.

114. Lyn Mikel Brown and Carol Gilligan, *Meeting at the Crossroads: Women's Psychology and Girls' Development* (New York: Ballantine Books, 1992), p. 2.

115. Ibid., p. 5.

116. Ibid.

117. Ibid., p. 166.

118. Ibid.

119. Interview with Cristin Newbold, April 4, 1998, Norfolk, Va.

120. Interview with Donnie Newbold, April 6, 1998, Norfolk, Va.

121. Interview (Self) with Clair T. Newbold, April 8, 1998, Norfolk, Va.

122. Interview with Brandi Hammock, June 4, 1998, Norfolk, Va.

123. Christina Hoff Sommers, *Who Stole Feminism? How Women Have Betrayed Women* (New York: Simon and Schuster, 1994), p. 152.

124. Pollitt, "Marooned on Gilligan's Island," p. 44.

125. Ibid.

126. Carol Gilligan, "On *In a Different Voice*:: An Interdisciplinary Forum," *Signs: Journal of Women in Culture and Society* 11, no. 21 (1986): 329.

127. Catherine G. Greeno and Eleanor E. Maccoby, "On *In a Different Voice,*" *Signs: Journal of Women in Culture and Society* 11, no. 21 (1986): 315.

128. Zella Luria, "On *In a Different Voice,*" *Signs: Journal of Women in Culture and Society* 11, no. 21 (1986): 306.

129. Linda K. Kerber, "On *In a Different Voice,*" *Signs: Journal of Women in Culture and Society* 11, no. 21 (1986): 306.

130. Luria, *Signs,* p. 316.

131. Kerber, *Signs,* p. 314.

132. Ibid., p. 304.

133. Ibid., p. 308.

134. Pollitt, "Marooned on Gilligan's Island," pp. 46, 47.

135. Ibid., p. 49.

136. Ibid.

137. Gilligan, *Signs*, pp. 324–25.

138. Ibid., p. 327.

139. Pollitt, "Marooned on Gilligan's Island," p. 55.

140. Gilligan, *In a Different Voice*, p. xiii.

141. Martha Saxton, "Are Women More Moral Than Men?" *Ms.*, December 1981, p. 66.

142. Carol Gilligan, "Joining the Resistance: Psychology, Girls and Women," *Michigan Quarterly Review* 24, no. 4 (1990): 529.

143. Ibid.

144. Pollitt, "Marooned on Gilligan's Island," p. 61.

145. Gilligan, *In a Different Voice*, p. 66.

146. Mary Field Belenky et al., *Women's Ways of Knowing: The Development of Self, Voice, and Mind* (New York: Basic Books, 1986, 1997), p. x.

147. Ibid.

148. Ibid. (back cover).

149. Sommers, *Who Stole Feminism?*, p. 152.

150. Ibid.

151. The AAUW Report, *How Schools Shortchange Girls*, p. 143.

152. Ibid., p. 159.

Appendix: Interview with Carol Gilligan, Harvard University, October 14, 1998

Dr. B.: You were born in New York City, right?

C.G.: Right.

Dr. B.: What part of the city?

C.G.: The West Side.

Dr. B.: Where did you go to school in New York City?

C.G.: I went to nursery school at the Walden School. Then, I went to Hunter Model School, the elementary school. And, then I went back to Walden for high school. I was in the middle of progressive education.

Dr. B.: Did Dewey influence you in any way? Besides being in progressive schools.

C.G.: I was influenced by Dewey's schools, not by Dewey as a philosopher. But, I went to progressive schools.

Dr. B.: What was the occupation of your parents?

C.G.: My parents are interesting because they were first-generation born in New York City. My father graduated from Cornell. When he graduated from Cornell he was a chemist. I think that's not right, it is going to be misleading. He went into business, then he went back to law school at night. You know this is the depression era. He became then a very successful lawyer. So, my father lived the Irving Howe story (of successful immigrant Jews in America). He was born in the back room of a dairy store. And he ended up as a successful and beloved Wall Street lawyer. During the war (WW II), my father was the warden for the block. My father was one of these who was loved by everyone.

My mother, you would probably be interested, also did a bunch of different things. She was artistic and she worked with an oriental rug person and she worked with fabrics and decoration and then she worked for the Menorah Journal and then she went to the Bank Street School for Education.

Dr. B.: She went to Bank Street. Did she get a degree?

C.G.: Yes, as a nursery school teacher. She worked at the Child Development Center at Bank Street and was a special object relations therapist.

Dr. B.: In your work there are two themes, the way I see it. One is that girls/women perceive moral issues differently than boys/men in terms of human relationships rather than abstract concepts; as you write an "ethic of care" rather than an "ethic of justice" that Lawrence Kohlberg found in his studies with boys. The other theme is that girls up to the "disconnect age" of eleven years/twelve years are confident, self assured and do well academically. Then they slide in self-esteem and in school. You also found in your research with these girls that the mother-daughter relationship at that stage in their lives is paramount. How did you relate at that age to your mother?

C.G.: It's interesting you ask this. I'll answer your question. It's only there are many questions you could ask me about my life at eleven and twelve. Given that I write about this as a break point. Given that I then pick up how many women have written about this as a break point—Charlotte Bronte, Toni Morrison, Jamaica Kincaid and on and on. Given that I then show what the break is among girls. That's the point where girls feel pressed to not know what they know. This brings girls into an intense relationship with women around the question of what do women know. And it shows the extraordinary, I guess I'd put it this way, challenge of authentic relationships between women and girls at this point. If I can go one step further that the world we live in, the structure of the society we live in and educate in which is patriarchal, that to me is a descriptive term, is in a sense maintained by a break in relationships between mothers and daughters. Why I say that then is that to have anything resembling an authentic relationship between a mother and daughter is going to challenge the perpetuation of the patriarchal order. We're talking about three millennia of patriarchy.

So I just want to place that relationship with my mother in that context. Then I'd say that I can remember at the time I was twelve and thirteen my mother and I began to struggle with each other around these issues. And I would say we were actively struggling with each other around these issues, I would say, through my adolescence. And it was a fight, probably on my side, for an authentic relationship with her. She was remarkable in the sense of hanging in there. But I think we were struggling to try to have a real relationship. I was going to say that what I came to when I did this work with girls and in schools I came to appreciate what was at stake for women teachers, mothers, and therapists to stay in relationship with, first of all, that part of their own history, which was, of course, revived for them by girls (students). It was easier to maintain a dissociation which was coded as development by most developmental scales—separation, independence, self-sufficiency, having good boundaries—were all seen as marks of progress. It was the girls saying I'm losing my relationships. You go to the novels, Jane Eyre saying I was a resistor, I refused to say I loved so and so when I didn't. I just wanted to say, yes, I struggled with my mother at this point. But it was a struggle and she was active in it, too. For want of a better word what would it mean for us to stay in a relationship. As I became an adolescent I saw further, felt more deeply, was more in touch with the realities of adult life, including her life.

Clair: I'm going through that right now with my daughter.

C.G.: I just want to say that I became tremendously in awe, because I have sons, and am sympathetic with and appreciative of what that relationship meant. Because the daughters today, and I think this was true for me, too, begin to see into their mother's lives in ways which most mothers welcomed and also felt you can't go there.

Clair: Exactly, I can relate to that, because I'm getting my Ph.D. at the same time and my daughter tries to cheer me up all the time. Well, you're getting your Ph.D., she says, that's a wonderful thing, you know. But she oversteps her boundaries sometimes and tries to delve into personal issues that are none of her business. So, she is trying to be an adult and she pulls back sometimes, then she reassures me.

Dr. B.: Did you have any siblings?

C.G.: I was an only child.

Dr. B.: How did you do in middle school?

Clair: How were your grades?

C.G.: I went to Hunter, you know (an elite school). I always did well in school. In fact, I would say that's why my mother as a teacher wanted me to go to Walden was because she really valued the central place of the arts in education at Walden and so I always was very involved in the arts. Modern dance. I was also a pianist. I always did choral singing if you want to understand my work in voice.

Clair: I play the piano, sing, paint.

Dr. B.: My oldest daughter has been in ballet from the age of five to now at thirty-three. She's an attorney. You have the arts forever.

C.G.: And then I'm a writer. I won prizes as a child for writing. I considered my mother's move to send me to Walden as a big decision.

Dr. B.: It was her decision?

C.G.: She was very pro-progressive education. My father, who was very demo-cratic, believed in public schooling because he had gone to Cornell on a regent scholarship.

Dr. B.: How were your teachers? Were there any special ones?

C.G.: I had wonderful teachers. In high school I had an English teacher named Raymond John. I just remember his classes. I had a Latin teacher named Lucille Cohen. And then in college, I went to Swarthmore and I had phenomenal teachers. I had a teacher named Sam Hines who was an English teacher and he influenced me profoundly. Those were the remarkable teachers. And all my friends' mothers were teachers.

Dr. B.: Were you precocious?

C.G.: I also spoke three languages. I was sent to a Hebrew School so I spoke Hebrew. Then my mother sent me, because I love good language, to an Israeli woman with whom I learned conversational Hebrew. I took Latin and I also spoke French. At Hunter we learned French in the first grade. You know I had a lot of dif-ferent languages. That was part of it, too.

I do remember that I loved books as a child. Just loved them. My mother used to read to me and sing to me and I love music and I love books. I love words, I guess.

Dr. B.: Did you have a literary bent? Did you want to write novels?

C.G.: Yes, which is what I'm doing now (in my research) (laughter).

Dr. B.: That's what I wanted to do, to write novels. Michael Harrington (the social critic) started by writing poetry, he wanted to be a poet. Jonathan Kozol (education author) published a novel first.

C.G.: I did it the other way around. I was never consciously aware of wanting to do it until fairly recent.

Dr. B.: How did you come to study girls and moral development?

C.G.: I came to feminism, like many people, through the civil rights movement and the anti-Vietnam war movement. But what I was aware of, and I was aware of this in graduate school, was there seemed to be a discrepancy between the way people lived their lives, which, of course, I knew from life, but also from literature, my education in human psychology, other than just from living, which is no small thing, as Virginia Woolf says you know what we could call psychology is that un-paid education in life through literature: I mean to Tolstoy and Dostoevsky, Virginia Woolf and Faulkner and everyone else. When I came to psychology as a graduate student, because I was the clinical type, I thought I wanted to be a thera-pist and it seemed very flat, the description of the human world. It seemed very re-duced in a way I didn't associate with gender at all. It seemed wrong to me. It just seemed too simplistic. This was true in my mind in the representation of men as well as women. I was teaching part-time as a post-doctoral student (at Harvard). I taught with Erikson and I taught with Larry Kohlberg. We taught this course on moral and political choice. The men students in the class, this was during the Vietnam War, didn't want to talk about the draft. So I thought, I would ask a group of graduate students, Do you want to do a study about how people make actual (moral) decisions? Not just hypothetical. You can say anything, words are cheap. So, I was going to study Harvard College men, although gender wasn't salient for me with the Vietnam draft. Nixon ended the draft, was it in '73? *Roe v. Wade* was decided (U.S. Supreme Court decision to legitimize abortion).

I started on my study again on decision making, on real life decision making, how the self appears in moments of conflict and choice where you have to say I'm going this way, not this way, how the personal pronoun "I" comes in. And sec-ondly, whether moral language guides that choice. So Roe v. Wade was total serendipity, that produced for me at that moment in history an all female sample. Which was the last thing I thought about was the fact that it was all women. Just as my previous study was all men. And then it was listening to women talk about this decision and hear the dissonance between what was the moral problem for women, that decision was embedded in a whole network of relationships includ-ing how do women get pregnant in the first place and then the decision about whether to continue or abort a relationship. It was completely at odds with the right to life, right to choice conversations. So when I wrote *In a Different Voice*, it was about changing the voice of the public conversation that was the conversation about psychology, the conversation about morality, the conversation about devel-opment, the conversation about what it meant to have a sense of self was to bring in women's voices meant changing the theme of conversation so you heard every-body differently. So it was this moment in history that happened and I think it is no accident that the abortion decision was so interesting because what had been seen as goodness for women was helplessness. To be responsible to others and to sort of put yourself last. But here what happened in that turning point the Supreme Court legitimatized women's voices where suddenly women said "Wait a minute. It's not responsible to be selfless: it's irresponsible. Because if you're selfless, you are not there and if you're not there, how can you take care of the child? So, it suddenly turned around the understanding of what responsibility means, what morality means, what it means to be a mother, a good mother, what it means to be in a rela-tionship. This notion that relationship means being selfless the women (in my study) were saying that's no relationship. So it was a real paradigm shift.

Clair: I think it helps out. It sheds light on other issues, too—like for example, spousal abuse or something like that because women still to this day deny their ex-perience. Something happens to them and they doubt their experience. They have to go to others, did he really do this to me, did he really say that. They doubt their own experience and I find your work sheds light on that whole area. If your feelings are valid, you don't have to have somebody else tell you.

C.G.: Yes, I would say that's the center of all of my work. It's about the sense of reality and the significance then of the developmental work on women and girls after *In a Different Voice* is that doubting of your experience comes in malevolent because it is very hard to hold onto your experience and enter into the social construction of experience. That's exactly it.

Clair: That's what I got out of all your work.

C.G.: That's it. That's the essence and that's the center of it. It's really about what's real. And to enter into what's said to be real, do I have to leave my experience behind.

6

John Ogbu and the Theory of Caste

Blacks in America constitute a pariah caste.

—John U. Ogbu

John Ogbu is a Nigerian-born anthropologist who has spent the better part of his academic career at the University of California, Berkeley, currently as the Chancellor's Professor of Anthropology. He has revolutionized thinking about the education of black Americans and has become a standard reference in the education and social science literature. One cannot omit the study of the education of African Americans in the United States without dealing with the research and theories of John Ogbu. Going beyond familiar interpretations of the academic failure among blacks (and other minority groups) such as class differences, Ogbu has posited a new theory that invokes the idea that African Americans are treated by the majoritarian society as an inferior caste, and they, in turn, often internalize the negative attitudes projected upon them by white America. This research has had a profound influence on American education.

Ogbu brings a fresh perspective to the issue of race and education. "As an African anthropologist," he informs us, "it is both very educational and very interesting to be doing research on American society and writing about Americans."[1] He finds that the "knowledge gained from . . . studying Western societies . . . could be very valuable in examining the nature and problems of Third World societies."[2] Yet, his main focus remains the education of blacks in America and he prescribes policy recommendations based on his research. He enjoys a tremendous reputation in American education. Carol Gilligan has called Ogbu one of her "heroes."[3] In September 1997, the academic journal, *Anthropology and Education*, devoted a whole issue with case studies by anthropologists in different countries testing out Ogbu's theories.[4] Indeed, in 1998 Ogbu received the Distinguished Contributions to Research in Education Award from the prestigious American Educational Research Association.

LIFE

Ogbu has a varied background. Born in a small village in Nigeria in 1939, he was the son of farmers. His father was polygamous and had seventeen children, seven of which were with Ogbu's mother. He was the second one of the family to go to school. His older brother had obtained a job with the government and at the age of seven Ogbu went to live with him and served as a "house boy."[5] He took an exam to obtain a scholarship to the Presbyterian high school in town about 100 miles away from the village and was one of the three highest scorers. The high school was a boarding school and the scholarship covered room, board, and fees. His brother paid for his books and transportation.

When he finished high school he "really wanted to be a doctor" but "because I had no money" he was not able to pursue his first career choice.[6] His desire to be a doctor was influenced by his high school principal, Dr. Francis Ibiam, who was one of the first Nigerians to obtain a medical degree and become a missionary. Ogbu singled him out as his "Uncle" (not a relative), who "influenced my outlook on life."[7]

Ogbu then went to a Presbyterian teachers college and taught Latin, math, and geography for two years in a missionary high school. He was interested in writing and "wrote poems" and participated in drama at school, especially Shakespearean drama which he loved.[8] He continues the practice of having poetry books "by my bedside" and "before I go to bed I read poetry."[9] His second career goal was to be "a minister in the Presbyterian Church."[10] He then decided to pursue a writing career in his studies for the ministry since "communication in writing is important in Africa today, not just preaching."[11]

Ogbu was sent to the Princeton Theological Seminary in the United States to further his studies. At Princeton Theological, a fortuitous "accident" caused him to switch his interest from the ministry to anthropology.[12] Seminaries in Africa concentrated on "church history, Greek or Hebrew" but at Princeton Theological, students were learning about American culture along with the theology. "To work for the church in Nigeria," Ogbu recalled in my interview with him, "I needed to know something about Africa, about my country."[13] So he "thought anthropology would be a good field since it was the only discipline here in the States, that would teach you something about Africa and African cultures."[14] Indeed, Ogbu had "never heard of anthropology" before he came to the United States.[15] He quickly dropped his English major at the University of California at Berkeley and "switched to anthropology."[16] He graduated from Berkeley with honors and then received his masters and doctorate degrees from that institution. Although Ogbu holds to development as a key to education, he does not recall reading any of John Dewey's work.[17]

Ogbu came to the United States in 1961 and became a naturalized American citizen. He began his professional career as an ethnographer in 1968–1969 with the Stockton, California, school system. It was during this time that he formed his provocative theory of caste. For most of his academic career he was associated with the University of California, Berkeley, and a visiting professor at the University of Delaware. He has been an advisor to the United Nations Education, Scientific ,and Cultural Organization (UNESCO).

OGBU AND THE CIVIL RIGHTS MOVEMENT

Ogbu has always been respectful of the civil rights movement. When he immigrated to the United States, he was witness to the movement at its height. He was able to see the many victories made possible at great expense accompanied by violence and bloodshed. Still, when describing America and racism, Ogbu clings to the concept of a racially closed society.

Let us examine the legacy of the civil rights movement. First, one could date the rise of the modern day civil rights movement with the 1954 U.S. Supreme Court Decision outlawing school desegregation. The National Association for the Advancement of Colored People (NAACP) had won a major legal victory that was to set the stage for another phase of the protest movement: mass demonstration. By 1956, the protest movement in the south had reached major proportions with the year-long boycott of public transportation in Montgomery, Alabama. Parenthetically, the Montgomery Bus Boycott was to introduce the major charismatic figure of the movement: Reverend Martin Luther King Jr.

By 1966, the movement developed another phase: black power. Moving away from the goal of integration, black power activists sought to control those institutions in which African Americans were a major part. The first test of this concept was in the community control movement in education in New York City (of which I was a part) in 1968.

As a result of this major domestic protest movement of the twentieth century, a number of positive changes took place. Racial discrimination in institutions was outlawed and African Americans were given the opportunity to vote. And, most important, a new concept of equality of results came to the fore. In his historic speech at Howard University in 1965, President Lyndon Johnson declared that "to fulfill these rights" of the civil rights movement, America must move from a "legal equity" of equality of opportunity to "equality as a result."[18] He was to flesh out the idea of "equality of results" with Executive Order 11246b that created affirmative action in schooling and jobs—in short, preference for African-Americans and other minorities in college admissions, jobs, and business contracts with the federal government. Affirmative action was not seen by its originator as a perpetual policy but one that theoretically would last three generations, enough to enable black Americans to improve their economic, social, and political position. Affirmation action was based on the progress of white ethnics in the first half of the century. Philosopher John Rawls in his 1971 classic book on social justice, *A Theory of Justice*, would suspend his doctrine of fairness where every participant has some measure of satisfaction. Rawls proposed a fifty year moratorium on his doctrine of fairness so that affirmative action could help blacks move up the social and economic ladder. Within a generation, the African American community profited by affirmative action.

The progress of African Americans in American society depends on the vantage point of the observer. Is the glass half full or is the glass half empty? One concedes the successes. But the black poor have been trapped in an economic web that has yet to be broken. On the one hand, as a result of thirty years of affirmative action, the black middle-class has quadrupled. There are four times as many black middle-class families with incomes over fifty thousand as there were more than thirty years ago.[19] Yet, one third of African American families are poor, and a third of black males in their twenties are in the criminal justice system.[20] There are more black elected officials in cities than before the civil rights movement but only a trickle in higher office: one state governor and few in the United States Senate. Most important, for most black Americans race has become an open wound that may never heal. Fifty-eight percent of African Americans (and 66 percent of the poor) surveyed in 1996 felt that "race relations will never be better than they are."[21]

A major scholar of black poverty has been the Howard sociologist, William Julius Wilson. Wilson's first foray into the racial condition of black Americans was his controversial 1978 book, *The Declining Significance of*

Race. In that tome, he argued that class superseded race as an explanation for black success or failure in American society. He wrote that "class has become more important than race in determining black access to privilege and power. It is clearly evident . . . that many talented and educated blacks are now entering positions of power and prestige and influence at a rate comparable to or, in some situations, exceeding that of whites with equivalent qualifications."[22]

Ten years later, Wilson would study the black poor. He found them "in a hopeless state of economic stagnation, falling further and further behind the rest of society."[23] In *The Truly Disadvantaged*, Wilson discovered an alarming situation: the exodus of the black middle class to the suburbs, further destabilizing the urban black ghetto. He wrote, "The exodus of middle and working class families from many ghetto neighborhoods removes an important 'social buffer.' . . . The very presence of these families . . . provides mainstream role models that help keep alive the perception that education is meaningful, that steady employment is a viable alternative to welfare, and that family stability is the norm, not the exception."[24]

Ruminating on this black exodus to the suburbs in 1996, civil rights leader Julian Bond lamented that "it . . . destroyed something we tend to romanticize but what was really an organic community with a wide variety of people . . . and where the community imposed a kind of standard of behavior."[25]

By 1996, Wilson would modify his views on race and class significantly. In an extremely important study, *When Work Disappears*, Wilson surveyed some 2,500 African Americans and Latinos in urban ghettoes in Chicago. He studied the employment patterns of urban ghetto residents and the employers in the area. After analyzing the data, he concluded that "it becomes clear that racism is far more important than I once believed."[26] Black males were the last hired by employers.

Still Wilson is preoccupied with class. Consequently, his main variable in analyzing urban poverty is jobs—or, more properly, joblessness. "For the first time in the twentieth century," he declared in the opening line of the book, "most adults in many inner city ghetto neighborhoods are not working in a typical week."[27] Although Wilson gives added emphasis to race, he sees the problem of the black and Latino poor to be complex. He sees social and economic "structural factors; cultural factors and social psychological variable."[28] Wilson argues for a "broader vision that includes all of the major variables."[29]

For Wilson, having a job provides "a framework for daily behavior and patterns of interaction because it imposes disciplines and regularities."[30] White employers complain about hiring black males for cultural reasons.

They mention a fear of crime; a need for drug testing; poor education of black males with an inability to read, spell or write, or speak standard English; tardiness and absenteeism, and poor dress—in short, the cultural expectations that go with middle class behavior. And, interestingly, black employers shared the same reluctance to hire poor black males. As a remedy, Wilson advocates an affirmative action policy and programs to mentor the urban poor for jobs. However, he blends issues of class and race in his "ideal affirmative action program" that "would emphasize flexible criteria of evaluation based on both need and race."[31]

Ogbu considers Wilson "a good friend of mine, but we decided to disagree."[32] Ogbu agrees "with his basic, original thesis" but does not believe that Wilson "studied the black community sufficiently."[33] Ogbu believes that Wilson and many other middle class African Americans misread the dynamics of the black community. He argues that the black middle class who have escaped black poverty "still do not have the center of experiences of the dominant group (White America)."[34] For example, he cites his research in the black community of finding who are their "committed heroes . . . Abraham Lincoln or Benjamin Franklin."[35] Instead he found that "their heroes turn out to be rebels, people who rebel against the system."[36]

Ogbu's views toward the leaders of the civil rights movement of the 1950s–1960s was that of "essentially an observer."[37] His assessment was that "people tended to support (Martin Luther) King to diminish the impact of Malcolm X."[38] He liked and admired King "but also saw the effectiveness of both."[39] For Ogbu, the civil rights movement made him "very happy" because "in the 1960s you had a choice."[40] He felt that blacks had "progressed" and that was a "period in which they moved up."[41] But he observed that the times when African Americans "achieved something have been in periods of crisis."[42] Despite American egalitarian rhetoric, what he calls "American Statues of Library theory," progress depends on "crisis" and challenges to the American system.[43] Ogbu considers racism still deep-seated in America.

OGBU'S CASTE THEORY

John Ogbu's great contribution to the research on African Americans (as well as other minorities) and schooling was twofold. First, he added to the theories on school success or failure. Second, he gave a plausible explanation based on the research of why African Americans have not done as well as whites on standardized tests scores and in the classroom. Ogbu's theories concern the impact of a majoritarian culture on minorities.

Ogbu is first and foremost an anthropologist. Moreover, he is an African anthropologist who reversed the trajectory of conventional anthropology. Rather than coming from a large developed country to study the village, he came from the village to study a large developed country. And his focal point is always the education of American blacks.

Ogbu's thesis is clear-cut. Ogbu proposes that the major influence in the education of African Americans (and some other United States minorities) is that they form a caste. Indeed, Ogbu argues American blacks form a "pariah caste."[44] As a caste, American blacks are prevented from two major areas of social mobility that are intertwined: education and jobs. In short, blacks receive an inferior education due to racism and are prevented even more so from advancing by a job ceiling that is set in place by the white majoritarian society.

And there is an important corollary to Ogbu's theory of caste. The majoritarian society views blacks as inherently inferior in every respect, including intelligence. "The dominant group," he writes, "usually regards (blacks) as inherently inferior."[45] Correspondingly, African Americans often internalize the negative opinions imposed upon them by the majoritarian society. For many black students, this translates into shunning learning in school for fear of becoming excluded from their peers for "acting white."

Ogbu's main book published in 1978 by Academic Press is *Minority Education and Caste: The American System in Cross-Cultural Perspective.* The book is a brilliant reconceptualization of minorities and education from the wider perspective of different cultures. It is a sophisticated review of innumerable studies with a fresh interpretation of the data. He interweaves this review of the literature with original data that he collected in Stockton, California.

Ogbu's first major foray into the education of African Americans was an ethnographic study in Stockton, California. The original study took place from 1968 to 1970 with follow-up visits in subsequent years. Stockton is a cross section of multicultural America with blacks, Latinos, Asians, and Indians.

Initially, in his interviews with black parents he found that black parents said "they stress education for their children because of the civil rights movement and affirmative action programs."[46] And their children "agree with their parents that good education or good school credentials are desirable for employment."[47] However, in later studies, Ogbu would find that despite such statements there was little support or reward system for academic success in the poor black communities. And Ogbu would discover in his Stockton study that "in spite of blacks' desire for good school credentials . . . black school performance in Stockton is relatively poor and has been that way for generations."[48]

Ogbu surveyed the education field for explanations of black school failure in Stockton. He interviewed "representatives of various segments of the city's population, listened to views expressed at public and private meetings on location educational issues and read location documents."[49] This process of triangulation in research led him to examine the main explanations for black school failure in the city. The most repeated explanation was that the "social class differences" accounted for academic disparity between black poor and middle class whites. This was followed by the theory that "the rural background of black parents" impeded their social mobility and educational level. Lastly, the theory that the cultural deficit traits of the black poor, such as limited English proficiency, was cited as a reason for lower school performance.[50]

Ogbu found these explanations inadequate, especially in light of the limited success of compensatory programs in education to remediate the educational shortcomings of the black poor. For Ogbu, "the problem originated in the involuntary incorporation of blacks into American society" and continuing racial discrimination whereby blacks are defined as an "inferior racial caste" and have "historically been given an inferior education to prepare them for their marginal roles."[51] Consequently, blacks do not think like the Chinese and Japanese counterparts in Stockton that "they can overcome barriers in employment by merely getting a good education."[52]

In *Minority Education and Caste*, Ogbu first examines the state of public education for African Americans and some other minorities. He then examines the effects of caste on other minorities in a number of other countries. "It is well known," he writes, that "black and white children differ in the linguistic, cognitive, and motivational skills they possess when they first come to school."[53] From that premise Ogbu analyzes the prevailing theories of why black children often fail academically and the concomitant strategies for school reform.

He reduces these theories to three major influences: "home environment, school environment, and heredity."[54] However, he finds these theories do not fully explain black and white differences in school performance. He writes: "I do not think that differences between black and whites in cognitive and other skills can be explained in terms of black resistance to acculturation, the failure of black parents to train their children as white middle class parents do, or to biological differences between the two races."[55]

For Ogbu, "what evidence there is suggests that blacks would have developed . . . if they had the same opportunities for more desirable social and occupational positions."[56] He perceives a "reciprocal relationship" between job opportunities and "the patterns of linguistic, cognitive, motivational, and other school related skills."[57] In short, the evidence suggests a caste system.

But Ogbu is careful to limit his study. He warns us that "it is not a study of what is wrong with 'public education' in general."[58] Nor does he deal with "the more general problem of social mobility."[59] It is a study of the interplay of education and economic opportunity for African Americans in late twentieth century America. In that regard, Ogbu makes a giant assumption that education is the crucial variable in social mobility. The prevailing scholars of the 1970s when he was writing—revisionist historians and sociologists such as Christopher Jencks—argued that education in America was not the crucial ingredient in social mobility. Ogbu makes a leap of faith back to the 1960s when romantic reformers made their mantra that education was the main avenue to economic success.

Ogbu concentrates on a subset of theories: cultural deprivation, cultural conflict, institutional deficiency, educational equality, and heredity. He finds these theories only partially explain black-white differences in school. He dismisses cultural deprivation since it does not explain the "success of lower-class children in learning their own culture."[60] He finds culture conflict also inadequate because it "does not automatically lead to . . . school failure" and he cites the success of the Chinese and Japanese school children in America as proof.[61] Regarding the impact of the school, Ogbu acknowledges that teachers and administrators have made "less serious efforts" for African American students.[62] And he does agree on educational equality that "lack of access to adequate school resources is undoubtedly one of the main reasons for the lower school performance of black children."[63] However, he argues that it cannot be shown that "better school resources are always associated with higher pupil performance."[64]

He dismisses the Arthur Jensen thesis that heredity is the basis for intelligence and that blacks appear to have less intelligence than whites. He cites methodological and theoretical problems with the heredity thesis. Moreover, he finds that Jensen's "proposed solution must be viewed with skepticism" and that "no school district has taken [it] seriously."[65] The problem with all these theories, Ogbu concludes, is that none "examines the nature of the American caste system and its possible influence on black school failure."[66]

Ogbu critiques the school reform movements that occurred after the civil rights movements of the 1960s. He genuflects to that movement acknowledging that this era "will long be remembered" for the "important social reforms intended to improve the social and economic status of black Americans and other minorities."[67] And he shares the same assumption of these reformers that "the strategy for reducing black poverty was to give blacks more and better education."[68] But he concludes that these school reforms were not adequate.

In his analysis of black school performance, he cites three factors inhibiting success: "the inferior education blacks have been given for generations"; the subtle "devices used in school by teachers who have low expectations"; and "the job ceiling" that stunts black student motivation.[69] He compresses these reform strategies into two categories: compensatory education programs, such as Head Start, and school integration. He omits discussion of the community control movement because he felt that there were "no adequate studies assessing their effectiveness in raising black school performance," although he conceded that community control did "probably succeed in enhancing black awareness."[70] (He did not know about Marilyn Gittell and my studies in 1972 and 1973, which used a combination of quantitative and qualitative methodologies to show the effectiveness of community control on academic achievement.)

Ogbu regards both the compensatory education and school integration strategies as only being "partially successful."[71] And he felt that these reforms were still "needed" but that they were "based on a partial explanation of the problem and represent only part of the solution."[72] According to Ogbu, the problem with school reformers is that they do not recognize that blacks "constitute a pariah caste" and that black "lower school performance" is an "adaptation to their lower social and occupational positions in adult life."[73] Ogbu then proceeds to investigate the conditions of other castes worldwide.

Ogbu examines the school performance and job opportunities of castes in six countries along two lines. The first category is castes in the same race in India, Israel, and Japan. The second category is comprised of castes of different races such as are in Britain, New Zealand, and the United States. He begins with castes of different races. In Britain, the West Indians constitute a caste; that is, they are perceived as inferior by the white majority in Britain and, correspondingly, internalize this prevailing attitude and do not perform well academically. They are also prevented from moving up socially and economically because of the invisible "job ceiling." According to Ogbu, West Indians form a colored minority whereby the color bar and job ceiling have a definite influence on the school performance of West Indian children in Britain.

The pattern repeats itself for the Maoris in New Zealand. Maoris are also treated as a caste and suffer "low teacher expectations and biased textbooks and curriculum" so that these "subtle devices" have "contributed to lower Maori school performance."[74] For the most best-known of castes, that in India, Ogbu finds a "gap in school performance between the scheduled castes and the upper castes."[75] According to Ogbu, this situation is "attributed to the fact that the education offered is generally inferior" and "that a job ceiling hinders their mobility."[76]

In discussing the same race castes, Ogbu finds that the Buruku in Japan, who number nearly three million people, also do poorly academically and job wise. However, when the Buruku migrate to the United States they are not treated as a caste and they do well in school. In the United States, he writes, "the outcasts appear to have increased their efforts in both scholastic and economic pursuits."[77] Ogbu concludes that they are "not overwhelmed by the traditional prejudices and discrimination" they faced in Japan.[78]

And Ogbu finds in his last example, the Oriental Jews in Israel, that the majoritarian society creates "barriers in school and society" contributing to "lowering their school performance."[79] Yet in comparing these six castes, he finds that "Oriental Jews in Israel are the least caste-like."[80] In the United States, Ogbu classifies some other minorities besides African Americans as caste-like minorities. They include Indians, Mexicans, and Puerto Ricans, who suffer some degree of discrimination and thus do poorly in school.

Ogbu prescribes generalized policy recommendations. First he perceives the solution to caste discrimination as "the elimination of caste barriers" so that there occurs "a total destruction of the caste system."[81] Although he can cite only one such instance of caste destruction in a small town in Peru, he believes that "all caste systems in the modern world contain the seeds of their own destruction."[82] The closest he comes to a specific strategy to insure the end of the caste system is to recommend affirmative action, "preferential treatment for caste-like minorities."[83]

Ogbu distinguishes between voluntary minorities and involuntary minorities, "immigrant or voluntary minorities." He writes "that immigrants are people who have moved more or less voluntarily to the United States—or any other society—because they desire more economic well-being, better overall opportunities, and/or greater political freedom."[84]

They tend to do well in school because of their "expectations." By contrast, involuntary minorities are those who were brought into United States society "against their will."[85] Ogbu says that minorities who are not in the United States because they expect better opportunities "experience greater and more persistent difficulties with schooling."[86]

Ogbu sought to quantify his theory developed from his reading of scholarly literature. Along with Herbert D. Simons he surveyed 2,245 minority students in grades 5 through 12 in sixteen schools in Oakland, California. Those minority students surveyed comprised 1,309 African-Americans, 429 Asian Americans, and 507 Latinos. He found that the voluntary minorities (Asians, Latinos) believe "that education is an important route to making it in society" and "are willing to conform to the dominant society's norms."[87] By contrast, the authors found that African American students "can best be described as ambivalent" with "exaggerated claims of success" with "less effort" in their studies than the other minorities.[88]

Some critics of Ogbu's caste theory offer a four-pronged attack. They contend that Ogbu cannot explain the "exceptions" whereby some involuntary minorities do succeed in school. They also claim that Ogbu neglects some major cultural differences among his caste examples. And they contend that he dismisses class as a contributing factor to poor school achievement. Finally, they question his emphasis on education as the sole means to social mobility. Richard J. Herrnstein and Charles Murray in *The Bell Curve* list Ogbu as proposing "a more specific version of the argument of cultural influence on IQ" that they argue does not have a significant effect on intelligence.[89] Most important, the initial reaction of many black educators to Ogbu's theory was that they consider the theory as "overly pessimistic."[90]

Minority Education and Caste was not reviewed in the general press or intellectual magazines. There were two scholarly reviews, one more positive than the other. Writing in *Contemporary Sociology*, Ray C. Rist credits Ogbu with one "of the most perceptive critiques of American race relations which challenges the conventional wisdom regarding education and inequality."[91] Rist's only reservation was Ogbu discounting "the contribution of school integration."[92] Otherwise he concluded that "the book is an outstanding contribution."[93] In the *American Anthropologist*, Jacqueline Mithum feels that "Ogbu must be credited for a very commendable job in tracking a complex problem."[94] However, she does not agree "with all the arguments against the (competing) theories he discussed."[95] Still she does "agree with Ogbu's conclusion as to the ultimate solution to the problem."[96]

One crucial subtext to Ogbu's theory of caste is what he calls cultural inversion. Cultural inversion is a process of internalization by the oppressed group of the negative perceptions of them by the majoritarian society. It is closely linked with the rather new concept of identity politics. For example, African Americans are hesitant to adopt the successful behaviors of the white majority for fear of betraying their own group. Consequently, they internalize the worst views of white society, and thus fail in school. "Cultural inversion," Ogbu writes, "is a process whereby subordinate group members come to define certain behaviors, events, symbols, and meaning as inappropriate for them because these are characteristic of their oppressors."[97] The African American often fears he/she "has lost his or her black identity and has 'assimilated' into white cultural identity or as evidence of disloyalty and collusion with the enemy."[98]

According to Ogbu, the areas which are perceived to be "white" were "first defined by whites themselves" and are ones "in which it was long believed that only whites could perform well, and few blacks were actually given the opportunity to try or were rewarded well when they succeeded."[99] Such areas are "intellectual performances (IQ test scores), scholastic performances, and performance in high-status jobs in the mainstream economy."[100] To bolster his point, Ogbu cites the testimony of "autobiographies, accounts of personal experiences, and research among blacks in academia and in the corporate world."[101]

The most celebrated documentation of Ogbu's cultural inversion theory was the "acting white" study by Signithia Fordham and Ogbu in 1986. Based on Fordham's doctoral dissertation, the study was a two-year ethnological analysis of poor black students in a high school in Washington, D.C. (Ogbu was the main adviser on Fordham's doctoral committee.) Ironically, this study has been often cited by conservative scholars and journalists as showing a lack of character among its subjects rather than the conclusion that the authors found—that the majoritarian society's oppression was the real cause of school failure.[102]

The students they interviewed were both high and low academic achievers. Capital High (a fictitious name) is 99 percent black and mostly poor. Students developed a "fictive kinship" by developing a "group loyalty by defining certain attitudes and behaviors as 'white' and therefore unacceptable, and then employing numerous devices to discourage one another from engaging in those behaviors and attitudes, i.e., from 'acting white'."[103] These white behaviors included speaking standard English, studying hard and obtaining good grades, listening to classical music, attending symphonies, reading and writing poetry, and visiting art museums. Those blacks engaged in such "white" behaviors were derogatorily called "brani-acs" and labeled as "not truly black."[104] Indeed, even black teachers were "often perceived to be 'functionaries' of the dominant society."[105] And Fordham and Ogbu saw the "acting white" syndrome to be characteristic of "other subordinate minorities in the United States."[106] But in interpreting the data, Fordham and Ogbu were careful not to blame the victim. They concluded that this problem arose partly

> because white Americans traditionally refused to acknowledge that black Americans are capable of intellectual achievement, and partly because black Americans subsequently began to doubt their own intellectual ability and began to define academic success as white people's prerogative, and began to discourage their peers, perhaps unconsciously, from emulating white people in academic striving, i.e., from "acting white."[107]

Fordham and Ogbu prescribe remedies. In order to change the self-perceptions of blacks in a white society, they argue that "the unique academic learning and performance problems created by the burden of acting white should be recognized and made a target of educational policies and remediation efforts."[108] This generalization, of course, lacks a specific strategy. In concert with school efforts, the authors admonish that "the black community has an important part to play in changing the situation" and "should develop programs to teach black children that academic pursuit does not equate into group betrayal."[109]

Fourteen years after the publication of *Minority Education and Caste*, Ogbu refined his ideas. In an article in *Educational Research*, Ogbu reinforced his theory of cultural inversion. "Among involuntary minorities," he writes, "school learning tends to be equated with the learning of the culture and language of White Americans, that is, the learning of the cultural and language frames of references of their 'enemy' or 'oppressors'."[110] Consequently, young African Americans often "fear that by learning the White cultural frame of reference they will cease to act like minorities and lose their identity as minorities and their sense of community and self worth."[111]

Most important, like African American sociologist William Julius Wilson, Ogbu feels that the African American community needs to play a more proactive role in the development of black youth. And like Wilson he is uncomfortable with the migration of the black middle class to the suburbs and the abandonment of the black poor left behind in the urban ghettoes. He accuses the black poor of only paying lip service to school achievement when he writes:

> Although making good grades is strongly verbalized by students, parents, and the community as a desirable goal, there is less community and family pressure to achieve it. For example, there is rarely any stigma attached to being a poor student and there are no community gossips criticizing a poor student or his or her ability. As for peer groups, their collective orientation is probably against academic striving. Therefore, peer pressures discourage making good grades.[112]

Ogbu argues that the schools cannot do it alone. It is a cultural problem for both majoritarian and minority communities. He finds that black children "do not succeed or fail only because of what schools do or do not do." Most important, he argues it is for the black middle class to "reevaluate and change its role vis-à-vis the community."[113] The black middle class must "reaffiliate with the community socially."[114] The black middle class sees "professional success as a 'ticket' to leave their community both physically and socially, to get away from those who have not 'made it'."[115] Ogbu beseeches this successful group to return, at least socially if not physically, to their roots and help mentor black youth. Moreover, he admonishes the ghetto community to provide "concrete evidence that its members appreciate and value academic success as much as they appreciate and value achievement in sports, athletics, and entertainment."[116]

By the mid-1990s Ogbu had further developed his theory. His corollary idea was that minority students bring with them to school their ghetto culture—what he called "a cultural frame of reference." "What the children bring to school," he writes, [such as] "their communities cultural models . . . are as important as within-school factors."[117] He then implored school administrators and teachers to learn that culture to be better able to understand and teach black poor children. "A cultural frame of reference," he writes, "refers to the correct way or ideal way to behave within the culture."[118] This frame of reference may include "attitude, behaviors, and speech styles that are stigmatized by the dominant group."[119]

First Ogbu critiques the move for cultural diversity in the schools as inadequate because "they are not based on a good understanding of the nature of the culture."[120] The two strategies that Ogbu dismisses are the move for a core curriculum and multicultural education. He argues that core curriculum advocates "are more concerned about U.S. economic and technological status in international competition" than they are in "assimilating culturally diverse groups into the mainstream cultures."[121]

As for multicultural education he observes that a clear definition does not exist. Although multicultural education "fosters pride . . . reduces stereotypes . . . and promotes intercultural understanding," it is not linked to improving "the academic performance of those minorities who have not traditionally done well in school."[122] And that, in essence, is "the crucial question."[123]

In the race versus class debate as to what most influences the educational and job progress of black Americans, Ogbu is firmly in the race camp. He writes that for many scholars, such as William Julius Wilson (whom he cites), "social class, rather than race, is now the important factor determining the life chances of black Americans."[124] He argues that "the shift from race to class explanation" of racial inequality "is attractive to both white and middle class black Americans."[125] For whites, it is "compatible" with their view of "society stratified by class."[126] For middle class blacks, "it reinforces their eagerness to distance themselves from those who have not made it or cannot make it."[127] But he maintains that "the inequality between blacks and whites is one not of class stratification but of racial stratification."[128]

According to Ogbu, the anthropological evidence confounds the class argument. "The problem with this view, he writes, is that anthropologists have documented the existence of caste and other forms of stratification in precapitalist societies and societies without corporate capitalism."[129] Despite the social progress of the civil rights movement with programs of affirmative action, Ogbu finds the bottom line is that in white America, blacks are still perceived, for the most part, as inferior. "Whites tend to believe," he writes in 1994, "that there is some undesirable biological, linguistic, cultural, and intellectual inferiority that sets blacks apart."[130] And despite the public rhetoric, "blacks still believe that there is an institutionalized discrimination against them."[131] Consequently, blacks in the ghetto "developed their own 'folk theory' of making it" that mostly involves a "collective struggle"—in short, identity politics.[132]

In 1991 Ogbu (along with Margaret A. Gibson) co-edited a book, *Minority Status and Schooling: A Comparative Study of Immigrant and Involuntary Minorities*, which consisted of a series of papers on the academic success of voluntary immigrant groups. First presented at the 1983 Anthropological Association, these papers, in the words of the editors, seek to discover with various case studies "why some minority groups do relatively well in school, in spite of fairly substantial barriers of race and culture."[133] At the time, there were few comparative studies in anthropology in education and minority groups. Most important, Gibson and Ogbu had a policy bent to their book. They had hoped that these case studies in different countries would "prove useful to educational policy makers, program planners, and school practitioners."[134] Moreover, they also hoped that minority group members "would also find this work useful in advancing their cause in education."[135]

What the editors proposed was a cultural model that would show that some immigrant groups were successful in education. They theorized that this cultural model would show an immigrant group that would be more adaptable to the rules and behavior of the majoritarian culture. The successful immigrant group, they maintained, would overcome barriers of race and culture more easily. One reason would be that the conditions in their homeland were more oppressive. For example, Ogbu contends the immigrant group "may not recognize the segregated and inferior schools as inferior, since their frame of reference is the education in the homeland," which was worse.[136] Consequently, the children of these successful immigrant groups perceive more opportunity and demonstrate more effort in school compared to the involuntary immigrant groups such as African Americans who are more cognizant of discrimination. The cultural frame of reference of immigrant minorities is significantly different than that of involuntary immigrants such as African Americans.

There were ten papers presented at this anthropological conference selected for this volume. The societies studied by the various scholars were Sikhs in Britain and the United States; Turks in Australia; Koreans in Japan and the United States; West Indians in the Caribbean; Mexicans in California; African Americans in California; Ute Indians in Utah; Maoris in New Zealand; and the Burkumin in Japan. The editors conclude that "the international and comparative literature shows clearly that minority youngsters of immigrant origin remain in school longer and meet with a greater degree of academic success than involuntary or nonimmigrant youths of similar social-class backgrounds."[137]

Ogbu's theories have been replicated by other scholars. In 1994, three researchers from the University of Minnesota employed a survey instrument to test Margaret Gibson's and John Ogbu's cultural model theory among St. Paul High School students whose families were voluntary immigrants from Laos. The Gibson-Ogbu theory holds that many voluntary immigrant groups hold positive "beliefs about social status and mobility in the newly adopted country that serve to promote reliance on education as a means of socioeconomic advancement."[138] The Gibson-Ogbu thesis posits that these groups feel that whatever "deprivation and discrimination they experience in the new country seem less onerous than former conditions in their country of origin."[139] Consequently, they "regard education as the best route to enhanced social status" and "adopt schooling strategies that promote the social adjustment and academic success of their children."[140] As a result, the children of these voluntary minorities do well in school, "because of the high degree of academic support from their families, their peer groups and their ethnic communities."[141]

The Minnesota scholars examined the belief of the Hmong parents and their children in high school and the latter's academic performance. They randomly surveyed 105 Hmong high school students and interviewed the parents of 80 of these students. The Hmong parents were farmers in Laos, had little work experience before coming to the United States, and occupied "low-paying service, clerical, and light manufacturing occupations."[142] They also were illiterate for the most part. Also, the Hmong children "received little or no formal education prior to their arrival in the United States."[143] Still, because of the encouragement and support of parents and peers, the Hmong students had higher academic aspirations, greater effort, and greater achievement than their non-Hmong peers in high school. The authors of the study conclude that the "Hmong refugees in the United States appear to have acquired most of the elements of a cultural model that Gibson and Ogbu see as typical of many immigrant groups."[144]

A more ambivalent assessment of Ogbu's caste theory was offered by Douglas Foley of the University of Texas, Austin. Foley credits Ogbu with presenting "anthropology's most powerful general explanation of minority school failure."[145] He finds that "John Ogbu's caste theory has served a very useful purpose in underlining the importance of institutional racism."[146] On the other hand, Foley is a micro ethnographer and is uncomfortable with a generalized overarching view. "Once an anthropologist tackles whole societies," he maintains, "however, they are in the domain of comparative historical sociology."[147] For all of the "power of caste theory he finds it too 'global' and 'ambitious' and based on rather limited evidence."[148] Nonetheless, such "policy-oriented explanations" of black school failure have "enriched the research discourse."[149] The task is for micro ethnographers with their case studies to "contextualize their studies more" to supplement Ogbu.[150] Foley concludes that "over the past twenty years (Ogbu) has also developed the field's most comprehensive explanation of why 'involuntary minorities' tend to fail in schools."[151]

CONCLUSION

John Ogbu has changed the way educators and social scientists talk about race when considering public schools. He has gone beyond most interpretations of black school failure to give, in one scholar's estimate, a "more complex" narrative. Consequently, no scholar or school practitioner can confront education and race without dealing with Ogbu's provocative theories. For example, in a September 1998 lead article in *Phi Delta Kappan,* the main journal of educational administrators, Mano Singham of the University Center for Innovation in Teaching and Education at Case Western University discusses the "canary in the mine," that is, "the achievement gap between black and white students."[152] Singham gives an extended analysis of Ogbu's work concluding that "the causes of black achievement identified by (Signithia) Fordham, (Claude) Steele and Ogbu cannot simply be swept away by legislation or administrative action."[153] And Singham bases his strategies for reform on these diagnoses.

As another case in point dealing with the same subject, sociologists Christopher Jecks of Harvard's Kennedy School of Government and Meredith Phillips of the University of California at Los Angeles published their book, *Black-White Test Score Gap,* the same fall and discussed Ogbu's ideas at length. They accept Ogbu's cultural theories concluding that "by linking black culture directly to oppression, Ogbu made it much easier for liberals to talk about cultural differences."[154]

Let us review Ogbu's main points. First, he has proposed a theory of caste whereby African Americans are perceived as inferior by the majoritarian society, thus crippling their educational and job opportunities. Second, he has discovered a pattern of cultural inversion whereby many African Americans internalize these negative opinions of the majoritarian society and fail to perform adequately in school for fear of "acting white." Third, he advocates that school personnel need to learn the culture of poor black students in order to facilitate better the learning of these students. Fourth, he admonishes the black community to play a stronger support role in promoting the education of African American youth.

Ogbu's work has changed the educational landscape for minority youth. He, too, has caused a major paradigm shift in American education.

NOTES

1. *Contemporary Authors* (Detroit: Gale Literary Database, 1998), p. 3.
2. Ibid.
3. Interview with Carol Gilligan, Harvard University, October 14, 1998.

4. *Anthropology and Education* 28, no. 3 (September 1997).

5. Interview with John U. Ogbu, December 3, 1998, Philadelphia, Pennsylvania.

6. Ibid.

7. Ibid.

8. Ibid.

9. Ibid.

10. Ibid.

11. Ibid.

12. Ibid.

13. Ibid.

14. Ibid.

15. Ibid.

16. Ibid.

17. Ibid.

18. Lyndon B. Johnson, "To Fulfill These Rights," *The Great Society Reader*, edited by Marvin Gettleman and David Mermelstein (New York: Random House, 1967), p. 254.

19. Hendrik Hertzberg and Henry Louis Gates Jr., "The African-American Century," *The New Yorker*, April 29 and May 6, 1996, p. 10.

20. Ibid.

21. Jervis Anderson, "Black and Blue," *The New Yorker*, April 29 and May 6, 1996, p. 64.

22. William Julius Wilson, *The Declining Significance of Race* (Chicago: University of Chicago Press, 1978), p. 2.

23. Ibid.

24. William Julius Wilson, *The Truly Disadvantaged: The Inner City, the Underclass, and Public Policy* (Chicago: University of Chicago Press, 1987), p. 56.

25. Henry Louis Gates Jr., "After the Revolution," *The New Yorker*, April 29 and May 6, 1996, p. 61.

26. Gretchen Reynolds, "The Rising Significance of Race," *Chicago*, December 1992, p. 128.

27. William Julius Wilson, *When Work Disappears: The World of the New Urban Poor* (New York: Alfred A. Knopf, 1996), p. xiii.

28. Ibid., p. xiv.

29. Ibid.

30. Ibid., p. 73.

31. Ibid., p. 99.

32. Interview with John U. Ogbu, December 3, 1998, Philadelphia, Pennsylvania.

33. Ibid.

34. Ibid.

35. Ibid.

36. Ibid.

37. Ibid.

38. Ibid.

39. Ibid.

40. Ibid.

41. Ibid.

42. Ibid.

43. Ibid.

44. John U. Ogbu, *Minority Education and Caste: The American System in Cross-Cultural Perspective* (New York: Academic Press, 1978), p. 102.

45. Ibid., p. 23.

46. John U. Ogbu. "Low School Performance as an Adaptation: The Case of Blacks in Stockton, California," in *Minority Status and Schooling: A Comparative Study of Immigrant and Involuntary Minorities,* edited by Margaret A. Gibson and John U. Ogbu (New York: Garland Publishing, 1991), p. 251.

47. Ibid.

48. Ibid., p. 252.

49. Ibid.

50. Ibid., p. 255.

51. Ibid., p. 252.

52. Ibid., p. 264.

53. Ibid., p. 201.

54. Ogbu, *Minority Education and Caste,* p. 2.

55. Ibid., p. 4.

56. Ibid., p. 5.

57. Ibid.

58. Ibid., p. 6.

59. Ibid.

60. Ibid., p. 46.

61. Ibid., p. 47.

62. Ibid., p. 51.

63. Ibid., p. 53.

64. Ibid.

65. Ibid., p. 65.

66. Ibid., p. 66.

67. Ibid., p. 11.

68. Ibid.

69. Ibid., p. 13.

70. Ibid., p. 69.

71. Ibid., p. 100.

72. Ibid., pp. 102, 212.

73. Ibid., pp. 247, 263.

74. Ibid., p. 285.

75. Ibid., p. 305.

76. Ibid.

77. Ibid., p. 320.

78. Ibid.

79. Ibid., p. 342.

80. Ibid., p. 343.

81. Ibid., pp. 357, 360.

82. Ibid., p. 361.

83. Ibid., p. 355.

84. John U. Ogbu, "Understanding Cultural Diversity and Learning," *Educational Researcher* 21 (August 1992): 8.

85. Ibid.

86. Ibid.

87. John U. Ogbu and Herbert D. Simons, "Cultural Models of Literacy: A Comparative Study," Springfield, Va.: Eric Reports, December 1994, pp. 19–20.

88. Ibid., p. 20.

89. Richard J. Herrnstein and Charles Murray, *The Bell Curve: Intelligence and Class Structure in American Life* (New York: The Free Press, 1994), p. 307.

90. Daniel Goleman, "An Emerging Theory," *New York Times*, Education Supplement, October 17, 1988, p. 22.

91. *Book Review Digest* 8, no. 1 (January 1979): 93.

92. Ibid.

93. Ibid., p. 94.

94. *American Anthropologist* (1979): 694.

95. Ibid.

96. Ibid.

97. John U. Ogbu, "Racial Stratification and Education in the U.S.: Why Inequality Persists," *Teachers College Record* 96, no. 2 (1994): 274.

98. Ibid.

99. Ibid.

100. Ibid.

101. Ibid.

102. Arthur M. Schlesinger Jr., *The Disuniting of America: Reflections of a Multicultural Society* (New York: W. W. Norton and Co., 1991), p. 105.

103. Signithia Fordham and John U. Ogbu, "Black Students' School Success: Coping with the Burden of 'Acting White,'" *The Urban Review* 18, no. 3 (1986): 185–86.

104. Ibid., p. 188.

105. Ibid., p. 185.

106. Ibid., p. 200.

107. Ibid., p. 177.

108. Ibid., p. 203.

109. Ibid.

110. Ogbu, "Understanding Cultural Diversity and Learning," p. 10.

111. Ibid.

112. Ibid.

113. Ibid.

114. Ibid., p. 13.

115. Ibid.

116. Ibid., p. 12.

117. Ibid., p. 5.

118. John U. Ogbu, "Cultural Problems in Minority Education: Their Interpretations and Consequences—Part One," *The Urban Review* 27, no. 3 (1995): 195.

119. Ibid., p. 196.

120. Ogbu, "Understanding Cultural Diversity and Learning," p. 5.

121. Ibid.

122. Ibid., p. 6.

123. Ibid.

124. Ogbu, "Racial Stratification and Education in the U.S.," p. 264.

125. Ibid., pp. 264–65.

126. Ibid., p. 265.

127. Ibid.

128. Ibid.

129. Ibid., p. 267.

130. Ibid., p. 271.

131. Ibid., p. 130.

132. Ibid.

133. Margaret A. Gibson and John U. Ogbu, eds., *Minority Status and Schooling: A Comparative Study of Immigrant and Involuntary Minorities* (New York: Garland Publishing, 1991), p. ix.

134. Ibid.

135. Ibid.

136. John U. Ogbu, "Immigrant and Involuntary Minorities in Comparative Perspective," in *Minority Status and Schooling: A Comparative Study of Immigrant and Involuntary Minorities*, edited by Margaret A. Gibson and John U. Ogbu (New York: Garland Publishing, 1991), p. 21.

137. Margaret A Gibson, "Minorities and Schooling: Some Implications," in *Minority Status and Schooling: A Comparative Study of Immigrant and Involuntary Minorities*, edited by Margaret A. Gibson and John U. Ogbu (New York: Garland Publishing, 1991), p. 358.

138. Miles McNall et al., "The Educational Achievement of the St. Paul Hmong," *Anthropology and Education Quarterly* 25 (1994): 44.

139. Ibid., p. 45.

140. Ibid.

141. Ibid.

142. Ibid., p. 50.

143. Ibid., p. 53.

144. Ibid., p. 59.

145. Douglas E. Foley, "Reconsidering Anthropological Explanations of Ethnic School Failure," *Anthropology and Education Quarterly* 22 (1991): 78.

146. Ibid.

147. Ibid., p. 70.

148. Ibid., p. 69.

149. Ibid., p. 72.

150. Ibid., p. 78.

151. Ibid., p. 82.

152. Mario Singham, "The Canary in the Mine: The Achievement Gap Between Black and White Students," *Phi Delta Kappan*, September 1998, p. 9.

153. Ibid., p. 12.

154. Christopher Jencks and Meredith Phillips, "America's Next Achievement Test: Closing the Black-White Test Score Gap," *The American Prospect* (September/October 1998): 50.

Appendix: Interview with John U. Ogbu, Philadelphia, Pennsylvania, December 3, 1998

Berube: Were you influenced by John Dewey's work?

Ogbu: No, I don't think I've read any of his work, actually.

Berube: You went for a short a time to the Theological Institute of Princeton.

Ogbu: Yes.

Berube: Do you think that had some bearing on the nature and direction of your work, in terms of the moral aspects of it?

Ogbu: Well, probably. Not so much Princeton, but I had started out wanting to be a minister in the Presbyterian Church in Nigeria. And I had gone to Christian schools, in grade school, high school, and so forth. I was teaching at a Presbyterian high school in Nigeria.

Berube: How did you get interested in anthropology? Why did you go from theology to anthropology?

Ogbu: Well, actually it was by accident. My desire was really to get an education in the United States, go back and work for the church, the Presbyterian church in Nigeria. But I was interested in writing too, because communication in writing is important in Africa today, not just preaching. So one of my ambitions was to be a writer. I had gone to Zambia, a Dominican center where they trained Africans in journalism and creative writing. And I had spent four or six months there before coming to the states. However, going to work for the church in Nigeria today and writing, I needed to know something about Africa, about my country. You see, what impressed me at Princeton, the seminary, was that I saw people who were going into the ministry, learning something about American society, because this was theology. You wouldn't learn that in Nigeria. Seminaries were teaching you the Bible, church history, Greek or Hebrew. Because of that, I thought anthropology would be a good field since it was the only discipline here in the states at that time that would teach you something about Africa, African cultures. I never heard of anthropology before I came here. So when I went to Berkeley, I sold my books in English, I was going be an English major, but I dropped that and switched to anthropology.

Berube: Did you think of writing a novel or just in terms of a being a scholar or a journalist?

Ogbu: I like writing in general. I'd say that I was interested in being a journalist, but also I wrote poems. But by my bedside today, I have all kinds of poetry books, which I read. If I don't listen to music before I go to bed, I read poetry.

Berube: That's a thread because both Gardner and Gilligan were interested in literature. Gardner wrote a novel and Gilligan said she is writing novels now with her research.

Ogbu: Oh, really!! I also like drama. I have all kinds of Shakespeare and other plays.

Berube: How did you finance your education in Nigeria? Or in the United States? Your parents were farmers, I believe.

Ogbu: Yes, then they went to school.

Berube: Were you on scholarship?

Ogbu: I was on scholarship. The way it worked out, I'm the second person in my family to go to school. My oldest brother did go, but not the others. My father was a polygamist. He had three wives, 17 children, o.k. so not everybody could go to school. And the schools. I did not get into them until it was very late. My brother was among the first in my village who went to school. He had to walk four miles every day to go to school. Anyway, when he finished and he went to the city to a small town, to work as a mechanic and be an apprentice in a government, they call them public works. And I was sent up to him to live with him when I was seven years old as a "house boy," cleaning things, and that's how I got to go to the Presbyterian school in town. And then, the Presbyterian mission from Scotland had a policy, they had a high school which took people by entrance exam all over west Africa, but mainly Nigeria. Their policy was, if you were among the first three they give you scholarship. And that's how I got it. I passed the entrance exam when I was in fifth grade, and they would take people in sixth grade. So when I was in fifth grade, I took the exam, and I was among the three—I don't know what I was, first, second or third—but I got an automatic scholarship to go there which covered my room, board, and fees. And my brother had to provide my transportation and books and so on. I spent five or six years at the boarding school during my high school.

Berube: How about when you went to Princeton Theological and Berkeley?

Ogbu: Well, when I finished my high school, I really wanted to be a doctor. But nobody would send me because I had no money to be a doctor, to get a government scholarship it was very competitive. And I didn't think I was very good in math, so I switched to arts. I could get A in Latin and arts. Which I did. And so, my high school sent me to normal school for tests. I went to a Presbyterian teacher's college for two years, and got credentials there, and went back to my high school and taught for two years. And the Presbyterian church sent me to Zambia. While I was teaching I began the school of music for high school kids. I used to produce a musical every week or every other week. And for that reason, I guess, they sent me to Zambia for this training. And I went there for six months, and it was there that I met some people who introduced me to the idea of coming to the states to study, you know, to go back and work for the church. So I came to the United States after I had been to Zambia, after I had taught high school. And I wanted to major in English, because I was interested in going back and continuing to work in the area of writing, or helping the church, or whatever they were doing.

Berube: Did you have any favorite teachers?

Ogbu: I really liked my English teachers. We worked together in producing Macbeth. I also liked my Latin teachers. By the way, there is somebody whom I should always say influenced me all of my life. That's my "uncle," Dr. Francis Ibiam. He was the first Nigerian missionary. He got his medical degree at the University of Aberdeen, and became a missionary doctor, which was very rare in those days, in the 30s or 20s. He passed away just two years ago. He later became the governor of the state. He was also the principal in my last years of high school. He influenced my outlook on life.

Berube: Was he an actual relative, when you say uncle?

Ogbu: He was not a relative, but he was one who felt like he was.

Berube: How many brothers or sisters did you have? Of course there's a quite extended family. . . .

Ogbu: As I said, 17, but on my mother's side, there were seven of us.

Berube: Do you go back to Africa or Nigeria frequently since you've been in the United States?

Ogbu: I went back in 1993, when I took my family, because my children are mostly grown. I wanted them to see my village. I've been back only a few times. It is very expensive. So, but I go like when, like when I work for UNESCO, I stop by in Nigeria.

Berube: You are very familiar with William Julius Wilson's work, and you've written about his work. He has argued that class is more important than race in determining opportunities for African Americans. He modified his position through the years, but how do you feel about his latest work, *When Work Disappears*?

Ogbu: I read it without agreeing with him, although he is a good friend of mine. I disagree with his basic, original thesis and I've written about it. He basically started at American institutions. I don't think he studied the black community. Sometimes I wonder how anyone who has lived in Chicago could say that race is a declining factor in the opportunities for black Americans. I did say that on national public I was reading this book on the plane coming here and people were citing him in a way that is misleading. I think what people miss, and not just Wilson, is to look at black Americans as they seem to be just like whites. When black people talk about making it, whatever it is, they forget that the black middle class of those who made it, still do not have the center of experience as the white majoritarian developed group. So that creates a problem. I try to look at it in much of what I've written, that I ask various groups who are the heroes, who are your role models. The Japanese will say engineers, doctors, and professionals. In the 1980s I asked blacks in the ghetto who are your heroes: Abraham Lincoln or Benjamin Franklin? No, their heroes turn out to be rebels, people who rebel against the system. O.K. Moral character, people who withstood punishment and all that, John Henry, fighting against the system and so on. Because in Stockton, California where there was confrontation between lower-class blacks and middle-class blacks. Because if you are black middle-class, you get there because you were lucky, because you were smarter than everybody else, or because you were an Uncle Tom. Those things have to be taken into account. Why people are not acting, not just because they are poor, because I can show you that in New Orleans, here are Vietnamese and blacks and so on, and in my study, blacks are the most educated and have the best jobs. Those things have to be taken into account.

Berube: Were you aware of the studies that Marilyn Gittell and I had done at that time in NYC in terms of school systems that were under community control?

Ogbu: Oh, yes. I think I bought the book. I read it. I read a couple of things by Gittell.

Berube: You did, but you didn't think we were that effective. I wondered if you changed your mind.

Ogbu: The trouble is, part of the problem, is that I'm not really from education.

Berube: You treat the civil rights figures evenhandedly. Who did you feel that you admired the most of the civil rights activists of the 1960s?

Ogbu: I would not answer the question in terms of whom I admired most. I took the position essentially as one of a observer. An observer in terms of my academic work. I used to ask, for example, look at King and Malcolm X. My assessment at that time was that people tended to support King to diminish the impact of Malcolm X. King was non-violent, and the Muslim group was perceived as the greater evil. If you look at where blacks have progressed, it appears that they have achieved something only in periods of crisis. They first moved up when there was labor shortage during World War II. And the movement in the 1960s was also a period in which they moved up, not so much because they accomplished a lot educationally. Despite American statutes of liberty theory, it was crisis created by the civil rights movement that made the difference. I was very happy. I've been here since 1961 and observed progress from the time when there was very little to a time when there was much. In the 60s, you had a choice. You had the Muslims, which were perceived by white America as destructive and very evil, or you supported non-violent people. So that's the way I saw it. You know I like King. and I admire King, but I also saw the effectiveness of both King and Malcolm X.

— 7 —

An Intellectual Legacy

Every thinker puts some portion of an apparently stable world in peril, and no one can wholly predict what will emerge in its place.
—John Dewey

The four intellectual giants that we have examined have left a deep and rich legacy for American education. Each exemplifies one aspect of progressive education—that most American of educational systems—education for intellectual, moral, social, and aesthetic growth. Dewey, the father of progressive education though, is seen in his impact on what constitutes thinking and his artistic influence on Abstract Expressionism; Gardner redefines the concept of intelligence; Gilligan brings the moral development of a neglected feminist constituency; and Ogbu reflects the social aspect of education in creating a more positive educational work for an oppressed African American minority.

There are commonalties. Gardner and Gilligan were imbued with Deweyan thinking. All believe in the concepts of process and development rather than a fixed, immutable genetic endowment. All have an artistic bent: Dewey the poet, Gardner the pianist, Ogbu, also a poet, and Gilligan the dancer. All have created major shifts in how we think about education. Some have had direct policy impact.

A large question looms on how the legacy of their thought and research can be translated into our everyday lives. The first effect, of course, is changing how we think. Nonetheless, the difficulty in having a greater impact on our educational lives illustrates the complexity of the relationship of thinking, research, practice, and policy.

Nowhere has this dilemma been more evident than in the agonizing debate within the counsels of the educational research community. Ever since Chester E. Finn Jr., then Assistant Secretary of Education in President Ronald Reagan's administration, challenged the educational researchers a decade ago to become more policy-oriented, there has been a constant stream of reappraisals of the role of research in the pages of the journals of the American Educational Research Association (AERA). Finn provocatively addressed the 1988 AERA conference with a challenge on "what ails education research."[1] He charged that the American public "regards our work with more than a trace of skepticism" that "tends to be associated with educational faddism on the one hand and pointy-headed intellectualism on the other."[2] Finn's major complaint was that educational research had "not fulfilled its role in the effort to improve our schools."[3] For Finn, education research had to be policy-oriented with a trickle-down influence to classroom practice.

Finn's charges resounded throughout the educational research community. For the next decade, the pages of *Educational Researcher* would carry articles by scholars on the role of education research. A sampling, for example, includes Carl Kaestle's "The Awful Reputation of Education Research" (1993); Penelope L. Peterson's "Why Do Educational Research," (1998); and Mary M. Kennedy's "The Connection between Research and Practice" (1997). In 1997, the journal would start a four-part forum for past presidents of AERA to examine "The Vision Thing: Educational Research and AERA in the 21st Century." Clearly, Finn placed education researchers on the defensive.

Unfortunately, most scholars responded to Finn on Finn's terms, that is, on the pragmatic policy implications of educational research. For example, Peterson agonized that "we must sometimes reinvent our identities and our methods" and "we need to rethink the audiences for our research."[4] Kaestle complained that the "field is politicized" by the federal government impeding the implementation of policy research.[5] Mark A. Constas observed that Finn's effect was to move education in research "toward politically oriented research and away from scientifically situated research."[6] Richard J. Shavelson and David C. Berliner criticized Finn's "narrow conception" of educational research and concluded that "prescriptions for education policy or practice are impossible."[7]

Perhaps the most comprehensive assessment of the role of research was Mary M. Kennedy's analysis. Her focus was to connect research and classroom practice. She rehearsed four main criticisms of why educational research does not have the same respect with the public at large that research in the hard sciences does. She concluded that perhaps the "research itself is not sufficiently *persuasive or authoritative*"; that it "has not been *relevant to practice*"; that the research has not been "*accessible to teachers*," and that "the educational system itself is intractable and unable to change."[8] The first two charges relate to problems with quantitative research designs and the introduction of qualitative (ethnographic) research. One no longer can conduct statistical designs in a classroom or school setting and expect to learn from a highly qualitative process of learning; ethnography is needed to complement the quantitative studies.

The last two charges relate more to the audience—the consumers of research, administrators and teachers. Few administrators and fewer teachers are sufficiently skilled to understand the research much less able to implement the research implications in their school systems or classrooms. The process normally goes as follows: research is presented at academic conferences, which often results in publication in referred journals. Some administrators and fewer teachers either attend or read these publications. They are normally the provinces of the educational research community itself who create the research in the first place. However, school superintendents need an educational agenda for school effectiveness and will rally to the particular body of research they find interesting, thereby creating a culture of faddism. Thus one pertinent recommendation on the "vision thing" in educational research was expressed by past AERA president John I. Goodlad, who saw as the chief priority "creating a future constituency for educational research" because "we have an incredible body of knowledge of high relevance to educational practice that is little used."[9] Other AERA presidents such as David Berliner went one step further and urged AERA to "be an advocate for creating the conditions under which our knowledge could possibly affect the lives of children."[10]

Moreover, there has been a long and deep tradition of anti-intellectualism in America. This strain of anti-intellectualism dates back to the origins of the republic. Nowhere has it been so ably traced and analyzed than in historian Richard Hofstader's classic 1963 study *Anti-Intellectualism in American Life*. Hofstader points out that the very idea of American democracy with its rhetoric of egalitarianism is at odds with intellectualism. The leveling process of democracy renders a goodly portion of American society distrustful and contemptuous of an intellectual elite. "Anti-intellectualism," he wrote, "is founded in the democratic institutions and the egalitarian sentiments of this country."[11] And "the intellectual class" is of "necessity an elite in its manner of thinking and functioning."[12]

Hofstader found that "anti-intellectualism in various forms continues to pervade American life."[13] For example he cites the rhetoric of education as a saving remnant. He observed that "one of the signal facts of our national experiment . . . [is] . . . our persistent, intense, and sometimes touching faith in the efficacy of popular education."[14] In his time, "the rhetoric of the past" did not conform to the realities of the present" and there was "something missing from the passion for education."[15] What had supplanted that passion, he argued, was a "cult of athleticism" whereby "the schools of the country seem to be dominated by athletics."[16]

Anti-intellectualism pervades the highest level in the land. A case in point was the 1992 presidential campaign. Perhaps one of the most disturbing aspects of the selling of the presidential candidates was the conscious attempt by the candidates to dumb themselves down. And, in the process, to dumb down the American public.

Neither presidential candidate nor his running mate wanted to present himself as the educated, sophisticated person he is. Rather, they blurred their educational and cultural credentials in hopes of appealing to the "typical" American. The "typical" American is one who never attended college and who is, presumably, more at home watching television than reading a book. He/she is suspicious of intellectuals and artists. No more than 20 percent of the voting public have attended four years of college.

Vice President Dan Quayle took the most direct approach. His attacks on a "cultural elite" in the universities and the media, whose values allegedly undermine America, was an appeal to that "typical" American. Attacks on cultural elitism resound well with Americans uneasy about the world of ideas and art. President Bush took a more indirect approach. Despite being a product of eastern elite schools and Yale University, he tried to subtly disguise his patrician background. A fan of both opera and country music, he was more likely on the campaign trail to appear with country music stars than with operatic divas. Indeed, President Bush fooled even the most skeptical of critics. In the 1988 campaign, journalist Gail Sheehy took Bush at face value when he informed her that he could not "remember a single book that influenced him."[17] She concluded that "clearly, Bush is not fired up by ideas."[18]

But the truth of the matter is that Bush is no intellectual slouch. He graduated from Yale Phi Beta Kappa. Moreover, he completed his course work in a mere 2.5 years—a remarkable feat of that most motivated of college generations, the returning World War II veterans. And his college major was economics, regarded as the "dismal" science of undergraduates, which he didn't find "dismal at all."[19]

Nor was Bill Clinton exempt from dumbing down. A Rhodes scholar who attended some of the world's great universities—Georgetown, Oxford, and Yale—he was quick to point out, in his acceptance speech at the Democratic convention, that these schools were no match for the values of his grandfather, with his rudimentary grade-school education. His grandfather, Clinton informed us, knew "more about equality than [Clinton's] professors at Georgetown," more about "the intrinsic worth of every individual than all the philosophers at Oxford," and more about "the need for equal justice than all the jurists at Yale Law School."[20] Supposedly, this played well in Peoria.

Clearly, a sophisticated education appears as a political liability for the highest office in the land. But can one imagine the scholarly president of France, Francois Mitterrand, minimizing his books? Or the former president of Czechoslovakia, playwright Vaclav Havel, dismissing his literary gifts? Indeed, one wonders how that supreme cultural elitist, Thomas Jefferson, would have fared on the campaign trail in 1992.

Unfortunately, the strategy of dumbing oneself down may be, in the short run, the correct one politically. America may yet have to outgrow that anti-intellectual tradition that historian Richard Hofstader described more than a generation ago. But for aspiring education presidents purportedly taking the long view, it was the wrong signal to send to the American people.

In Hofstader's day, the appellation "intellectual" covered a broad range of people, from scholars in universities to journalists writing for intellectual magazines with small readerships. But it was a clear term in that "intellectual" designated a person dedicated to a life of ideas. And he felt that intellectuals were beginning to have a measure of recognition, "to enjoy more acceptance" despite a history "where alienation is the only appropriate and honorable stance for them to take."[21]

Yet even as Hofstader was writing, a division was occurring within intellectual ranks. With the rise of mass education after the GI Bill of Rights in 1944, many intellectuals in small magazines, such as the famed New York Intellectuals of the 1930s and 1940s, were scurrying to the groves of academe for financial security. Thus the distinction between scholar and intellectual journalist became blurred. By 1987, Russell Jacoby would bemoan the passing of these "last intellectuals" whereby "nonacademic intellectuals are an endangered species."[22] He criticized academics for allegedly writing only for themselves for career purposes of tenure and promotion and ignoring the general public producing an inconsequential scholarship.

Despite a serious misreading, Jacoby identifies a vexing problem within the arcane world of scholarship. Indeed, "public intellectuals" who address a general public, albeit in traditionally small intellectual magazines, have become few and far between. This divorce has caused further agonizing within the academic community and the public at large, who need simple translations of complex thought. Moreover, Jacoby writes about the province of literary studies rather than the world of data based research in the social and hard sciences.[23] Indeed, it is only within the last thirty years that such research has proliferated and become more methodologically complex.

Perhaps Jacoby is uncomfortable with the new public intellectuals who have developed in the last decade. In 1995, Michael Bérubé identified "a new generation of black thinkers" who are "becoming the most dynamic force in the American intellectual areas since the fifties."[24] Bérubé argues that "like the New York intellectuals, the new black intellectuals are, to varying degrees public figures, and, like the New York intellectuals, they seek to redefine what it means to be an intellectual in the United States."[25] Their venue are best-selling books that are bought, for the most part, by a new and rising black middle class. Their matrix is a new brand of "cultural politics" that seeks to change minds rather than public policy. "Cultural politics," Bérubé writes, "is a kind of compensation for practical politics."[26] Yet Bérubé is quick to point out that neither did the "celebrated New York intellectuals" have a policy bent so that "Lionel Trilling had no hand in Truman's Far East policies, nor did Philip Rahv enforce Brown v. Board of Education."[27] But to their credit, Bérubé contends the "black public intellectuals are doing their work at a time when the very idea of the 'public' has become nearly unthinkable in national politics."[28]

Dewey, Gardner, and Gilligan are public intellectuals. Ogbu has not yet achieved that status of "crossover intellectual" but he is constantly referred to in these public journals. Gardner and Gilligan can be found occasionally in the OP-Ed pages of the *New York Times*, among other venues, discussing current topics. They are household names to a literate public. Dewey wrote regularly for *The New Republic* and other general magazines. And Dewey, Gardner, Gilligan, and Ogbu are equally at home in the work of cultural politics as they are in policy-oriented practical politics.

Ideas are power. These four eminent educators have transformed American education.

NOTES

1. Chester E. Finn Jr., "What Ails Education Research," *Educational Researcher* (January/February 1988): 5.

2. Ibid.

3. Ibid.

4. Penelope L. Peterson, "Why Do Educational Research? Rethinking Our Roles and Identities, Our Texts, and Contexts," *Educational Researcher* (April 1988): 7, 4.

5. Carl F. Kaestle, "The Awful Reputation of Education Research," *Educational Researcher* (January/February 1993): 29.

6. Mark A. Constas, "The Changing Nature of Educational Research and a Critique of Postmodernism," *Educational Researcher* (March 1998): 26.

7. Richard J. Shavelson and David C. Berliner, "Erosion of the Education Research Infrastructure: A Reply to Finn," *Educational Researcher* (January/February 1988): 10.

8. Mary M. Kennedy, "The Connection Between Research and Practice," *Educational Researcher* (October 1997): 4.

9. John I. Goodlad, "The Vision Thing: Educational Research and AERA in the 21st Century, Part 2," *Educational Researcher* (June/July 1997): 13.

10. David C. Berliner, "The Vision Thing: Educational Research and AERA in the 21st Century, Part 2," *Educational Researcher* (June/July 1997): 12.

11. Richard Hofstader, *Anti-Intellectualism in American Life* (New York: Alfred A. Knopf, 1963): 407.

12. Ibid.

13. Ibid., p. 393.

14. Ibid., p. 299.

15. Ibid., p. 300.

16. Ibid., pp. 300–301.

17. Gail Sheehy, *Character: America's Search for Leadership* (New York: William Morrow, 1988), p. 160.

18. Ibid.

19. Ibid.

20. *New York Times*, July 17, 1992, p. A14.

21. Hofstader, *Anti-Intellectualism in American Life*, p. 393.

22. Russell Jacoby, *The Last Intellectuals* (New York: Basic Books, 1987), p. 7.

23. Ibid.

24. Michael Bérubé, "Public Academy," *The New Yorker*, January 9, 1995, p. 73.

25. Ibid.

26. Ibid., p. 79.

27. Ibid., pp. 79–80.

28. Ibid., p. 80.

Bibliography

BOOKS

The AAUW Report. *How Schools Shortchange Girls*. New York: Marlowe & Company, 1995.

Addams, Jane. *Twenty Years at Hull House*. New York: Macmillan Co., 1945.

Alexander, Thomas M. *John Dewey's Theory of Art, Experience, and Nature: The Horizons of Feeling*. Albany: State University of New York Press, 1987.

Armstrong, Thomas. *Multiple Intelligences in the Classroom*. Alexandria, Va.: Association for Supervision and Curriculum Development, 1994.

Ashton, Dore. *The New York School: A Cultural Reckoning*. New York: Penguin Books, 1992.

Belenky, Mary Field et al. *Woman's Ways of Knowing: The Development of Self, Voice, and Mind*. New York: Basic Books, 1986, 1997.

Bennis, Warren, and Burt Nanus. *Leaders: The Strategies for Taking Charge*. New York: Harper & Row, 1985.

Breslin, James E. B. *Mark Rothko: A Biography*. Chicago: University of Chicago Press, 1993.

Briner, Bob. *The Management Methods of Jesus: Ancient Wisdom for Modern Business*. Nashville, Tenn.: Thomas Nelson, Inc., 1996.

Brown, Lyn Mikel, and Carol Gilligan. *Meeting at the Crossroads: Women's Psychology and Girls' Development*. New York: Ballantine Books, 1992.

Burns, James MacGregor. *Leadership*. New York: Harper & Row, 1978.

Campbell, James. *Understanding John Dewey*. Chicago: Open Court, 1995.

Carnegie, Dale. *How to Win Friends and Influence People*. Rev. ed. New York: Pocket Books, 1982.

Contemporary Authors. Detroit: Gale Literary Database, 1998.

Coughlan, Neil. *Young John Dewey*. Chicago: University of Chicago Press, 1975.

Covey, Stephen R. *Principle-Centered Leadership*. New York: Simon and Schuster, 1991.

———. *The Seven Habits of Highly Effective People*. New York: Fireside, 1990.

Cremin, Lawrence. *The Transformation of the School: Progressivism in American Education 1876–1957*. New York: Vintage, 1961.

Cunningham, William G., and Donald W. Gresso. *Cultural Leadership: The Culture of Excellence in Education*. Boston: Allyn and Bacon, 1993.

Deal, Terrence E., and Allen A. Kennedy. *Corporate Cultures: The Rites and Rituals of Corporate Life*. Reading, Mass.: Addison-Wesley, 1982.

De Kooning, Willem. *The Collected Writings of Willem de Kooning*. New York: Hanuman Books, 1988.

Dewey, John. *Art as Experience*. New York: Capricorn Books, 1934.

———. *Democracy and Education*. New York: The Free Press, 1916.

———. *How We Think*. Boston: D. C. Heath, 1910.

———. *Moral Principles in Education*. Cambridge, Mass.: The Riverside Press, 1909.

Dykhuizen, George. *The Life and Mind of John Dewey*. Carbondale: Southern Illinois University Press, 1973.

Elfand, Arthur D. *A History of Art Education: Intellectual and Social Currents in Teaching Visual Arts*. New York: Teachers College Press, 1990.

Fitzgerald, F. Scott. *The Great Gatsby*. Cambridge, Eng.: University of Cambridge Press, 1995.

Flam, Jack. *Motherwell*. New York: Rizzoli International Publishing, 1991.

Fraser, Stephen, ed. *The Bell Curve Wars*. New York: Basic Books, 1995.

Gardner, Howard. *Art, Mind and Brain*. New York: Basic Books, 1982.

———. *Artful Scribbles*. New York: Basic Books, 1980.

———. *The Arts and Human Development*. New York: Basic Books, 1973.

———. *Creating Minds*. New York: Basic Books, 1993.

———. *Frames of Mind: The Theory of Multiple Intelligences*. New York: Basic Books, 1993.

———. *Leading Minds: An Anatomy of Leadership*. New York: Basic Books, 1995.

———. *Multiple Intelligences: The Theory in Practice*. New York: Basic Books, 1993.

———. *To Open Minds*. New York: Basic Books, 1989.

———. *The Unschooled Mind*. New York: Basic Books, 1991.

Gettleman, Marvin, and David Mermelstein, eds. *The Great Society Reader*. New York: Random House, 1967.

Gibson, Margaret A., and John U. Ogbu, eds. *Minority Status and Schooling: A Comparative Study of Immigrant and Involuntary Minorities*. New York: Garland Publishing, 1991.

Gilligan, Carol. *In a Different Voice: Psychological Theory and Women's Development*. Cambridge, Mass.: Harvard University Press, 1982, 1993.

———, et al., eds. *Making Connections: The Relational Worlds of Adolescent Girls at Emma Willard School*. Cambridge, Mass.: Harvard University Press, 1990.

———, et al. *Mapping the Moral Domain*. Cambridge, Mass.: Harvard University Press, 1988.

Greenberg, Clement. *The Collected Essays and Criticism of Clement Greenberg 1957–1969*. Vol. 4. Chicago: University of Chicago Press, 1993.

Herrnstein, Richard J., and Charles Murray. *The Bell Curve: Intelligence and Class Structure in American Life*. New York: The Free Press, 1994.

Hirsch, E. D., Jr. *Cultural Literacy: What Every American Needs to Know*. New York: Houghton Mifflin, 1987.

Hofstader, Richard. *Anti-Intellectualism in American Life*. New York: Alfred A. Knopf, 1963.

Jacoby, Russell. *The Last Intellectuals*. New York: Basic Books, 1987.

James, William. *The Varieties of Religious Experience*. New York: Longman, Green & Co., 1902.

Kingsley, April. *The Turning Point: Abstract Expressionists and the Transformation of American Art*. New York: Simon and Schuster, 1992.

Kohlberg, Lawrence. *The Philosophy of Moral Development*. Vol. 1. New York: Harper & Row, 1981.

Machiavelli, Niccolo. *The Prince*. New York: Oxford University Press, 1984.

Mattison, Robert Saltonstall. *Robert Motherwell: The Formative Years*. Ann Arbor, Mich.: UMI Research Press, 1986.

McCluskey, Neil G. *Public Schools and Moral Education*. New York: Columbia University Press, 1958.

Mens-Verhulst, Janneke Van, et al., eds. *Daughtering and Mothering*. London: Routledge, 1993.

Motherwell, Robert. *The Collected Writings of Robert Motherwell*. New York: Oxford University Press, 1992.

Naifeh, Steven, and Gregory White Smith. *Jackson Pollock: An American Saga*. New York: Clarkson N. Potter, 1989.

O'Conner, Francis V., ed. *Art for the Millions*. Boston: New York Graphic Society, 1973.

Ogbu, John U. *Minority Education and Caste: The American System in Cross-Cultural Perspective*. New York: Academic Press, 1978.

Pollitt, Katha. *Reasonable Creatures: Essays on Women and Feminism*. New York: Knopf, 1994.

Presseisen, B., et al., eds. *Topics in Cognitive Development*. Vol. 2. New York: Plenum Press, 1977.

The Random House Dictionary of the English Language. New York: Random House, 1967.

Reinhardt, Ad. *Art-as-Art: The Selected Writings of Ad Reinhardt*. New York: The Viking Press, 1975.

Rosenberg, Harold. *The Tradition of the New*. London, Eng.: Thames and Hudson, 1962.

Rost, Joseph C. *Leadership for the Twenty-First Century*. Westport, Conn.: Praeger, 1993.

Ryan, Alan. *John Dewey and the High Tide of American Liberalism*. New York: W. W. Norton and Co., 1995.

Sadker, David and Myra Sadker. *Failing at Fairness: How America's Schools Cheat Girls*. New York: Charles Scribner's Sons, 1994.

Schapiro, Meyer. *Modern Art: Selected Papers—19th and 20th Centuries*. New York: George Braziller, 1979.

Schlesinger, Arthur M., Jr. *The Disuniting of America: Reflections of a Multicultural Society*. New York: W. W. Norton and Co., 1991.

Schlipp, Paul Arthur, ed. *The Philosophy of John Dewey*. New York: Tudor Publishing Co., 1951.

Seitz, William C. *Abstract Expressionist Painting in America*. Cambridge, Mass.: Harvard University Press, 1983.

Sergiovanni, Thomas J. *Value-Added Leadership*. San Diego: Harcourt Brace Jovanovich, 1990.

Sheehy, Gail. *Character: America's Search for Leadership*. New York: William Morrow, 1988.

Sommers, Christina Hoff. *Who Stole Feminism? How Women Have Betrayed Women*. New York: Simon and Schuster, 1994.

Tawney, R. H. *Religion and the Rise of Capitalism*. New York: Harcourt, Brace and Co., 1926.

Westbrook, Robert B. *John Dewey and American Democracy*. Ithaca, N.Y.: Cornell University Press, 1991.

Wills, Gary. *Certain Trumpets: The Call of Leaders*. New York: Simon and Schuster, 1994.

Wilson, William Julius. *The Declining Significance of Race*. Chicago: University of Chicago Press, 1978.

———. *The Truly Disadvantaged: The Inner City, the Underclass and Public Policy*. Chicago: University of Chicago Press, 1987.

———. *When Work Disappears: The World of the New Urban Poor*. New York: Alfred A. Knopf, 1996.

ARTICLES

Anderson, Jervis. "Black and Blue." *The New Yorker*, April 29 and May 6, 1996.

Anthropology and Education 28, no. 3, September 1997.

Beinecke, John A. "The Investigation of John Dewey by the FBI." *Educational Theory* (winter 1987).

Berliner, David C. "The Vision Thing: Educational Research and AERA in the 21st Century, Part 2." *Educational Researcher* (June/July 1997).

Bérubé, Michael. "Public Academy." *The New Yorker*, January 9, 1995.

Book Review Digest 8, no. 1 (January 1979).

Buettner, Stewart. "John Dewey and the Visual Arts in America." *Journal of Aesthetics and Art Criticism* (summer 1975).

Campbell, Patricia. "What's a Nice Girl Like You Doing in a Math Class?" *Phi Delta Kappan*, March 1996.

Constas, Mark A. "The Changing Nature of Educational Research and a Critique of Postmodernism." *Educational Researcher* (March 1998).

Eastman, Max. "John Dewey." *Atlantic*, December 1941.

Eddy, Phillip. "Kohlberg and Dewey." *Educational Theory* 38, no 4 (fall 1988).

Eisner, Elliot W. "A Symposium on *Multiple Intelligences: The Theory in Practice*." *Teachers College Record* (summer 1994).

Finn, Chester E., Jr. "What Ails Education Research." *Educational Researcher* (January/February 1988).

Foley, Douglas E. "Reconsidering Anthropological Explanations of Ethnic School Failure." *Anthropology and Education Quarterly* 22 (1991).

Fordham, Signithia, and John U. Ogbu. "Black Students' School Success: Coping with the Burden of 'Acting White'." *The Urban Review* 18, no. 3 (1986).

Gardner, Howard. "Lofty Ideas That May Be Losing Altitude." *New York Times*, November 1, 1997.

———. "The Need for Anti-Babel Standards." *Education Week,* September 7, 1994.

———. "Reflections on Multiple Intelligences: Myths and Messages." *Phi Delta Kappan,* November 1995.

———. "Remembering AL." *Education Week,* May 14, 1997.

Gates, Henry Louis, Jr. "After the Revolution." *The New Yorker,* April 29 and May 6, 1996.

Gilligan, Carol. "Joining the Resistance: Psychology, Girls and Women." *Michigan Quarterly Review* 24, no. 4 (1990).

———. "Remembering Larry." *Journal of Moral Education* 27, no. 2 (1998).

Goleman, Daniel. "An Emerging Theory." *New York Times,* Education Supplement, October 17, 1988.

Goodlad, John I. "The Vision Thing: Educational Research and AERA in the 21st Century, Part 2." *Educational Researcher* (June / July 1997).

Hertzberg, Hendrik, and Henry Louis Gates Jr. "The African-American Century." *The New Yorker,* April 29 and May 6, 1996.

Jacobson, Leon. "Art as Experience and American Visual Art Today." *Journal of Aesthetics and Art Criticism* (Winter 1960).

Jencks, Christopher, and Meredith Phillips. "America's Next Achievement Test: Closing the Black-White Test Score Gap." *The American Prospect* (September / October 1998).

Kaestle, Carl F. "The Awful Reputation of Education Research," *Educational Researcher* (January–February 1993).

Kennedy, Mary M. "The Connection Between Research and Practice." *Educational Researcher* (October 1997).

Kohlberg, Lawrence, and Carol Gilligan. "The Adolescent as a Philosopher: The Discovery of the Self in a Postconventional World." *Daedalus* 100, no. 4 (1971).

Kohlberg, Lawrence, and Rochelle Mayer. "Development as the Aim of Education." *Harvard Educational Review* 42, no. 4 (November 1972).

Kultermann, Udo. "John Dewey's '*Art as Experience*': A Reevaluation of Aesthetic Pragmatism." *Art Criticism* (1990).

McNall, Miles, et al. "The Educational Achievement of the St. Paul Hmong." *Anthropology and Education Quarterly* 25 (1994).

Ogbu, John U. "Cultural Problems in Minority Education: Their Interpretations and Consequences—Part One." *The Urban Review* 27, no. 3 (1995).

———. "Racial Stratification and Education in the U.S.: Why Inequality Persists." *Teachers College Record* 96, no. 2 (1994).

———. "Understanding Cultural Diversity and Learning." *Educational Researcher* 21 (August 1992).

"On *In a Different Voice*: An Interdisciplinary Forum." *Signs: Journal of Women in Culture and Society* 11, no. 21 (1986).

Peterson, Penelope L. "Why Do Educational Research?: Rethinking Our Roles and Identities, Our Texts, and Contexts." *Educational Researcher* (April 1988).

Pollock, Jackson. "My Painting." In *Possibilities 1: An Occasional Review.* Problems of Contemporary Art, No. 4. New York: Wittenborn, Schultz, 1947.

Pratte, Richard. "Reconsiderations." *Educational Studies* (summer 1992).

Reynolds, Gretchen. "The Rising Significance of Race." *Chicago,* December 1992.

Riner, Phillip S. "Dewey's Legacy to Education." *The Educational Forum* (winter 1989).

Rose, Frances. "Confident, Composed at 16." *New York Times Magazine*, January 7, 1990.

Rothko, Mark. "A Symposium on How to Combine Architecture, Painting and Sculpture." *Interiors*, no. 10 (May 1951).

Saxton, Martha. "Are Women More Moral Than Men?" *Ms.*, December 1981.

Shavelson, Richard J., and David C. Berliner. "Erosion of the Education Research Infrastructure: A Reply to Finn." *Educational Researcher* (January/February 1988).

Singham, Mano. "The Canary in the Mine: The Achievement Gap Between Black and White Students." *Phi Delta Kappan*, September 1998.

Sternberg, Robert J. "A Symposium on *Multiple Intelligence: The Theory in Practice.*" *Teachers College Record* (summer 1994).

VanGelder, Lindsy. "The Importance of Being Eleven." *Ms.*, July/August 1990.

FILM/TELEVISION/RADIO

Bragg, Melvyn, ed. *Portrait of an Artist: Jackson Pollock.* (Film). London, Eng.: South Bank Show, 1987.

de Antonio, Emile. *Painters Painting.* (Film). New York: New Video, 1972.

Hughes, Robert. *American Visions: The Empire of Signs.* (Episode 7). (Television). Public Broadcasting System, 1997.

Public Broadcasting System. *Robert Motherwell and The New York School: Storming the Citadel.* (Television). New York, 1991.

Snyder, Robert. *Willem de Kooning: Artist.* (Film). Pacific Palisades, Calif.: Masters & Masterworks, 1994.

Talk of the Nation. National Public Radio, October 26, 1994.

INTERVIEWS

Interview with Carol Gilligan, October 14, 1998, Harvard University.
Interview with Brandi Hammock, June 4, 1998, Norfolk, Virginia.
Interview with Cristin Newbold, April 4, 1998, Norfolk, Virginia.
Interview with Donnie Newbold, April 6, 1998, Norfolk, Virginia.
Interview with John U. Ogbu, December 3, 1998, Philadelphia, Pennsylvania.

LETTERS

Dore Ashton to Maurice R. Berube, May 23, 1996.
Norman Bluhm to Maurice R. Berube, July 14, 1997.
Fielding Dawson to Maurice R. Berube, July 28, 1997.
Larry Hickman, Director, The Center for Dewey Studies, to Maurice R. Berube, June 24, 1996.
Pat Passlof to Maurice R. Berube, November 18, 1996.

Philip Pavia to Maurice R. Berube, October 17, 1996.
Richard Rorty to Maurice R. Berube, May 10, 1996.

NEWSPAPERS/MAGAZINES

Boston Globe, August 20, 1995; November 5, 1995.
The Christian Century, December 27–29, 1982.
Harper's, December 1983.
Mother Jones, February 1996.
New York Review of Books, October 27, 1983.
New York Times, December 25, 1983; May 2, 1988; December 20, 1993; October 9,
      1994; October 27, 1994; March 4, 1996; March 16, 1996; April 10, 1998; May 2,
      1988.
Phi Delta Kappan, January 1997.
Time, December 20, 1993; June 17, 1996.

UNPUBLISHED MATERIAL

Gilligan, Carol. "Responses to Temptation: An Analysis of Motives." Doctoral dis-
      sertation, Harvard University, Cambridge, Mass., 1963.
Ogbu, John U., and Herbert D. Simons. "Cultural Models of Literacy: A
      Comparative Study." Springfield, Virginia: *ERIC* Reports, December 1994.
Pavia, Philip. "The Records of The Club." Archives of American Art, Smithsonian,
      Washington, D.C., 1965.
Pollock, Jackson. "The Papers of Jackson Pollock." Archives of American Art,
      Smithsonian, Washington, D.C., 1975.
Reinhardt, Ad. "The Papers of Ad Reinhardt." Archives of American Art,
      Smithsonian, Washington, D.C., 1940s.
Rothko, Mark. "The Scribble Book." Archives of American Art, Smithsonian,
      Washington, D.C. (circa: late 1930s).
Scott, Oscar, Jr. "Multiple Intelligences and the Gifted: Identification of African-
      American Students." Ph.D. dissertation, Old Dominion University, Norfolk,
      Va., 1996.

Index

About the Author

MAURICE R. BERUBE is Eminent Scholar of Educational Leadership at Old Dominion University, Virginia and author of many books, all published by Greenwood/Praeger.

ISBN 0-313-31060-2

90000>

EAN

9 780313 310607

HARDCOVER BAR CODE